THEODORE PRATT
A Florida Writer's Life

TAYLOR HAGOOD

Pineapple Press
Palm Beach, Florida

 Pineapple Press

An imprint of Globe Pequot, the trade division of
The Rowman & Littlefield Publishing Group, Inc.
4501 Forbes Blvd., Ste. 200
Lanham, MD 20706
www.rowman.com

Distributed by NATIONAL BOOK NETWORK

British Library Cataloguing in Publication Information available

Library of Congress Cataloging-in-Publication Data Available

ISBN 9781683343622 (cloth : alk. paper) | ISBN 9781683343639 (ebook)

♾™ The paper used in this publication meets the minimum require-
ments of American National Standard for Information Sciences—
Permanence of Paper for Printed Library Materials, ANSI/NISO
Z39.48-1992.

For Mary Faraci

CONTENTS

CONTENTS

PROLOGUE
Journey to Dreamland

In 1934, Ted and Jackie Pratt had been through the wringer for almost half a decade. Their married life together was supposed to start as an adventure in Europe, but the stock market crashed historically three days after their wedding. Off they had gone to Europe anyway, but that ended in the debacle of an international incident on the island of Majorca. They returned to find the country deep in the Great Depression. Suffering in the New York cold, the couple needed sunshine. They decided to seek it in the Sunshine State.

The Pratts made the long drive down the coast on US Highway 1. Along the way, the air softened with the accents. By the time they reached Georgia, the land spread in languid salt flats of ochre grasses, and the wide St. Johns River made an apt introduction to the quiet, understated beauty of Florida. The Pratts drove through the old Spanish city of St. Augustine to Daytona and Melbourne. As they made their way down the peninsula, the vegetation shrank in height to a verdant clumped jungle, more and more palms mixing with the pines. The atmosphere grew sleepy and remote, an enigmatic quality increasing with the exotic beauty.

Finally, they reached coastal South Florida. They arrived in West Palm Beach and looked across Lake Worth Lagoon to Palm Beach Island. On that playground of the rich stood the fabulous Spanish-style homes designed by recently deceased architect Adison Mizner. The couple could appreciate these stone and mortar incarnations of romantic dreams. It was easy to dream here in the subtropics.

But it was the primitive feel, natural beauty, and real Floridians that struck Ted most—the Spanish moss, the pine trees, the palms, and the uncouth, unique, yet endearing inhabitants, human and otherwise. And there was the ocean, teal, vast, and calling.

Ted knew material for writing could be found in Florida. Other writers showed that. Ernest Hemingway—with whom he was destined to have a vexed indirect connection—was living in Key West. Marjorie Kinnan Rawlings had just last year published *South Moon Under* about Cracker culture in the north Florida scrub. This year saw the publication of Zora Neale Hurston's *Jonah's Gourd Vine*. Ted immediately saw possibilities on the South Florida coast for himself. As he put it twenty years later, "I took one look and said, 'This is for me to write about.'"[1]

And write about it he did. Ted went on to publish thirteen novels set entirely in Florida and several more partially set in the state or with some reference to it. Eventually, journalists would give him the title "Literary Laureate of Florida." In the process of becoming a chronicler of what the poet Elizabeth Bishop called "the state with the prettiest name,"[2] Ted embraced not only the tantalizing dreams Florida offers but also its many ugly sides. He put himself in the way of harm from hurricanes, shipwrecks, irate locals, and other perils. He delved deeply into Florida history and culture, mining the memories of pioneers, the ways of Seminole Indians, the vagaries of cockfights and holiness revivals, and Cracker and Bahamian lifestyles.

Most memorably, he dramatized the historical post office practice peculiar to South Florida of mail deliverers walking the beaches from the Jupiter inlet to Miami. Ted's writing about one of those unshod postmen helped elevate the figure into a local folk hero. Many people actually believed him to be *the* "Barefoot Mailman," the name he gave to his most famous novel and the skiff it bought him.

Theodore Pratt's importance to Florida literary history stretches far and wide. He was arguably the original writer of Florida detective fiction later practiced by the likes of Brett Halliday, Charles Willeford, Les Standiford, James W. Hall, and Ted's friend, John D. MacDonald. His first serious Florida novel, *Big Blow*, grappled with race and violence in the South as earnestly as two pillars of the genre published the same year—Margaret Mitchell's *Gone With the Wind* and William Faulkner's *Absalom, Absalom!* Ted championed civil rights in his writing and political activism, supporting the segregationist-turned-civil rights advocate Florida Governor LeRoy Collins. He formed friendships with other Florida writers, including Rawlings, Hurston, MacDonald, and the Miami environmentalist Marjory Stoneman Douglas. Like writers contemporary with and after him—from Carl Hiaasen to Randy Wayne White—Pratt witnessed and decried the increasing urbanization of Florida and the ruining of its distinctive natural beauty.

As important as Pratt is in Florida literary history, his significance reaches wider still in illuminating mid-twentieth-century US culture. Several of his works were made into films that featured some of the most significant actors of Hollywood's golden era, including Ann Sheridan, Ronald Reagan, Robert Cummings, and the legendary Edward G. Robinson. *The Incredible Mr. Limpet*, starring Don Knotts and based on Pratt's novel, has become a beloved live-action animated film classic. Moreover, Pratt lived and wrote in a transformative time in publishing, embracing the paperback revolution to both his monetary gain and his critical reception's detriment. His original paperbacks with their lurid covers appeared on drugstore shelves in the 1950s. In those novels, he not only told ripping yarns but also engaged such controversial issues as euthanasia and rape with clear-eyed and sometimes disconcerting honesty.

Herein lies a story, then, of interest to anyone who loves and/or loathes Florida. Also herein lies a man's journey through the middle of the twentieth century in America. The story's hero encounters major figures of American culture, from Norman Rockwell to Rita Hayworth to Desi Arnaz to Burt Reynolds, while writing books that distill that historical moment. His books display some of the prejudices and blind spots of their time, but they also argue for concepts progressive in their era. Those books are always the products of a writer seeking some understanding of truth.

And Pratt found that truth most often and with the greatest clarity in the green glades, purple shadows, and blue waters of the Sunshine State. He became a boater, a fisherman, and a diver in the coastal waters even as he followed a predilection for natural history into the alligator-haunted hammocks and stately sheet flow of the South Florida interior. Patiently recording these experiences, Pratt lived out what can be called the quintessential Florida writer's life.

CHAPTER 1

Minnesota Born, New York Raised (1901–1915)

The story of Theodore Pratt begins far from Florida and the writing life he committed to so passionately. He would be known for his ability to capture subtropical land and seascapes, but he first saw daylight in the cold North.[1] Where he would come later to write of Seminoles and Crackers, his own family was Gallic and Germanic. His were practical people, intrepid and determined, living in places only recently tamed by pioneers. The pioneer drive would always be a part of Pratt, and its spirit would drive him to a southern frontier.

His father, Thomas Amede Pratt, was Canadian, born June 15, 1867, in Stanbridge East, Quebec.[2] Thomas immigrated to the United States in 1892, where he gained expertise in silk wholesaling with the Wyman-Partridge Holding Company.[3] The young salesman was handsome, svelte, dark-haired, and dark-eyed.[4] He combed his hair up and back in a style his son would later emulate. He waxed his moustache into slightly curling handlebars and sat for photographs wearing high collars and neat neckties.

In his twenties, Thomas met Emma Rosetta Hineline, an Irish-German woman born August 29, 1870, in Minneapolis. The child of a Bavarian father and an Irish mother, she was more cute than beautiful. Her nose spread a little too wide, and her forehead was low. But she had a well-formed mouth that turned upward naturally in a hint of a smile, and her cleft chin was distinct. Her eyes, which she bequeathed to her son, were dark and a little frank and knowing.

Thomas and Emma married in 1898. A photograph presents the newlyweds along with friends of theirs, Mr. and Mrs. Lew North.[5] Posed in a woodland setting, the Pratts come off as the more dashing of the two couples. The Norths look roughhewn where the Pratts wear outfits of striking color and symmetry: white long-sleeve shirts, dark belts, skirt and pants of similar hue, both man and wife with dark ties.

The couple was living in Minneapolis when their first child, Theodore George Pratt, was born on April 26, 1901, the day of William Shakespeare's baptism. The Catholic couple had *their* son baptized on May 12 by Reverend George Arctander, Pastor at the Church of St. Charles in Minneapolis.[6] Theo—as his family would call him—favored his mother in photographs of him as an infant and young child. He was four when his sister, Isabel Agnes Pratt, was born on Halloween, October 31, 1905. Both children would be raised as devout adherents to the Catholic faith, which settled into a particularly deep reverence bordering on terror in Theo.

The family lived in a house on Zenith Avenue, southwest of downtown Minneapolis. The name "Zenith" stands out conspicuously in a literary context, for it would later take on significance as the fictional city in numerous writings by fellow Minnesotan, Sinclair Lewis. The second-floor exterior of the Pratts' white clapboard house was painted a darker color, and it had a capacious screened-in porch with ionic columns. Nearby was Lake Harriet, which featured a pavilion called the Casino for outdoor concerts.[7] The lake was a beloved spot, with the family recording trips to its Casino photographically. It was on this lake that Theo first became interested in reading while lying in an aimlessly drifting boat. The book he read was *Little Women*.[8]

It was unsurprising that Theo would discover a love of reading on the water. Minnesota is not coastal, but it ranks ninth in total water surface.[9] Theo's enchantment with water derived not only from Lake Harriet but also Lake Minnetonka, fifteen miles southwest of Minneapolis where the Pratts stayed during the summer months.[10] Just as Ernest Hemingway developed a love of nature in Michigan's Walloon Lake, so Theo spent his childhood enjoying the pleasures of boating and fishing in Minnesota waters. His sense of identity developed in connection with woods and prairies, lakes and streams. He learned to paddle and steer a canoe and other small craft on nearby Minnehaha Creek. That stream bore a literary connection with Henry Wadsworth Longfellow's *The Song of Hiawatha*. Theo likely saw Jacob Fjelde's statue of Hiawatha and Minnehaha, which was placed by the stream just above the falls in 1912.

It may already have been by this time that Theo's uncle, Eugene Pratt, had moved to Miami. The story of a pioneer moving from the far north to Florida would capture Theo's imagination and never lose its hold. It may be that already the stirrings of a future Florida writer had begun in him. His growing identity shaped into a sense of being both a city mouse and a country mouse, a hybridity attainable in Minneapolis where the frontier perched on the doorstep. All his life he would respect and even fear nature.

Theo's interest in writing started as early as he could remember.[11] Artistry, of the writing variety or any other kind, was not commonplace in his family. He later wrote, the "statistics of my immediate ancestors are therefore, and hereby, limited to the fact that none of them possessed a nature that would seem to breed a writer."[12] But writing fascinated him: he made his first stab at an autobiography when he was ten, although he did not get past page three.[13] He had just not yet lived enough life to write about. Still, he pursued his passion and soon enjoyed the excitement of having his first publication in a school paper. "I remember seeing it and I remember the thrill I got out of seeing it that preserved, for all time it seemed, in ink on paper," he later wrote.[14]

Theo was not the only developing writer from Minnesota. He may already have been hearing about and reading the aforementioned Sinclair Lewis, who by Theo's fourteenth year was regularly publishing short fiction and the first novel under his own name, *Our Mr. Wren*. It would not be long until the Sauk Center native would turn to the small-town Minnesota-inspired material that would make him famous. Meanwhile, a teenage F. Scott Fitzgerald had returned from the East with his family in 1908 and the next year published his first short story in St. Paul Academy's student newspaper. While direct cross-pollinating between Fitzgerald and Pratt is as unlikely as the twin cities were apart in their rivalry, the two young men's being young Catholic writers in the same urban area made for striking parallels.

Those parallels extended into other dimensions. Just as Fitzgerald's father took a job as a salesman at Proctor and Gamble in Buffalo, New York, when his wicker furniture business failed in St. Paul, so Thomas accepted a position as sales manager at a silk manufacturing company in New York City in 1915.[15] The move was traumatic for Theo. To him, the city was frighteningly far away. Minnesotans who had gone there said it was all right to visit but not a place to live. Theo pleaded to be able to stay but "was dragged downtown to get my first manicure and then forcibly made to accompany the family to the train."[16] As the train pulled out of Minneapolis, Theo cried and determined that he would, like a Horatio Alger character, make a fabulous fortune in New York and return in triumph to live again in his home city. Fate had other plans; that dream would never be fulfilled.

The train ride terminated in Jersey City, and Theo saw New York for the first time from a ferry. It scared him to death. "It was a huge Babylon, dangerous and awful, the windows of its buildings spitting fire from a setting sun," he remembered. Brooklyn Bridge and the Hudson formed only "mild interest" for him as the family took a cab to an aunt's brownstone on MacDonough Street in Brooklyn. The boy, accustomed to the less urbane and cramped setting of the middle West, was horrified at the tiny backyard.

But Theo beheld the magic of Manhattan when his cousin took him to see the Woolworth building. The elevator scared him even as he enjoyed five lollypops. But the view from atop the tower fascinated the boy. In fact, the budding New Yorker quickly began to think of Manhattan as superior to Brooklyn. He was glad when the family moved to a suite in the Endicott Hotel on 81st Street and Columbus Avenue for the daunting but boast-worthy sum of a hundred dollars a month. Theo's father laughed off his wife's concerns about the high rent with a jolly, "That's New York."

Now Theo found himself in the epicenter of urban life. This new home unnerved him when the elevated train ripped by and sent everything inside rattling.[17] But he found Central Park delightful—not quite Minnesota but close enough. When the parks lakes froze over, he proudly showed off his skating skills. Gliding over the ice, he swelled with pride that a boy from Minnesota could do something better than New Yorkers.

More than anything else, he fell in love with the Natural History Museum. He would go three to four times a week, walking its length and memorizing its contents. As he put it, "I became an enthusiastic, living but slightly tiresome catalogue of its engrossing contents."[18] Years later, a psychoanalyst told him his "inferiority complex came partially from standing too long in awe before the fourteen-hundred-year-old redwood tree."

Theo learned about the wide world in the museum, and his fascination with natural history fueled him throughout his career. His greatest talent and accomplishment would lie in his ability to capture the natural environs of Florida in vivid, compelling, and unforgettable ways.

Theo had not gone to school during the winter because it was the middle of the year, so fall saw him entering sixth grade at Public School Number 87 on Amsterdam Avenue at 77th Street.[19] There, he had an experience that taught him a valuable writing lesson. When he wrote a story as part of an assignment in an English composition class, the teacher selected his as an example of creating distinctive characters.[20] He took to heart the teacher's stressing the importance of making the people he created interesting via distinctive details. He would always call it one of the best lessons in writing fiction of his life.

Just as Theo was beginning to settle into New York, his father announced in the winter that they were moving yet again. Their new home would be New Rochelle, in Westchester County. Now the boy did not want to leave the city. But the family's furniture and Buick were brought east out of storage, and the Pratts moved into a house at 96 Locust Avenue. Theo's father assured him that New York City was only a short train ride away.

Founded near the end of the seventeenth century by Huguenots, New Rochelle had long ago lost its pioneer flavor.[21] Its most illustrious early citizen, Thomas Paine, had been a fiery writer in support of the Revolution. By the time the Pratts arrived, the town had become a playground for the wealthy. Theo understood about playgrounds: where he had lakes and streams to explore in Minnesota, now he had access to the Long Island Sound. Beyond those recreations, New Rochelle also boasted a stable of writers and artists. It was a fortuitous relocation for a boy who wanted to become a writer.

CHAPTER 2

Teenage Newspaper Man
(1916–1920)

Theo's first extensive foray into the world of letters took the form of a self-published newspaper called *The All News*.[1] The one-page daily featured its title hand-lettered across the top along with the volume, issue number, and price of "One Cent." Printed on only one side, the text was set in type in three columns, with lines indicating section breaks. The first issue appeared on August 30, 1916, announcing an impending freight train strike, a "Citizens Meeting," and that mail would not be delivered on Labor Day. It also included a dark joke on infantile paralysis, an epidemic that was claiming lives daily.

The second issue made it clear that the "Editor, Reporters, Staff, Financier, printer, typesetter, and newsboy are all in one namely—Theodore Pratt." This lone-operating publishing juggernaut invited outside contributions in the way of jokes that, if deemed worthy of publication, would be "paid at the rate of 50¢ each." By the end of the fifth issue, Theo ceased the project, with no one having bought a copy. The paper may not have been a commercial success, but, as he put it later, it "was an expression of some yearning to write and be published."[2]

By fall, the Pratts moved into a white clapboard house at 25 Sickles Place. At the time, the neighborhood featured a mix of first- or second-generation immigrants as well as descendants of Huegenots.[3] Theo enrolled in New Rochelle High School, housed in a neoclassical columned building only a few blocks away that is now City Hall. Soon he was writing pieces and submitting them to the school paper, *The Parrot*.[4]

When the United States entered the Great War in April 1917, the freshman Theo tried to enlist in the Marines. Lying about his age failed to fool a recruitment officer, so Theo decided instead to pursue what he believed to be the glamorous lifestyle of journalists. His model was Richard Harding Davis, a dashing, handsome man who had his break covering the Johnstown flood in 1889. Davis, who had died in 1916, wrote in a brilliant style about such controversial issues as suicide and abortion.[5] Incidentally, Sinclair Lewis would refer to him in his 1924 novel, *Dodsworth*. The teenage Theo envisioned himself as just such a bold adventurer-writer who could take on the most immense events of the world.

To put his plan of glory into action, Theo looked to the local paper. He rode his bicycle to the Main Street headquarters of the *New Rochelle Daily Star*, which were housed in a white frame house not that dissimilar from his own. Editorial rooms were located upstairs while downstairs the linotype machine and flatbed press rattled the glass vases in the florist shop that shared the building. The editor of the *Daily Star*, Robert Forbes, determined that the teenager could type well enough and hired him for eight dollars a week. Theo was thrilled: he would always remember with excitement and nostalgia the "click-clack of the linotype machine" and the "sweet, rather sickish smell of printer's ink."[6]

Like Hemingway, Theo's writing career was deeply shaped by his training as a reporter. Forbes sent the boy to his sister,

Amy Forbes King, who instructed him on the techniques of writing stories for the newspaper. She showed him how he must get the "Who, What, When, Where, How, and Why" into the lead and how to forge an eye-catching headline to fit into the allotted space. The boy quickly learned newspaper lingo as he both worked in the offices and rushed out to cover everything from fires to weddings. He thrilled at each by-line, and the compositor, seeing his excitement, made him a piece of lead with his name on it. When Theo picked up the hot lead, it burned him, sending the compositor into peals of laughter. Enduring the hilarity, Theo picked it back up when it cooled and kept it the rest of his life as a paperweight.

As a reporter, Theo also found a way to engage directly with the war-time moment. Caught up in patriotic fervor, the boy was shocked when on one of his assignments he heard a city official refer to departing soldiers as fools.[7] His disillusionment with the war deepened with the discovery that some young men paid doctors to give them diagnoses that could keep them out of the military. Before long, he was being sent to cover the news when telegrams arrived informing parents of their sons being killed in Europe. Theo never lost his patriotism, but it became more refined and complex as he developed doubts about war. When a second world war erupted later, he would fashion a character who voiced his own struggles with warfare.

By 1918, the country was in the grip of the influenza pandemic as well as war, and on one summer day Theo arrived at the newspaper offices to find Forbes and King sick at home.[8] It was up to Theo to get the paper out. He wrote like crazy, ignoring the reporting rule of being concise. Instead, he made generous use of a different rule of small-town papers—to print as many residents' names as possible. Practically every name in town appeared in that issue along with an extraordinary amount of boilerplate. Despite the compositor's skepticism,

Theo got the job done. That issue of the *Daily Star* hit the stands only half an hour late. "If there was ever any one point where I formally decide to be a writer," he wrote later, "it was then."[9]

With this real-life newspaper experience, Theo saw the high school paper's flaws and limitations. So, in the 1918/1919 school year he instigated a move to end *The Parrot* and start a new paper. A contest was held for its name, and it was retitled *The Purple and White*.[10] Theo became the editor-in-chief of this nicely edited and printed publication, each issue of which was made up of heavy slick paper.

Theo could now boast of being a professional reporter and editor, but the call of fiction sounded in his ears. Under his leadership, the newly initiated paper set up a short story contest, and Theo published fictional pieces in it. "John Brockwood's Return" and "At Five in the Morning" were among his first published short stories. While both bear obvious marks of a teenage imagination, they also anticipate Theo's later, mature fiction. The writing is clear and concise, the descriptions controlled and not overwritten. The youngster successfully executed a storyline that led to a moment of seeming disaster followed by a last-minute, if not altogether believable, happy ending. He would write such happy endings throughout his professional career. When the spring term ended, he clipped the two stories along with a third piece and pasted them into a little volume entitled *Short Stories* by Theodore G. Pratt, editor of *The Purple and White*.[11]

Even as Theo channeled energy into writing, he was also fascinated with other creative people and resources in town. Cartoonist Clare Briggs had just built a mansion at the Wykagl Country Club. In a similar graphic vein, New Rochelle was home to a cadre of illustrators, including Joseph C. Leyendecker, Courtney Allen, Coles Phillips, and a young man who in 1916 sold his first ever cover to the *Saturday Evening Post*: Norman

Rockwell. The now-legendary illustrator also that year started renting a barn on Prospect Street where he set up his studio, a move that stuck in Theo's imagination. Writing for a local magazine called *The Chesterfieldian*, Theo interviewed Rockwell, Leyendecker, Phillips, and Briggs as well as other artists in Fairfield and Westchester Counties, including Frederick Dana Marsh, Orson Lowell, and Lucius Wolcott Hitchcock.[12]

Theo also took note of New Rochelle's drama scene. Not far from his house lived the playwright Augustus Thomas. Although not well remembered now, Thomas was celebrated in his own time, his play *The Copperhead* igniting the career of Lionel Barrymore on both stage and screen. The still new and raw film industry also had a presence in New Rochelle in the form of the Thanhouser Film Company, founded by Edwin Thanhouser in 1909. One can imagine how fascinated the teenage Theo would have been by the glass-house studio, constructed to maximize light for the cameras of the time. Theo even referenced the studio in *The All News* when he recorded that a child of an unnamed actor in the studio had contracted infantile paralysis.

But the short story occupied Theo's attention most, and he longed to interact with professional writers of fiction. *The Chesterfieldian* sent him to interview minor writers in the area whose names have since been lost. He hoped in interviewing them that they would show him their manuscripts because he believed he could learn something about writing from examining them. None of the writers ever offered. Disappointed, Theo made up his mind that if he ever made it as a writer, he would make his manuscripts available to young writers.[13]

Theo took his fiction writing development into his own hands when the 1919 school year ended. He enrolled in a summer session at Columbia University, paying for it out of his newspaper savings. Perhaps riding on the train with his father to the city, he made his way to the campus in Harlem to take a course named "Technique of the short story," receiving a B. From this instruction and with his own determined drive, Theo wrote and submitted stories to magazines. Drawing on his passion for history fueled by his trips to the Museum of Natural History and inspired by his history teacher, Henry Durfree, Theo wrote a story entitled "The Man With the Odd School." Another early story was a western entitled "The Bad Man of Cactus City," published in the Sunday magazine section of the *Chicago Ledger*.[14] These and other stories deepened Theo's commitment to fiction.

He graduated from New Rochelle High School on June 24, 1920.[15] That year turned out to be a banner one for Minnesota writers. March saw F. Scott Fitzgerald's first novel, *This Side of Paradise*, published by Scribner's. The book not only brought Fitzgerald enough success to claim the hand of Alabama socialite Zelda Sayre, it inaugurated an era, kicking off the decade soon to be called "The Jazz Age." Later in the year, Sinclair Lewis's *Main Street* exploded into the public, presenting the American small town in a level of artistry wholly new. The book would go on to win the Pulitzer Prize and become the bestseller of 1921, a publishing phenomenon that swept the country. It must have seemed to Theo the most logical thing in the world for Minnesotans to find success as writers. Certainly, he was committed to that path, and he set about to further his education and contacts in that direction.

CHAPTER 3

College Playwright
(1920–1924)

In 1920, the influenza pandemic had passed, the war had ended, women had been granted the right to vote, Prohibition had begun, and Theo—or "Ted," as he now preferred to be called by people outside his family—enrolled at Colgate University in Hamilton, New York.[1] A high school friend had gone on before him to the bucolic campus, inspiring Ted's choice. Now Ted walked among the collegiate buildings as a student himself.

Ted's first semester went well enough, with an A in "Short Story" and Bs in English literature, rhetoric, and philosophy.[2] The next semester, he slipped, with Cs in geology, history, and biblical literature, and another B in English literature. Perhaps extracurricular activities interfered with his studies, as he joined Phi Kappa Psi and got on the staffs of the daily newspaper, a humorous magazine, a literary magazine, and the yearbook.[3] Student life held little attraction for him otherwise—he especially despised organized sports, with extra hatred for football. He was not and never would be a physical specimen, although he enjoyed playing tennis. On the shorter side, his dark hair always neatly groomed, he was quiet, reserved, yet opinionated.

He was initiated into Phi Kappa Psi. The fraternity's secrecy and exclusivity rankled with him as did the inconsistencies he saw in upperclassmen who ostensibly upheld high ideals but blithely went about throwing their weight around as they caroused.[4] The hazing ritual of beating freshmen sickened him; he had a strong natural repugnance to bullying and to people of lower status being taken advantage of. His disillusionment with fraternities marked an early sign of what would become a disillusionment with and distrust in rites, ultimately including Catholicism.

Despite his disgust with the fraternity, Ted got in good with its upperclassmen when he started writing their papers for rhetoric at five dollars apiece.[5] The teacher, Professor Crawshaw, called him into his office about the suspicious similarities among the papers. Ted replied that the papers resembled each other because the fraternity brothers had been discussing Crawshaw's lectures so fervently. Not fooled, the professor told the boy never to let it happen again and ordered him out. Embarrassed as he was, Ted ever-after had admiration and affection for Crawshaw.

The fall of Ted's sophomore year turned out worse yet. Not only did he receive Fs in economics and French, there was no number value assigned to the grades, suggesting he may never even have attended those classes. He received a C in general literature. His one accomplishment was another A in "Short Story," but even that was bittersweet, for one of his fraternity brothers laughed uproariously when Ted read one of his stories aloud. The next semester was better, but still average, with Cs in psychology and sociology and Bs in general literature and rhetoric.

It may be that Ted lost interest in the college scene, generally. He later wrote that the culture of the institution at the time stigmatized diligent studies. The library offered him his real education. There in the stacks he read Oscar Wilde, Leo Tolstoy,

Joseph Conrad, George Bernard Shaw, Theodore Dreiser, Anatole France, Gustave Flaubert, Honoré de Balzac, Walt Whitman, and his fellow-Minnesotan, Lewis.[6] He also discovered W. Somerset Maugham, Ford Madox Ford, and H. L. Mencken. Ted would come into proximity with each of the latter three. His association with Mencken would bring him serious trouble.

Ted also developed a passion for the Little Theater movement then coming into vogue. One of the fruits of this interest came in the form of a collaboration during his time at Colgate. Working with a classmate named Krause Crofoot, Ted wrote a play entitled "A Study in Furniture" produced along with two other plays as part of Colgate's "Little Theatre" on May 4, 1922, under the auspices of the Masque and Triangle Club.[7] The *Colgate Maroon* described the play as "a farce of the trials of a college youth who secured funds from his father on the pretense of buying furniture for his room and spent the money in revelry."[8]

Ted left Colgate after two years. He claimed the institution simply did not offer the writing courses he needed, but he may have left under the pressure of the poor grades and distractions. He transferred to Columbia University, where he shared the campus with such later-famous figures as Lou Gehrig, Amelia Earhart, and Langston Hughes. He just missed taking classes at the same time as his future friend and fellow Florida writer Zora Neale Hurston. Ted's student records list no courses in the 1922/1923 academic year, but in 1923/1924 he took three.[9] One was an advanced course in playwriting in both the fall and spring semesters in which he earned an A and B, respectively. In the fall, he enrolled in stage craft and stage direction, earning Bs in both. He did not receive a degree.

Overall, Ted's Columbia experience proved worse than Colgate. He bristled under the tutelage of short story writing instructor Blanche Colton Williams, whose textbook he found "limiting and didactic."[10] Amid his disappointment with her teaching, Ted shifted his attention toward drama. He did so under the influence and encouragement of Hatcher Hughes, a North Carolina native who had joined the Columbia faculty in 1912. At the moment, Hughes was working on a play entitled *Hell-Bent Fer Heaven*, a melodrama set in the Blue Ridge mountains that would be staged in 1924 and win a Pulitzer Prize.[11] Ted regarded Hughes as a real-life practitioner instead of just a teacher, and North Carolina would become important to Ted in adulthood.

Ted's excitement about theater spread beyond Columbia's campus. He studied at the American Academy of the Dramatic Arts and submitted plays to Broadway.[12] He also attended a number of professional productions, including Eugene O'Neill's *The Emperor Jones*, starring Paul Robeson, at the Provincetown Playhouse.[13] Finally, he joined a theatrical troupe in New Rochelle called the Huguenot Players. Their organizer and leader was a mover and shaker in the Little Theater movement named Walter Hartwig. In him, Ted gained a mentor who had significant clout and connections.

It was with the Huguenot Players that Ted made his first mark of any significance: a 1923 one-act play entitled *The Revolt of the Mummies*. A "Comedy in One Act" Ted developed from one of his Columbia courses, the play draws on Howard Carter's 1922 discovery of Tutankhamun's grave and Ted's own days spent in the Museum of Natural History.[14] For the action of the play, Ted used a framing device of two maintenance men who are decidedly unimpressed with a museum's rotting old mummies. When the men leave the Egyptian section of the museum, the mummies come to life. There are five of them, designated as The Slave Mummy, The Melancholy Mummy, The Lively Mummy, The Pharoah Mummy, and a woman named Valeeta, who happens to have been married to all the others at different times. Angry over being trapped on display and at Valeeta for pining after an animated marble statue of Socrates, the male mummies threaten to destroy the museum. But Valeeta crushes their impulse, and they all return to their display cases as the maintenance men return to close the play with further comment about how uninteresting the mummies are.

The play was entered into a New York Drama League Competition, where it was directed by Hartwig and broadcast over the radio.[15] The competition took place on May 7, 1923, at Bayes Theatre on 44th Street, west of Broadway as part of "Little Theatre Tournament" competing for the David Belasco Trophy.[16] The Huguenot Players performed the play again along with three other one-acts at the New Rochelle High School on June 19 and 20.[17]

Ted enjoyed his first ever reviews. The *Evening Standard* gushed with the headline, "Hugeunot Players Shine Broadway in Fantastic Play." The *New York Sun* reviewer stated, less enthusiastically, "Timely." The mighty *New York Times* deigned to declare the play "Clever."[18] The *Daily Star* gave a portrait of the performance, describing the set as "weird—just a dark drapery curtain open in the middle, disclosing the entrance to a museum" while the "only light on the stage was a faint blue glow illuminating the entrance through which the actors appeared and disappeared" and the mummies wore "brown, stained wrappings."

Riding the wave of his Little Theater involvement, Ted wrote a number of other one-act plays in 1923. *Socrates* (Ted had a fascination with the ancient philosopher) was published in a magazine entitled *Poet Lore*. Another, *Inside Stuff*, was published in *Plays for Strolling Mummers*, edited by Frank Shay, owner of the Greenwich Village bookshop on Christopher Street famous for its door signed by great literary figures of the day. *Inside Stuff* saw multiple performances in small venues as did *Escape*, yet another one-act Ted wrote and published in Shay's *Fifty*

More Contemporary One Act Plays.[19] A few other one-acts Ted destroyed in dissatisfaction.

Also that year Ted developed a Columbia class project into an adaptation of Oscar Wilde's *The Picture of Dorian Gray.* Ted submitted the full-length play to producer Sam Harris, and it somehow made its way to Jeanne Eagles, a one-time Ziegfield girl now starring in the role of the prostitute Sadie Thompson in *Rain*, which was based on a Maugham story. According to Ted, Eagles invited him backstage after a performance of that hit play and told him she wanted to play the role of Dorian.[20] Although Eagles then leaked her desire to the gossip columns, Harris had no interest in producing the play. Ted claimed he then received a letter from a woman claiming to represent Russian director Vsevolod Meyerhold, who had made a now-lost film of Wilde's novella.[21] Ted sent her the script and never heard anything back. He later read that Meyerhold had indeed staged a dramatization, perhaps based on Ted's play.

Over the next five years, Ted wrote some fourteen more plays. *The Professor* was staged by the Huguenot Players on February 28, 1924, at Payson Assembly, Locust Avenue.[22] But none of the others were produced and many were destroyed, although he later developed material from at least one into a novel. After 1928, he gave up playwrighting altogether for a decade.

His lack of success as a playwright convinced Ted that surviving monetarily as a writer meant diversifying. Not only did he continued working for newspapers, now he attempted to get on the editorial staff at *Variety*.[23] Still under the leadership of Sime Silverman, who had founded it in 1905, the weekly covered Manhattan's theater scene. Ted had been working with the magazine as a correspondent for Broadway try-outs, but Silverman did not think the young man up to the job. Instead, he offered Ted work selling advertising on a commission basis.

While Ted appreciated the money to be made from selling advertising, he neither liked the job nor showed any promise at it. He found more congenial work as a "reader" for motion picture companies, making outlines of books to submit to companies for possible production. This work he did freelance with then-New York–based Paramount and Metro-Goldwyn-Meyer. Ted excelled at this job—"I could read fast, type fast, and write a synopsis fast."[24]

From these combined income streams, Ted made as much as seventy-five dollars a week, which he took straight to Guaranty Trust Company to exchange for French francs at a rate of four cents to the franc, which he then deposited.[25] He was saving to go to Europe. Originally, the plan had been for his uncle, Louis Pratt, to bankroll the trip. But his uncle suffered financial losses, so Ted's parents agreed to pay for the steamship passage if he could save up enough money to afford to live in Paris for a period of time.[26] Ted managed to save fifteen hundred dollars in francs by the fall of 1924, and Thomas and Emma bought the ticket.

A newspaper notice of his trip simply stated that he was going to Paris to study "French dramatic literature" at the Sorbonne, but there was considerably more involved.[27] In one sense, the trip was a no-brainer for a writer because Paris's Left Bank was in its Modernist heyday, with Gertrude Stein's Saturday night salon being a center for writers such as Hemingway and Fitzgerald. But Ted did not tend toward a Modernist sensibility. His conception of the city apparently derived instead from columns by Richard Le Gallienne for *The New York Evening Sun*.[28] These articles presented the city in all its glittering glory but not necessarily canted toward a Modernist sensibility.

Ted's greater motivation, however, lay in a desire to get away from his parents' strict religious observance. After a childhood of terrified obedience to Catholicism, by age nineteen he had lost his fear, become bored by the liturgy, and now distrusted the church's motives. He declared the Catholic church a "medieval dictatorship."[29] It did not help that he could not see the church condoning his desire to write about sex. Knowing his lack of faith would disappoint his parents, he had continued to go through the motions of faithful practice until now, aged twenty-three, he felt guilty about deceiving them. Leaving for Paris would, he believed, take him far from the constrictions of his life.

CHAPTER 4

Paris, Jackie
(1924–1929)

In November 1924, Ted embarked on old French *paquebot*, *La Savoie*, on what was to be the ship's final voyage.[1] Ted suffered through a storm, but the perilous journey proved less memorable than a life-changing encounter with a man Ted later referred to by the fictional name of Dan.

This fellow, a little older than Ted, was devoting his life to carnal pleasures.[2] Already twice divorced, Dan required a variety of women and believed sex to be better without romantic involvement. He told Ted he had slept with two hundred women and had set a goal of a thousand. He was returning to Paris because he believed that romantic city the best place to achieve that goal. His ultimate hope was to die "in the arms of a lovely girl" for whom he had made provision in his will, whoever she may be.

Needless to say, in Ted's eyes Dan soared as a heroic figure to be emulated. However much he may have rejected Catholic teachings, Ted's experience with lovemaking was practically nonexistent. Dan offered to initiate him into the world of French cocottes.

Upon arriving in Paris, Dan secured lodging for them in connected rooms at Hôtel Des Principautés Unies on Rue Servandoni. Here, Dan explained, D'Artagnan had lived in Alexandre Dumas's *The Three Musketeers*.[3] Situated on the Left Bank, the hotel put the young writer in the heart of bohemian Paris. Dan took him to the expatriate hangout Café-des-Deux-Magots for an *apéritif*.[4] It is tantalizing to imagine a young Ernest Hemingway in the corner of that café or some other one during Ted's stay. But there is no evidence that the two Midwesterners ever met in the city.

After a drink, Dan whisked his protégé off to see other sites. Soon, Ted found himself in Montmartre at a *bal musette* watching six entirely nude women sing onstage.[5] Later, Dan took Ted to a shop selling *articles d'hygiene* to equip him for his adventures. These Ted put to use in his first experience with a cocotte, whose name was Dédé. Afterwards, Ted imagined he could hear the sword of D'Artagnan clashing on Rue Servandoni in celebration of his initiation.[6]

An even more consequential encounter came in the form of a more expensive cocotte named Lucienne Monteaux, commonly referred to as Lulu. Whereas Dan set up Ted's meeting with Dédé, Lulu approached Ted in the lobby of Folies-Bergère during a performance intermission. Lulu was no mere girl of the streets. She was fabulously beautiful—Ted's ideal of the perfect woman—and she commanded the high price of twenty-five francs.[7] Ted talked her down to twenty, marveling that he should come to a point in life of such bargaining. When the time came for business to transpire, Ted realized he had forgotten to bring his hygienic equipment. Such was Lulu's beauty that he went through with it anyway, then worried to death that he would get a disease. None ever materialized.

Ted developed a different disease, though. He was in love. He convinced Lulu to write down her address, and he soon went unannounced to the rooming house where she lived. It took three days finally to catch her at home. At first, she did not remember him. When she did, she let him in and they talked about her life and the fact that she was actually one of the six women who sang at the *bal musette*. The idea made him jealous. She had him take her out for dinner and a show before returning for an encounter fully equipped this time but for no charge. They continued with several such evenings, with the exception that one night she took him to a large room fully lit where, unbeknownst to him, people watched their lovemaking through peepholes.[8]

Ted was of course destined for heartbreak, and his effort at having a lasting relationship with Lulu failed. Years later, he would think of Dédé and Lulu with tender nostalgia, wondering what had become of them. "Walking around Paris today and running into them," he reflected, "would I recognize them in perhaps that old crone who sold me a newspaper at the corner kiosk, or possibly the faded beauty with the still perfect profile waiting on customers at the zinc bar in the *bistro* on the *Place Blanche*?"[9] Ted's experiences with them affected the rest of his life, igniting a passion in him for the nuances of physical affection that flirted with coarseness but that was always colored by a perpetually adolescent excitement. He would forever believe that a more open approach to sex was healthy and important for society, an idea that would come to form a major component in his writing. It would not be inaccurate to call him an evangelist of sex education.

Eventually, Dan left Paris with a group of artists on a painting trip to Algiers, and Ted relocated to the Hotel de la Grille on Rue Jacob. After staying there for a time, Ted took a trip to Italy and Switzerland. Then, with funds running low, he returned to Paris and rented a tiny room on Rue Cardinale next to the church of St. Germain des Prés, the oldest in the city.[10] Despite having left Catholicism behind, he loved the sound of the church bells.

Maybe a lingering nostalgia for some of that religion's pag-
eantry was what led him also to attend Christmas mass at St.
Suplice. While he avoided so touristy a thing as ascending the
Eiffel Tower, he made sure to visit Oscar Wilde's grave as well
as Napoleon's. All the while, he spent hours in the Louvre and
other museums.[11]

What Ted conspicuously did *not* do was engage with the
Modernist scene. When his friend Dan returned to Paris after
several months, he tried to initiate Ted into a love for Modern
art. But Ted did not go for it, declaring abstract art to be "one of
the greatest frauds ever conceived."[12] He particularly disliked
Picasso, unsurprisingly for someone not enticed by the Stein
salons. It was a curious thing about Theodore Pratt that while
he embraced the sexual daring of bohemian life, he never pursued the artistic and philosophical movement that accompanied
and drove it. For that matter, he seems to have left his sexual
escapades behind in Paris.

Indeed, compared to the Modernists, Ted was a blue-collar
writer. He was a get-up-and-go-to-work-early everyday laborer
who happened to labor in words and stories. To that end, he
embraced the many dimensions of writing as a job instead of
pursuing writing as a quasi-religious high calling disdainful of
readers, sales, and critics. The idea of producing rarified literary
art for relatively few readers made no sense to him. Too much
of that practicality of his businessman father lingered in him for
that, however rebellious Ted may have been.

Ted's workmanlike approach should not be taken as a sign
of his being conventional. That he was not. His marked independence of mind, liberal views on sex, disgust with much of
popular culture (again, especially sports), and determination to
live a life not dominated by the time schedules and strictures
of corporate America all placed him squarely in the category

of artist. He simply did not become an artist in the Modernist mold. If anything, he may be seen as distinct for becoming a writer who embraced an aesthetic in opposition to Modernism. His heroes—Maugham, Lewis, and the like—wrote directly instead of experimentally. Ted would not hesitate to use allegory or other literary devices, but he loved a clean, simply presented, well-told story.

Still, when the sad time came to return to the United States after about a year in Paris, Ted had little to show for in support of his claim to Parisians that he was an *ecrivain*. Back in New York, he moved into a second-floor, one-room flat at 1 Minetta Lane in Greenwich Village.[13] There, he lived far enough away from his parents that he could hide his lapsed faithfulness to Catholicism.

He got back to work supporting himself and saving money to return to Paris. Employed by *Variety* again, he began writing a weekly section he called "Art Theater," covering the smaller theatrical productions in New York.[14] This job paid a lowly twenty dollars a week, so he went back to freelance reading for MGM, Paramount, and now Fox for an additional sixty dollars per week. Soon, he had an in-office job with Fox for eighty-five dollars a week. To all of this activity, he added a third job as a play reader for producer Winthrop Ames.

By September 1926, Ted took an office reader job, similar to the one at Fox, with the Pathe Motion Picture Company.[15] The company was originally launched in 1904 as a subsidiary of the French-based Pathé company, founded by brothers Charles, Émile, Théophile, and Jacques Pathé, who had acquired the Lumiere brothers' patents and further developed film technology. Although the American Pathe was at first located in Buffalo, by the time Ted started working for the company, its offices were at 35 West 45th Street in Manhattan. He worked through the company's being acquired by the Keith-Albee-Orpheum theater chain, but resigned in August 1927 before the company was acquired by Joseph P. Kennedy, father of the future president of the United States, John F. Kennedy.

During all this time working with motion pictures, Ted had two memorable experiences. One was *not* getting to meet W. Somerset Maugham during a film collaboration. The other was rejecting a screen treatment written by Eugene O'Neill, who later turned it into his play, *The Fountain*.[16]

Taxing as working three jobs could be, Ted still found time to write stories and articles. He began placing pieces with *The New York Times*, *The New York Sun*, *The Telegraph*, and *The World*.[17] It was likely during this time that Ted had the opportunity to interview vaudevillian Eddie Foy. The star lived in New Rochelle, and Ted wanted to write his biography. He approached an agent but discovered that another writer had beaten him to the punch.[18]

A more successful venture came in Ted's writing for the newly founded *New Yorker*. His articles received the painful carving-up of famously fastidious editor Harold Ross, who taught him "how to write a simple declarative sentence, the most difficult thing to do in the English language."[19] Ross was also a stickler for the facts and harassed Ted about his series on little-known details about New York, past and present. From the experience, Ted learned how to do solid research. He also made the acquaintance of E. B. White, Katherine Angell, and James Thurber.[20]

It was, in fact, a grand time to be a writer in New York. This was the era of Alexander Woollcott and Peter Arno. The Jazz Age was still roaring, even if Fitzgerald's *The Great Gatsby* had failed to sell well in 1925. Sinclair Lewis had followed his smash-hit *Main Street* with *Babbitt* (1922), *Arrowsmith* (1925), and now his tale of a con-artist preacher, *Elmer Gantry* in 1927. Neighbors of Ted's at Minetta Lane, DeWitt and Lila Wallace, were publishing *The Reader's Digest*, which they had started in 1922 as a conservative magazine that would later publish some of Ted's pieces.

During this prosperous moment, cash flowed for Ted. His income allowed him to move to a better apartment on Twelfth Street and then again on Horatio Street in Greenwich Village. And he could still save money to return to Paris.

Ted also found love. It came in the form of a young lady who worked as an assistant to a director in a theatrical casting office.[21] Rosabelle Mary Jacques was born on November 4, 1902, in Sturbridge, Massachusetts.[22] Her parents, Joseph and Marie, were both from Quebec. By 1910, the family was living in Sterling, Massachusetts, where Joseph worked out of his home as a shoemaker.[23] Marie died the next year. Rosabelle was one of sixteen children, six of whom died in childhood.

She went by the name "Jackie." A photograph of her taken around the time she met Ted features a young woman with haunting, penetrating dark eyes that might hold a secret. Her dark hair falls in ringlets to daringly bared shoulders. Her lips are parted a little, as though she has just laughed at something and the last shadow of a smile remains. She exudes an earthy appeal rather than a glamorous one, and she had a no-nonsense personality to go with her appearance. She had the kind of strength Ted found attractive.

Ted and Jackie met on a blind date, perhaps set up by mutual friends in their line of work.[24] Their courtship is preserved in a series of his letters to her. The earliest is dated June 9, 1927, on blue DeMille-Pathe Story Department letterhead sent to her at "The Cottage," Eltingville, Staten Island.[25] Already through the summer he was calling her "Dearest Jackie," inviting her to plays, and worrying over having to go a full week without seeing her. Her French-Canadian background surely appealed to him as a Francophile, and he occasionally inserted French into his letter. Before long, he was calling her his little peanut and himself her pumpernickel.

By spring of 1928, however, a crisis arose between them. In a letter dated May 10, Ted wrote of his sadness at watching her leave on a train and having to accept that he "couldn't very well spend my time trying to be a God damn writer and have you, too."[26] It was a note that would sound many more times to come—that writing took priority over her. Jackie went all way to Hollywood, perhaps working for a motion picture company.

On June 1, Ted wrote trying to get her back.[27] Addressing her as "Buttercup," he told her how much he missed her and ventured, "When I look back and think how sweetly we got on for the most part I wonder if we didn't make a mistake separating as we did. What do you think?" His missing her continued when he went to Farmington, Maine, with a stock group. On September 1, he sent her a telegram telling her he realized how "terribly much I love you and feel we are too closely bound together to give each other up things will be as you say when you return don't want to make things hard for you but for your happiness advise let love and affection rule the day."[28]

In the end, love and affection did rule the day. Jackie made her way back East, the relationship repaired despite her concerns about writing interfering. Ted had managed to save over three thousand dollars to return to Europe, and the couple planned to marry and enjoy an extended honeymoon there.[29]

Ted was meanwhile turning his attention to writing novels. Always interested in transformation, he had written a novel entitled *Soft Marble*, about statues coming to life in the vein of *Revolt of the Mummies*.[30] He started shopping the manuscript. A reader at Simon & Schuster liked it but could not convince the press to publish it. Other presses turned it down too. On the way to one of the publishers to retrieve his manuscript, a bizarre episode took place.

Walking on Fifth Avenue, Ted encountered an old school-mate who told Ted he was flush with inheritance money and had purchased an estate in Virginia. The man had become a master of hounds, keeping his own pack and nearly thirty horses. He was carrying books signed by famous riders, and he took Ted to Spaulding Sporting Goods Store, where he ordered riding clothes and equipment. He also showed Ted a copy of the hunting yearbook with his name and estate listed.

Ted invited his old schoolmate along to the editor's office. When they arrived, the schoolmate and the editor both started talking about foxhunting. The two men forgot all about Ted and his manuscript until the schoolmate offered to underwrite Ted's book. The editor explained that his press did not allow such funding, but he called a vanity publisher to set up publication at a thousand dollars' cost. Having arranged that, the schoolmate offered the ecstatic Ted his estate for the upcoming honeymoon before they parted company.

Not long after, as Ted awaited confirmation of his novel's publication, the editor called Ted to his office and informed him that the schoolmate was a complete fraud. The man had no estate, no hounds, no horses, and had likely never ridden a day in his life. He had submitted his name and estate along with the fee to be included in the yearbook and signed the other books himself. The equipment and costume order had been cancelled. Worst of all for Ted, *Soft Marble* would not be published. In fact, it would never make it into print. Ted determined right then that he would never rely on anyone other than himself again. Certainly, he would never pay to be published.

Ted and Jackie married on October 26, 1929. The ceremony took place at the New York City Municipal Building.[31] The newlyweds interviewed with a priest to be married in a Catholic church, but the priest doubted their faith. As a matter of fact, both Ted and Jackie wanted to end any pretense of interest in religion. Still, they told their parents they had been married in a church. Ted's parents seemed unconvinced by the story, but they gave their blessing and five hundred dollars as a wedding gift.

The couple set sail for Naples two days later on an Italian liner named the *Vulcania*.[32] The next day the stock market crashed. Ted, who had left two thousand dollars in the bank in New Rochelle, read the *Variety* headline "Wall St. Lays an Egg." But the newlyweds had their faces turned toward sunny Italy, full of excitement and leaving all problems and encumbrances far behind.

CHAPTER 5

Majorca
(1929–1933)

As the *Vulcania* sliced through the Atlantic's blue waves en route to Naples, Ted and Jackie Pratt found themselves competing in an informal international shuffleboard tournament.[1] It took some convincing to get the deck steward to allow a woman to play, but Jackie and Ted won their way to the championship game against a pair of Italians. The contest was held on October 28, the anniversary of Benito Mussolini's march on Rome, and it became a stand-off between representatives not only of two countries but two opposing political systems. The Italians' buttonhole pins of fasces signaled their national and political pride at stake. The Italian ship actually slowed its pace to lessen the rocking as an aid to the Italian team. The game came down to a final shot that Ted could easily make and win. But he feared doing so might literally precipitate an international incident, so he sent the shot wide, giving the Italians victory.

The moment presaged what was to come for the Pratts in Europe.

But for now, the newlyweds plunged into life in France, settling in Cagnes-sur-Mer. Situated on the country's southeastern coast, Cagnes-sur-Mer sat atop a hill overlooking the Mediter-ranean. Le château Grimaldi, a blocky medieval castle, stood on the town's highest point, and cobblestone streets threaded through the congregation of lovely tile-roofed houses. The very road upon which Hannibal drove elephants over the Alps in antiquity still wound past the village toward the snow-capped peaks beyond.

Ted and Jackie moved into their home, which bore the name *Le Perchoir, Planastel,* "The Nest in the Open Places."[2] The pink, two-storied house boasted one of only two bathtubs in town. The Pratts' monthly rent was twenty dollars. Ted drew on their saved funds and got paid to write a story a month for *The New Yorker* and travel articles for *The New York Evening Sun* as well as some European magazines.[3] Like Hemingway and the protago-nist of his 1926 novel *The Sun Also Rises,* Ted was working as a foreign correspondent. Certainly by now, Ted had his eye on his Midwestern contemporary.

Cagnes-sur-Mer had a distinct history of fostering creatives. August Renoir lived the final twelve years of his life there, and Ted actually met the Impressionist painter's still-living favorite model.[4] Modigliani spent some time in the town as well. Most recently, Harry and Caresse Crosby, two of the most notorious carousers of the 1920s and the founders of Black Sun Press, had resided in the town. Now Ted and Jackie joined the current crop of artists and writers, most of them Americans. Their initiation into the expatriate colony was marked by a drunken food fight.[5]

Indeed, where Ted missed out on the bohemian scene in Paris, he now got it in spades in Cagnes-sur-Mer. The par-ties were endless, and not a little obnoxious. There were lewd dances, roaring music, and lengthy discussions of art and litera-ture that could grow vicious. If townspeople dared to complain, they were apt to be greeted with disdain, one party-going Amer-ican responding to a shopkeeper with a display of his genitals and a long piss. When the percussive composer George Antheil moved into a house next door to Ted and Jackie, some people asked him if he was concerned about the noise. Antheil replied that he doubted Ted's typewriter would be a problem for him.[6]

Unsure as he was about some of the more extreme behavior, Ted enjoyed the scene well enough. He and Jackie grew fond of Lincoln Gillespie, a writer who regarded himself as James Joyce's equal and who was given to verbose rhapsodies of extemporaneous prose.[7] The famous actress, socialite, and collector of millionaires Peggy Hopkins Joyce showed up one night.[8] On another evening, the normally outrageous crowd sat in tender vigil for D. H. Lawrence, who lay ill in nearby Vence. Ted would always remember the lights flickering and then a phone call coming to announce the great writer's death.[9]

While the artist and writer crowd provided great stories and characters for Ted, their view of success did not match his own. These writers talked constantly about novels they never actually wrote. If writers' works did get finished and published, they usually appeared in little magazines that sprang up for a brief time and did not pay. When Ted got pieces published in paying magazines with large circulations, the others shamed him for his commercialism.

Still, when a call from the heights of literary greatness came, Ted responded. On one of Ted and Jackie's trips to Paris, they met a friend of Ford Madox Ford who agreed to show him some of Ted's writing.[10] The Modernist was impressed and initiated a brief correspondence with Ted that culminated in an invitation for the couple to visit Ford's farm in Toulon. Upon arriving, the Pratts mistook Ford for the gardener and were taken aback when he asked them for money. Ted enjoyed the older writer's cooking and useful writerly advice. But he felt dismayed when he discovered that Ford had lost several pages of Ted's manuscript. A search revealed them to have been dropped behind the couch.

From the visit, Ted developed a story entitled "Visit with the Master," which was published in the October 1932 issue of *Story*. The "Master," an older writer named Alfred Pillsbury, is dirtier than even the apparently "dirty" Ford, both in hygiene and in his keeping a young lady who is likely a prostitute. Pillsbury tells Ted's alter-ego, George Pendleton, frankly that his novel is bad. When the younger writer discovers that Pillsbury has used some of the lost pages of his manuscript for toilet paper, Pendleton throws his novel into the sea, apparently never to write again.

The story is important in Ted's career and life. It is tempting to read its conclusion as Ted fictionally abrogating "literary writing" forever, but that is probably a little too academic and easy since he never actually embraced Modernism anyway. More poignant in the larger arch of his life was the fact that he should in a sense confer a part of himself into the ocean, a fitting and prophetic gesture. He would always regard the story as among his very best. It was reprinted in *The Best Short Stories, 1933*, edited by Edward O'Brien.

Years later, Ted remembered Ford glowingly and criticized writers who abused Ford's generosity. Ted particularly took his text on Hemingway's harsh treatment of Ford in *A Moveable Feast*.[11] But Ted's own story reads unkindly, and he rightly felt abashed when Whit Burnett outed the model for Pillsbury upon reprinting the piece in *A Story Anthology* in 1933. By the time Ted wrote his own autobiographical guide for younger writers late in life, he claimed that Ford had inspired him to offer advice, guidance, and nurture.

By the end of two years in Cagnes-sur-Mer, the Pratts were ready to move on. The parties had grown tiresome. It would be nice to go home, but Ted and Jackie were hearing horror stories about the Depression in the United States. Ted's father moved their money out of one bank into another for fear of the first one failing: it did. Easier to stay in Europe where they could live cheap, although it apparently meant missing Ted's sister, Isabel, marrying Louis Walter Dempsey on April 16, 1931, in St. Gabriel Roman Catholic Church in New Rochelle.[12]

Seeking a fresh start in a new European place, Ted and Jackie decided on the Spanish island of Majorca. Typically spelled Mallorca today, this Balearic Island rising out of the Mediterranean is a posh tourist spot. In Ted and Jackie's time, it was only beginning to take on a touristic flavor, but it had already harbored some heavy-hitting creatives. The writer Robert Graves was living in the village of Deià with his mistress, already at work on his powerful fictional biography, *I, Claudius*. When Graves asked Gertrude Stein her thoughts about living there, she replied, based on her experience, "It's a paradise—if you can stand it." Almost a hundred years earlier, Frédéric Chopin and George Sand lived together in the western village of Valldemossa. The couple at first loved the Mediterranean climate and atmosphere of the island, but when winter set in they were miserable. Chopin composed his moody "Raindrop Prelude" there, and Sand wrote a travel memoir critical of the Majorcans as crude, unintelligent, and inept in agriculture.[13] That bright-dark, love-hate response was about to repeat for Ted and Jackie.

The Pratts' timing for this move portended trouble from the beginning. In April, the Spanish King Alfonso XIII was deposed, bringing an end to centuries of Spanish monarchical rule and setting up a Republic for which the country was ill prepared. When securing their Spanish visa in Nice, Ted and Jackie asked if there was much threat of unrest and revolution and were assured there would not be. The Spanish Revolution began five years later, bringing Hemingway to the country and inspiring his epic *For Whom the Bell Tolls*.

Still, Majorca impressed at first. Arriving in Palma, the Pratts saw the gothic Cathedral of Santa Maria Palma, generally referred to as La Seu. Equally impressive stood the magnificent Royal Palace of La Almudaina, an Alcázar that featured a mash-up of Romanesque arches, crenelated walls, and Moorish towers. This home of monarchs likely offered Ted's first glimpse of a style of architecture that later played an important role in his life and career.

Ted and Jackie took a train northward out of Palma, grateful for a heated canister for their feet in the lingering cold of spring.[14] Halfway into the trip, they transferred to a *diligence* for their destination, Puerto de Pollensa. This northerly port sits on the Bay of Pollensa, a circle of blue water hugged by mountainous arms. Puerto had already harbored its own share of artists, including Atilio Boveri and Hermenegildo Anglada Camarasa. In less than a year from the Pratts' arrival, Agatha Christie would visit and, after returning a few years later, would be inspired to write "Problem at Pollensa Bay."[15]

The Pratts moved into a stone farm cottage with a walled garden for ten dollars a month.[16] Water must be drawn from the well, and charcoal provided the fuel for cooking. Ted liked the arrangement just fine—a romantic place close to the water at a price just right for a writer. Although he and Jackie had studied Spanish, here they encountered Mallorqui, which has been described as "the local Catalan dialect, which sounds like a mishmash of Spanish, Portuguese, and eating marbles."[17] They gained a strong enough grasp of the language to get by, and soon Ted had a nickname among the natives: "El Sandalio," the Sandaled One. He used the nickname when he started writing for *The Palma Post*, one of the English-language newspapers in Palma.

Puerto's expatriate community included Americans, British, and Germans. Most of the Americans came in search of cheap living and a way out of the Depression. Many opened bars, although one bred dachshunds (the Pratts bought a puppy and named her Diana Murphy, "Dinnie" for short).[18] Jackie herself proved resourceful in this community, roasting, packaging, and selling the island's almonds.[19] It was one of a number of industries she would undertake to make ends meet during the first two decades of their married life; Ted would always be grateful for her ability to generate income. The German population included a particularly obnoxious Nazi, but also a surgeon who had fled Germany because he had a Jewish mistress.[20] When the surgeon nursed Ted through a case of hepatitis, he quipped that Adolf Hitler had inadvertently saved his life. Ted later reworked the sentiment into one of his most famous books.

As for books, Ted went to work on his second one, a novel about the Great Depression. He wanted to capture the terrifying encroachment of poverty as conveyed in the stories he was hearing from home. The narrative he fashioned amounted to a take on Paul Gauguin, who in the wake of an 1882 stock market crash in France left his wife and children to dedicate himself to painting. Ted emulated Maugham's Gauguin-inspired *The Moon and Sixpence* while also drawing on his own experiences interviewing artists and illustrators in and around New Rochelle, including Norman Rockwell.

Set in fictional Denison, Connecticut, the novel follows the fall and rise of protagonist Charlie Day. The story begins with Charlie's employer, Phoenix Bank, closing. Charlie's wealthy in-laws offer to work out a new position for him, but their stiflingly conventional ways rankle with him and his secret desire to be an artist. When Charlie's ex-coworker commits suicide, leaving Charlie a note with twenty five dollars plus interest to pay back a loan, he resolves to pursue a life in art. He goes to New Haven, Connecticut, then to New York City, Schenectady, and Utica, where for the first time he gets paid for his drawings. Even as his wife begs him to come home, Charlie accepts a female artist's invitation to go to Woodport, New York, to live in an art colony. There Charlie works in a barn studio conspicuously like Rockwell's in New Rochelle, and Charlie displays more talent as an illustrator than a studio artist. But when offered a large sum for his illustrations, Charlie refuses, determined instead to be a serious artist. He returns home dedicated to success in the field of art.

Ted titled the novel *Spring from Downward*. He likely had it in the hands of the New York–based agent Virginia Rice in 1932, maybe about the time his first niece, Isabel Therese Dempsey, was born on January 15. Rice eventually got the manuscript to a London agent who placed it at 15 percent commission with the British publisher Selwyn and Blount.[21] Ted signed the contract in July 1933, with a publication date in the fall. Its happy ending, signaled from the beginning in the name "Phoenix," Ted surely meant to be a balm in the midst of the Depression. But no American publisher could imagine people reading about the misery they were living, happy ending notwithstanding.

In his moment of publishing triumph, Ted's life crashed. The controversial and outspoken journalist H. L. Mencken, whom Ted had discovered in college, commissioned him to write an article as part of a series of hit-jobs for his magazine *American Mercury*. In the tradition of Sand, Ted criticized Majorcans for their cruelty to animals, their general crudeness, and their gleeful embrace of American consumerism that, as he saw it, only wrecked their own culture and brought devastating price-gouging. Entitled "Paradise Enjoys a Boom," the article appeared in the July 1933 issue and hit the right note of Menckenian irony, for the economic "boom" of paradise actually brought a bust on a human level.

Unfortunately for Ted, the editor of a Majorcan paper, *La Ultima Hora*, translated the worst parts of the article into Spanish and denounced El Sandalio as an ingrate and traitor. Ted and Jackie were surprised when a policeman came to the house requesting their joint passport for examination. Immediately after the policeman left with the passport, a Spanish friend came to the house with a copy of *La Ultima Hora* warning Ted and Jackie to lock the windows and doors against the possibility of a demonstration that night.

By ten o'clock, a crowd of around three hundred had gathered outside. Ted remembered the sound of their murmuring resembling that of lynch mobs in westerns.[22] An explosion sounded from either a small bomb or a stick of dynamite in the front yard. Ted believed the house itself would have been destroyed had not a Majorcan owned it. Two Guardias Civils prevented the mob from breaking in and harming the Pratts.

The next morning, the policeman from the day before escorted Ted and Jackie to Palma. People lined the streets as they rode out of town. The Pratts spent the first night in a downtown hotel, but the next day they were thrown out. An American artist named Clair Van Scoy took them in at the behest of Ted's lawyer friend, George London, who went to work straightening out the mess.[23] London discovered that the American consul was already in Palma dealing with a case of American arrests he saw as resulting from American misbehavior. Worse yet, *The Palma Post* had been criticizing the consul, and he took his frustration out on Ted by refusing to help.

With the consul failing to offer aid, London told Ted to give him all his money so he could make a deal with the government. Ted gave him the five hundred dollars he had in Majorca, keeping secret the one thousand dollars still in the states. Half the money went to legal fees, half to bribes. London obtained a deal with the government that Ted apologize for his article, say the things he wrote were not true, and promise not to write about Majorca again in the future.[24] Ted refused to declare his comments to be untrue, so London went back to the governor and returned with a new offer that if Ted explained that he had not intended to offend Majorcans Jackie could have the joint passport returned. That would obviously allow them both to go back to the United States. Ted accepted this offer but maintained that the translation had misrepresented his article.[25]

As soon as Jackie recovered the passport, she and Ted bought passage on the American Export Lines ship *Exchorda*. In confirmation of one of Ted's criticism of Majorcans, an official informed them that they could not take their dog Dinnie under the pretext that she had no ticket. As the ship was pulling away from the harbor, the official called out that he would have Dinnie's eyes put out.[26] Although the horrified Pratts later learned that the Majorcans did not carry out that threatened cruelty, they never saw their dog again.

CHAPTER 6
Florida
(1933–1935)

Ted and Jackie returned to the United States as the famous figures of an international incident. News first reached the United States with articles in the *Herald Tribune* on July 18, followed by press releases in Savannah, Fort Worth, Newark, Baltimore, Omaha, and Memphis, to name just a few.[1] Within days they were front-page news across the county. Now, when the *Exchorda* arrived in Boston, the press scrambled to interview the couple. But even that went wrong because Ted could not provide them with alcohol here in the midst of Prohibition and in all the excitement had not thought to bring liquor from Europe. Without that expected gift, the press turned on the Pratts, crafting headlines suggesting Ted had committed a crime and been duly punished.

Newspaper photographs of the returned couple presented Ted in trim form, his pencil-thin moustache and dark hair giving him a Latin look. His pocket square jutted like a row of teeth from his breast pocket. Jackie appeared in the photos in a white dress, shoes, and hat, her eyes unsurprisingly showed signs of wear, her hands on her hips almost in defiance.[2]

Ted and Jackie stayed for a time in a garage apartment near Ted's parents and Isabel and Walter, who were expecting their second child, Rita Ann (born on November 30, 1933).[3] This apartment was the best the couple could afford, as was the case with so many people at the time. Although they were on good terms with the family, Ted and Jackie no longer attended mass. Ted knew his decision grieved his parents, but they said nothing. After their deaths, he described them as being "nice, pleasant, gentle people, what the French call *gentil*."[4] He also wrote that they and his sister "gave me something priceless: They let me be."[5]

Living with low rent, Ted and Jackie got on well enough. Money did not come steadily, but Ted managed to sell some pieces for five hundred dollars to slick magazines that could not afford the two thousand dollars their normal contributors demanded. In a time when five dollars could cover groceries for a week, those checks went a long way.

Meanwhile, Ted started writing a new novel. Fresh off his international incident, he set this story on a Spanish island he called Saracen. It concerns a young American named Philip Stout, who seeks financial support from his expatriate family so he can realize his dream of becoming a film producer. He also happens to be in love with a young actress named Nancy Stewart, who has come to Puerto for a stay as well but cannot marry because of a clause in her contract. Philip and Nancy fall in with American expatriates, who correspond closely to the real-life Cagnes-sur-Mer set. One of that group is Ernest Fisher, whom the island natives have dubbed El Borrachón, The Drunkard.

It turns out that Fisher is Nancy's father, a source of grief and embarrassment to her, especially when he opposes her marrying Philip. Like his creator, Fisher writes a scathing article about the natives of Saracen, parts of which get translated into Spanish and disseminated, bringing down the wrath of the people. Meanwhile, Philip's adventurer Uncle Ben, presumed dead, reappears on the island. Thrilled to see and support his nephew's career goals, he razzes his siblings and their pieties. The family worries that Uncle Ben puts Philip in his will, but when Uncle Ben dies, Philip reveals that he had no money to leave behind. However disappointed Philip's career may be, he still has Nancy, and they will marry and name their first child Ben.

Ted entitled the book *Not Without the Wedding* in reference to the disapproval Philip's family shows for his extramarital relations with Nancy. He placed the book, apparently again through Virginia Rice, with Selwyn and Blount for an early 1934 publication date, presumably under the same conditions as his first novel.

As for that first novel, *Spring from Downward* was published by Blunt and Selwyn in October 1933. His royalty check from the sales amounted to $106. Ted reckoned the daily income of the year's worth of writing the book to come to thirty-three cents per day and four cents per hour.[6] Proud as he was of having his first novel published, the economics of it more than gave him pause.

The novel received a review in the *Times Literary Supplement* that appeared on the same page with a review of Erskine Caldwell's *Tobacco Road*.[7] "This first novel shows some uncertainty in its handling of emotional situations," the anonymous reviewer wrote, "but it is interesting and promising for a soberly drawn picture of the depression in America." In the United States, the Ossining, New York, *Citizen-Register* announced, "English Hail New Book by Theodore Pratt."[8] According to the reviewer, "the English are hailing the book as an American parallel to the famous German novel, 'Little Man What Now?'" Ted seems to have advised the reviewer, for the review shows acquaintance with him, even advertising his story, "A Visit with the Master." It ends with an especially intimate bit of information, and a fateful one: "Mr. Pratt and his wife, who have been visiting his parents in New Rochelle, expect to leave shortly for Florida, where they will spend the Winter."

Ted's family had gone to Florida in past winters without him.[9] His Uncle Eugene and Aunt Louisa were living in Broward County, but it is not altogether clear that they were a draw. It takes little imagination to envision someone in New Rochelle in the brown dead of winter in the middle of the Great Depression seeking a change of scenery. Ted's own explanation for the decision to go to Florida succinctly combined vocation and lifestyle: "In 1934 we decided to adopt the only advantage an author has, which is carrying his office in his head and being able to live anywhere he wants, and go to Florida. It turned out to be the best thing we ever did."[10]

The couple made the trip in their Ford Model A in a golden time for travel in America.[11] A year later, Ted wrote up a list of the sites and stops along the way that captures the experience of taking to the road in that era.[12] "Fifty miles to Grean Leaf Tourist Camp," Ted began, citing a now long-vanished roadside attraction. Here, the amenities included Yum-Yum Coffee and Doc's Log Cabins along with signs announcing "Ye Oldish House" and "Cow Crossing" and the slogans "You Will Like Our Home Cooking" and "Justa Tourist Camp." During your stay, you could see George Washington and a Minute Man. Pets cost twenty-five cents; Ted and Jackie had now acquired a new puppy they named Timothy Brace.

Entering Virginia, the menus offered corn cakes, barbecue, and ham. Places to stop included such nostalgic-sounding places as Home Comfort Inn, Tourist Town, Little Log Cabin in the Lane, and Tight-Wad Inn, although the reality of segregation arose in the announcement that they sectioned off certain rooms for "Colored Tourists." Signs along the way announced mules for sale and that you should drive slowly because three were killed here. At "White Oak Quail Farm, Visitors See Birds by Appointment." A plaque somewhere mourned, "Beneath This Stone Lies Elmer Gush, Tickled to Death by His Shaving-Brush."

Traveling further southward on Highway 1, their luggage stowed in the rumble seat, Ted and Jackie entered North Carolina with more promise of barbecue and a billboard asking, "Where Will You Be in Eternity?" They may have stayed at Pee-Dee Camp, which "Our Guests Say the Best from Maine to Maine" rather than the "White Only" Wise Tourist Camp. They were surely glad to take advantage of "Pat's Hot and Cold Showers, the Best in Dixie." The state marked a midway point where they would more than linger—they would spend enough time in North Carolina in the future to be seen as seasonal locals.

"Hello, Buddy, Welcome to South Carolina," greeted the Palmetto State. Here the politics sharpened. "No New Deal but a Square Deal" sang out one slogan, while a coal establishment proclaimed, "We Are in a Black Business but We Treat You White." The couple might have stopped to try and buy one of the "Cutest Log Cabins on the Coast," making Ted the Literary Laureate of South Carolina instead of Florida. But they pressed on through Waterboro, which guaranteed the "Hospitality of the Old South with the Advantages of the New."

The Pratts had entered the full-blown Deep South. They crossed the state line into Georgia. Soon they were six miles from Palmetto Camp where they could "Stop and See the Snakes." Another mile could take them to "Pecans, See Them Growing." A jingle jingled,

> *He Had the Ring*
> *He Had the Flat*
> *She Felt His Chin*
> *And That Was That*

Hams could be obtained pit-cooked and eaten to the sound of a radio in every cabin at one place. Somewhere Ted and Jackie saw a sign announcing, "Jesus Said Ye Must be Born Again" and elsewhere, "Please Do Not Shoot the Ducks."

Finally, "Welcome to Florida." At the state line they could stop and send a box of Indian River fruit home if they chose. The places to stay here included King Edward Tourist Court, Cane Juice Inn, Duck Inn, C'Mon Inn, and Nestle Inn. The couple was told when they could get their "First View of the Tropics" and, soon enough, "Hot Fishing and Cold Beer" and "Welcome to Our Ocean."

When Ted pulled into West Palm Beach, he knew they had arrived in a very different place from anything he had known before. He may have dallied with cocottes in Paris, but when he parked on Clematis Street in downtown West Palm and sat waiting in the car while Jackie went into a store, a prostitute gave him her card and invited him to her "tearoom."[13] He claimed he never visited, but the incident spoke to one of Ted's biggest passions. Here in this languid subtropical seaside town where voluptuousness made itself forward, this quiet man found himself in-between the vast ocean to the east and the vast jungle with its own waterways to the west. Florida took his love of water, naughtiness, and exploration and made it all bigger, rawer, and more vivid.

As he himself put it, he could have a "turbulent love affair" with this place. "There she goes," he wrote of Florida, "right off from the rest of the country, sailing on her independent own for more than five hundred miles into the blue-green waters of the West Indies, almost as if she wanted to get away from the United States, perennially seceding."[14] In one of the biggest compliments he could give, he explained, "She is one of the few places that lives up to her color photographs" but also asserted "that Florida is different and colorful enough for the truth to be told about her rather than lies which only disappoint people when they see the real thing."[15]

The West Palm Beach Ted and Jackie arrived in still lingered in the real estate bust in the midst of the Depression. The population numbered over twenty-six thousand, many of whom lived in Spanish bungalows on gridded streets stretching north and south of downtown. The town played second fiddle to illustrious Palm Beach, which lay across the Intracoastal Waterway as the winter homeplace of the ultra-wealthy. That island then and now can create a drive in people, a desire to find a way across the bridges into the upper echelon of wealth and society. The contrast between the two places and between places and populations in South Florida generally struck Ted. He later wrote that the "first day he set foot in the state it impressed him as a writer's paradise. On the coasts he saw a suburb of the north trying to be civilized and modern; within spitting distance of the coast there was a fine, wild, lusty, virgin territory into which practically no one had poked his nose."[16]

The Pratts did not make West Palm their home, however. Instead, they rented a place just south in Lake Worth at 1428 North Lakeside Drive, close to the Intracoastal.[17] In the present day, Lake Worth maintains an artsy atmosphere that mixes well with a quasi-Caribbean feel. Its north-south running streets between Federal Highway and Interstate 95 are marked only by letters, its east-west ones by numbers. The town had what is now thought of as an aura of "Old Florida," and in 1934 it surely felt less northern suburban-y than did West Palm.

Whatever rent Ted and Jackie paid, they also finagled a way for Ted to find a writing room in town. Despite her qualms with his vocation, Jackie supported Ted's writing. She readily offered feedback on his work, which he sometimes found harsh. But she could not stand the incessant pecking of the typewriter. Their fights over that maddening sound throughout the day soared into the stratosphere of viciousness. Finding a room to write in spared them the stresses of awful shouting matches and allowed him to focus on his writing. Ted almost certainly found such a room gratis since the Depression and the low income of a writing career required extreme thriftiness—at which, incidentally, Jackie excelled.

Ted's first book written in a Florida writing room had nothing to do with Florida. Instead, he wrote a novel totally new and different from what he had done before but that drew on a topic much on his mind: abnormal sexual appetite as a psychological disorder. This novel marked a massive step forward for Ted. While there was complexity to the protagonist of *Spring from Downward*, the first two novels showed a disappointing lack of roundness in the characters. The new book showed serious writing about a very taboo subject.

That content went a step too far for publishers. Virginia Rice could not find a taker for the manuscript, which was entitled "The Tormented." Over the course of the next fifteen years of intermittent submission, thirty-three publishers rejected it.[18] It would prove to be one of Ted's most discouraging runs with a project, and many times he would grow so hopeless about it as to quite shopping it out altogether. Thankfully, however, he now had a big new subject to write about.

CHAPTER 7

Timothy Brace, Florida Crime Writer (1935)

T ed took up learning about Florida with the same passion he had for learning as a child at New York's Museum of Natural History. As he put it, he was "absorbing" the state, deepening his knowledge to accompany his "immediate affinity for the flora and fauna."[1] He observed the varieties of palm trees, the clumping walls of sea grapes, the Spanish moss hanging gray and listless from live oak limbs. He learned the shades of blue and green peculiar to South Florida 's section of the Atlantic along with the fish that swam there and current techniques for catching them.

The newcomer to South Florida also learned about the area's heat and humidity, which became so torturous in June he could not work.[2] He and Jackie headed back north to New Rochelle for the summer. But the Florida sand and sea had entered his bloodstream. The couple returned in autumn, Ted with a new writing project.

This new book was a mystery novel. At its center stood an amateur detective and big game fishing enthusiast named

Anthony Adams, who lived on a yacht named *Fisherman*. Ted seems to have been inspired by Nick Charles, the sleuth of Dashiell Hammett's *The Thin Man*, published in 1934. Instead of a wise-cracking wife, Nora, Ted pairs Adams with a somewhat nervous and colorless manservant named Thurber who more closely resembled Sherlock Holmes's Doctor Watson.

For any reader of Florida crime fiction, elements of Ted's mystery scenario look familiar. John D. MacDonald's Travis McGee, developed three decades later, would be a semi-professional sleuth living on a boat called the *Busted Flush*. James W. Hall's character Thorn does not live on a boat, but he does live in a shack in Key Largo where he ties flies for fishing guides until disaster strikes and he solves and avenges the crime in an amateur role. Randy Wayne White's Doc Ford is a marine biologist and retired National Security Agency agent living on Florida's west coast. With his first novel in a series of four predating Brett Halliday's (née Davis Dresser) first Mike Shayne novel by three years, it may well be that Ted invented Florida's distinct version of crime novel, which might aptly be called "Florida Noir."

Drawing on his own interest in fish and fishing, Ted entitled the first novel *Murder Goes Fishing*. For it, he devised a particularly diabolical mode of murder. Lonzo Cayberry, the richest Palm Beacher, is found strangled on the Palm Beach fishing pier on a morning when an extraordinary number of people who know him and/or stand to gain from his death are also present. Police Chief Ernest Chase summons Adams from his yacht, and the dilettante sleuth discovers an unusual cut in the victim's neck and bulging eyes that suggest a poisoned sharp instrument. It is not until one of the suspects is killed in the same way, but to a more gruesome degree—with the throat literally sliced open—that Adams realizes the murder technique. The murderer fashioned a noose of fishing line and slipped it over the sleeping first victim and the drunk second one. Then the murderer baited a hook attached to the opposite end of the line. When fish took the bait and ran, the nooses tightened and strangled the victims. The greater violence of the second murder resulted from a barracuda biting the bait and tugging much more viciously than the kingfish that took the first one.

For the novel's denouement, Adams brings all the suspects to Bimini in his yacht, getting them in a room together Nick Charles–style in order to solve the case. He cinches the case by identifying who wrote the last of a series of notes sent to Adams throughout the book. These quotes came from William Shakespeare and Thomas Gray and presented themes of fish feeding on humans. Adams had planted slightly different colored paper in each stateroom in order to identify the perpetrator. When the murderer finally realizes the game is up, he dashes out to the yacht's rail where sharks have been circling, declares they are his friends, and throws himself to them to be eaten.

At first glance, the murderer's motive might seem a poor pay-off for reading the entire novel. Instead of the motive being malice specifically against the victims, it is a general malice resulting from the character's psychosis at having tragically lost his wife and child, resulting in a persecution complex that transferred to sympathy for fish. This psychological complex developed into an irrational anger at anglers and a desire to have them feel what it is like to be a hooked fish. Thus, the fish catches and kills the angler by depriving him of oxygen just as the fish is deprived of its life-giving water.

Taken in the context of later developments in Ted's career, the motive and the novel's ending are striking. Here is a story of identification with fish, a desire for revenge, doubt about humanity's superiority to fish, and ultimately a desire to join fish and even to imagine oneself as being one living out a life underwater. Such an affinity for water had characterized Ted's life and always would. These ideas would come together again in a lighter-hearted novel to bring Ted his arguably greatest success and longest legacy.

Already, here in his very first Florida novel, Ted showed his ability to capture the atmosphere of the southeastern part of the state. He discusses some of the more technical aspects of fishing, including the Florida technique of attaching kites to outriggers. He rightly identifies a densely foggy night as a rarity in South Florida and exploits its mysterious vagaries with skill and effectiveness. And he describes catching a five-hundred-pound marlin with splendidly tactile detail and motion. In his growing fondness for a certain Florida writer, Ted even has Adams explain during a fishing outing, "I agree with Ernest Hemingway . . . that the popular idea of sails tapping the bait to kill or stun it and then coming back to take it, is nonsense."[3] It would not be the last time Ted would mention his fellow Midwesterner-Floridian in a novel.

Murder Goes Fishing began a run of four crime novels written under the pseudonym Timothy Brace (the name of their new dog). Ted later claimed he wrote each novel in "a month or less."[4] This first novel, however, shows a level of care and creativity that suggests he took longer on it. Exactly when he began and finished the book is not clear, but he presumably signed a contract for it in 1935 with a 1936 publication date.

The beginning of 1935 brought reviews of the American edition of *Not Without the Wedding* published by E. P. Dutton (Selwyn and Blount had released it strangely titled *Without the Wedding* the year before). The press Ted had received over the Majorcan affair garnered attention for the book. The Baltimore *Evening Sun* simply titled the review "Majorca" and on a page that included a review of Nobel Prize–winning Italian writer Luigi Pirandello's work the reviewer groused about Ted's novel: "Neither sharp enough for the classes nor dull enough for the masses, the story falls in no man's land, a sacrificial record of the

Majorcan invasion."[5] On a more positive note, in Ted's original hometown paper, the Minneapolis *Star Tribune*'s reviewer, Jay Bee, cooed about the fine experience of reading the book "while relaxing in the warm glow of a coal fire."[6] The review sported a caricature of Ted drawn by Georges Schreiber.[7]

A paper in Ted's new home state, the *Miami Herald*, was less kind. "A thoroughly unpleasant book, from any angle," the reviewer said, complaining that "there are only two characters in the book who might by any stretch of the imagination exist in real life and they are so colorless that they might be portraits of any young couple."[8] It is hard to imagine a reviewer in present-day Miami grieving over bacchanalian carryings-on, but this one complained that Ted "insists on making the account of [the characters'] shameful orgies amusing, a treatment of the situation which results in a sense of extreme discomfort for the reader."

A West Palm Beach reviewer offered a much gentler response for the Lake Worth resident. Although the "characters in themselves are none too vital, the majority too cut to pattern," the reviewer allowed that "the ensemble effect is pleasing and creditable enough to warrant more than perfunctory notices from the critics" and that the "book seems admirably adapted to movie adaptation."[9] In a gentle outing of the author's true identity, the reviewer explained that there was "special interest" from the community in Ted's career since he had joined the "winter colony" of Palm Beach County. As for Ted's other place of residence, New Rochelle, the *Standard-Star* reviewer wrote that he "has mingled comedy and near-tragedy very entertainingly in a book frankly designed for the label of 'light fiction.'"[10] The reviewer also hoped that Ted would "sit down and devote himself to some full-length portraiture."

Amid the noise of the reviews, Ted expanded his exploration of Florida. At first, he could figure out only how to get just beyond the edge of civilization, which brought "endless things that fascinated me."[11] At a carnival, he saw a "hermaphrodite, exhibited fully and openly" and commented, "I had never seen anything like *that* during three years' residence in France where I often investigated the naughty nuances of that supposedly wicked but actually very proper country." He was not in Minnesota anymore, nor was he seeing the static antiquity and dead things in a museum. In this new phase of inquisitiveness, he encountered a living and operating real place filled with species of plant, animal, and human life new to him. And with this new information he began working on his first serious and in-depth treatment of South Florida . It would prove to be one of his most significant and underrated books.

CHAPTER 8

Big Blow

(1935–1936)

Timothy Brace wrote about coastal Florida, but Ted Pratt positioned himself to write about Florida's interior. He now began to learn about the state's watery prairies dotted with hardwood hammock islands. He learned the distinctive calls of its alligators and birds. He gathered his first knowledge about the Seminole Indians and may even have met some of them. He also began to wrestle with his identity as an outsider to both the state and the larger region of the South.

Ted found himself particularly drawn to Cracker culture. He wanted to know everything about these people—how they spoke, how they thought, how they viewed their world, how they made their world. As he worked his way deeper into the Florida hinterlands, he discovered juke joints where people gathered to dance to fiddle, guitar, and banjo music. One night at such a place he saw a woman slit the throat of another woman having an affair with her husband. He went to holiness tent meetings, sitting on hard wooden benches while music and preaching whipped people into rapturous spasms followed by the passing of collection plates. He witnessed medicine shows, with their pitches for alcohol-laced concoctions to cure a full range of ailments. He took himself to the country stores where old men sat chewing tobacco and drawing their penknife blades across wooden sticks to form perfect pigtail shavings. He attended cock fights, one time actually holding the cash as bets were made.

In these experiences, Ted learned the literal tastes of Florida. He ate yearling deer at a cookout, tasted alligator and turtle, and attended fish fries. He already knew from Marjorie Kinnan Rawlings's writing about orange groves; now he saw them and other exotic crops with his own eyes. He grew fascinated with the topsy-turvy nature of agriculture in South Florida where the growing season strangely began in the fall and ended in the spring. Moreover, crops matured so quickly here that several could be sewn and harvested in succession in a single season. Ted began to inquire about the soil's make up, the kinds of farm implements used in his moment and in the past, and the particular challenges to farmers in this unusual part of the country.

Ted also began to realize he was seeing a species of southern culture, which he could recognize from reading the likes of William Faulkner and Erskine Caldwell. That meant not only witnessing Cracker life but also African American culture. One night when Ted accompanied Palm Beach County Sheriff John Kirk on his rounds in the Everglades, the sheriff defused a tense stand-off at an all-Black joint and gave Ted a knife he confiscated for a souvenir.[1] Ted also observed race relations between poor whites and poor Blacks, and he felt himself keenly aware of living in a region where lynchings took place.

How did all of these subjects of study and investigation respond to this interloper? His Majorca experience had already taught him what could result from candid writing about locals. To the extent that he presented himself as a writer, some people in Florida seemed wary while others embraced the idea of their stories being told. Ted wrote a piece in which the wife of a holiness preacher worries that a stranger wishing to visit a tent meeting might be a writer. "We don't want no goddam writers around here," the preacher's wife says irreverently.

> *We took him in to our bosom, which is just like the bosom of the Lord, and let him attend all the meetings, and he didn't put as much as a single dime in the collection box. And then he went off and wrote about us for his paper. He called us some pretty hard names. Said we was low-down religion playing on people's ignorance.*[2]

Ted would feel this resentment to writers in this state he loved just as he had in Majorca.

Interestingly, the first Florida protest against Ted came not from a local Cracker but from a fellow northern transplant. This episode surrounded the catastrophic hurricane that swept through the middle Keys on Labor Day 1935, one of the deadliest natural disasters in Florida history. After fleeing the heat the previous summer, Ted and Jackie had determined to stay in South Florida the entire year so he could understand the region's unique seasons. Hurricane season starts in June, but August, September, and early October often see the most storms. Ted and Jackie learned that a hurricane approached Lake Worth, forecast to arrive at four o'clock in the afternoon on Labor Day.

Ted had by now formulated an idea for a novel based on what he was learning about Florida, and he envisioned a hurricane at the book's center. He decided to see what the ocean would look like ahead of the storm, so he and Jackie drove their Model A over the wooden bridge across Lake Worth. After getting a glimpse of the churning slate-colored waters, they started back only to find the bridge had been drawn up to allow boats through and could not be lowered against the strong winds. The storm struck sooner than expected, so the Pratts bore the brunt of it. They learned later that the storm had shifted and they had experienced only its outer bands. Still, it traumatized Ted.

The trauma did not quite come through in the public notices Ted relayed, however. In the *Buffalo News* section "A Line on Books," on July 13, came a flippant mention that Ted was waiting for a hurricane in order to write about it in his new book. Ted joked, "The local hurricane experts say they'll try to put one on for me, but they're not sure it can be done."[3] When the Labor Day hurricane had blown on through, on September 4 Ted got his picture on the front page of the *Standard Star* in New Rochelle, telling how he had hoped the storm would come his way in order to write about it.[4] The Mamaroneck *Daily Times* carried a notice on November 5 that "Theodore Pratt's friends hope he is enjoying the Florida hurricane. When the New Rochelle author and his wife left for Miami to spend an Autumn holiday he announced that one reason he chose that locality was the hope that he would encounter an autumn hurricane."[5]

It turned out that where Ted had merely tasted the storm's periphery, Ernest Hemingway in Key West experienced its more intense winds. After riding out the hurricane, Hemingway made his way up to the middle Keys to help with the cleanup and witnessed the horrific aftermath of its center. There he saw destruction of buildings, bloated dead bodies, and other hideous sights. Moved to malice against a government that would leave veterans stranded in such a storm, he penned an article for *The New Masses*. He directed most of his ire toward the government, but about three-quarters into the article, he took a different turn.

So now you hold your nose, and you, you that put in the literary columns that you were staying in Miami to see a hurricane because you needed it in your next novel and now you were afraid you would not see one, you can go on reading

*the paper, and you'll get all you need for your next novel;
but I would like to lead you by the seat of your well-worn-
by-writing-to-the-literary-column pants up to that bunch of
mangroves where there is a woman, bloated big as a balloon
and upside down and there's another face down in the brush
next to her and explain to you they are two damned nice girls
who ran a sandwich place and filling station and that where
they are is their hard luck. And you could make a note of it for
your next novel and how is your next novel coming, brother
writer, comrade s————t?[6]*

Exactly how Hemingway got wind of Ted's notices about
the hurricane is not clear. Perhaps a newspaper-insider friend
made some comment about them. Whatever the case, the flip-
pancy of the notices hit Hemingway all wrong. As for Ted,
when he saw the *New Masses* article he sat down and wrote
his distant Florida neighbor. "My pants aren't shiny from
writing letters to literary columns," Ted's September 27 letter
addressed to "Mr. Hemingway" in care of Scribner's begins.[7]
"That one appearing after your New Masses blast but before I
saw it was my first sin and my last."

Ted conceded his actions to be "a low-down procedure for
anyone attempting to be an honest writer." Still, he went on,
"you blasted it in too hard without knowing my actual attitude
on what happened in the hurricane. I've had enough lousy luck
myself to wish any on somebody else. I wrote an entire article
about what happened in the Keys with the same kind of indig-
nation you had in yours." Going on to justify the concept of
experiencing a hurricane in order to write honestly—the very
essence of the Hemingway approach, although Ted refrained
from saying so—Ted ventured, "I know you didn't name me,
but some people probably knew who you meant, and perhaps
my skin isn't toughened entirely yet—so this letter to you."

For all the letter's defensiveness, the final paragraph reveals that Ted was actually happy for an excuse to contact Hemingway. He shifted to a tone designed to make Hem his pal: "I've admired nearly everything else you've written, including the fishing stuff. My best is usually from the beach here, but the hurricanes have driven the bluefish in earlier than usual and I got two nice once [sic] the other day." If Ted hoped to start a correspondence with Hemingway, he was disappointed. No record exists of a reply or any further correspondence between the two. The silence seems to have rankled with Ted, and he later took his own shots at Hemingway in published writing.

The attack did not stop Ted from finishing the novel. He even gave it the hurricane-inspired title *Big Blow*. But it was far more than just a book about a hurricane. In the novel, he distilled all he had learned about Cracker life and forged it into a provocative take on a distinct brand of southern culture as witnessed by an outsider who is both entranced and horrified.

That outsider is Wade Barnett, who moves from Nebraska to South Florida with his mother Sarah and his Aunt Jane. Having bought an ill-fated piece of land near the town of Chobee (presumably Okeechobee), Wade comes into contact with Crackers. Where the cast of zany characters in *Not without the Wedding* were thin to the point of brittleness, in this novel Ted sinks his teeth into far more complex people. He does so, though, with a level of caricature akin to Erskine Caldwell's depictions of poor whites in *Tobacco Road* and *God's Little Acre*. Readers of the moment might have recalled Caldwell's sexualized characters when Wade meets Myrtis Peeple. This Cracker woman who has had sexual encounters with practically everyone in the county hoists her skirt to Wade, revealing no clothing underneath.

Wade struggles with the people and the land of his new home as he begins an agricultural venture that requires him to replace his entire store of previous knowledge and experience. Surprised and delighted at first to learn that multiple successive crops could be grown during the season, Wade brushes aside the information that the former owner completed suicide because he could not get his crops to make. But as crop after crop fails, Wade's spirits fall. The situation gets worse when his girlfriend from back home, Helen Carrington, breaks up with him after being disappointed in his prospects for success. Meanwhile, Wade finds himself at odds with his dishonest neighbor, Ony Mell, and the town bully, Carney Jelks. Even Wade's Aunt Jane antagonizes him, constantly taunting him for making this doomed move to a foreign land.

On a brighter note for the young man, he befriends Clay, an African American man who lives on the land as a friend and supporter of a young Cracker woman named Celie Partin. Celie herself is suspicious of Wade and his "foreigner" family, whom she sometimes also calls Yankees. But an attraction grows between the two young people, which further drives Carney Jelks, who has set his own eyes on Celie, to torment Wade. In one scene, Jelks uses the fervor of a Pentecostal camp meeting to lead a dazed Celie away to rape her. Wade foils him, further raising Jelks's ire. Shortly thereafter, Wade's mother passes away and Carney and his lackeys come to buy his land and warn him to leave. But Wade and Aunt Jane have fallen in love with Florida and determine to stay.

The novel builds to a dramatic conclusion set in motion when Aunt Jane kills a Seminole named Charlie Willie. Her anti–Native American attitudes have persisted through the novel, born of her father and grandfather having been killed by Indigenous people in the Midwest. Wade fears her killing Willie will give the community an excuse to attack him. But the sheriff declares the killing a social good because Charlie Willis was wanted. The sheriff gives Aunt Jane and Wade reward money.

At this point, a massive hurricane approaches. Amid preparations for it, Myrtis Peeple tries to rope Clay into a sexual encounter. Though he resists her advances, Clay cannot escape notice. Jelks gets up a posse to lynch him. As Wade frantically tries to board up his home, Clay appears at the doorstep, sent by Celie to explain his dangerous situation. When Wade attempts to flee with Clay, the men catch them and tie Wade up and hang Clay. By now, though, the hurricane interferes with visibility, and Celie arrives to untie Wade and cut down Clay before he dies. Wade, Celie, and Clay hole up in his cabin with Aunt Jane just as the storm hits in full force. When it does, it kills Jelks, Ony, and their group. Jelks actually gets cut in half by a flying sheet of metal.

Ted evidently took Hemingway's descriptions of the devastation of the 1935 hurricane to heart because he uses similar ones when Wade ventures outside as the hurricane's eye passes over. Wade "came upon the man who had been thrown against the tree. His body had dropped to the ground, released by the lull. It was wholly naked, the force of the wind having torn the clothes from it."[8] Further on, in the cabin, "Wade saw other nude bodies besides those still partially clothed. . . . When their bodies were not broken and twisted into shapeless things, splinters were driven into them, sometimes inches deep. So many protruded from one that the corpse gave a porcupine effect."[9]

After these lurid scenes, the back end of the storm hits. Wade barely makes it into the house in time. The barometric pressure drops so low the inhabitants struggle to breathe. Soon water floods into the house. Death and destruction loom, but the people survive. When the worst of the storm passes over, Wade goes into the bedroom and lies down with Celie. Despite protestations, they finally come to a silent understanding. The final pages offer an intriguing blending of storm, sexuality, interrelations of men and women, and the large question of land possession. "There was you that could not deny itself," Wade realizes as he holds Celie. "With this he could beat the land here and make it the alien, to be directed by him. . . . He had won the difficult earth with its coy riches by conquering her. She, of this earth while he was not, made him of it."[10] The moment seems a hackneyed repetition of the old colonial idea of the earth as a woman to be tamed.

But then the text reverses on itself as Celie opens to him emotionally and awakens physically. "There was no shyness and no withdrawal. Rather there was a full direction. Capitulation, if at all, for her was complete and without reservation."[11] Though the moment seems to continue the idea of the conquering "superior" male, "Her impulses and the conducting of them, as they had been all her life, were her own, to be used to suit her needs, guarded by her sure instinct."[12] Faced with the immensity of her own volition, "it was he who drew back, questioning and hesitating" and "he stared deeply into her waiting and ready eyes. Then he met her as she offered to meet him."[13] Much like the young Ted Pratt mastered and guided by the cocotte in Paris, this earthy young woman secures the upper hand against young Wade. From the other room, Aunt Jane wryly says, "I like to know young folks is enjoying themselves."[14]

Ted's mixing a racy dimension into his happy ending brings the book to a cessation particular to his passions. But the surprisingly female-empowered sexuality pales next to the intensity of Ted's presentation of Florida. He details the local plants, including the delicacy of the cabbage palmetto heart. He includes bird calls, such as that of the chuck-will's-widow. He shows readers a turkey-shoot, a cockfight, and a Holiness tent meeting. He presents intricacies of farming techniques in the difficult Florida sand at a time when agriculture formed an important topic in public policy and writing from New Deal policies to the writing of such agricultural advocates as Louis Bromfield.

And Ted captures the stiff resistance of this southern poor white culture to outsiders in a year that saw landmark statements about the South from insiders. William Faulkner's *Absalom, Absalom!* was published in May 1936 and the next month saw the publication of Margaret Mitchell's *Gone with the Wind.* These two novels took on racism, slavery, narrative-historical processes, and the roles of women in the South from white southern perspectives. *Big Blow* displays neither the profundity of the first novel nor the sweeping breadth of the latter. But it did articulate a version of the South that was fresh and from a different viewpoint. Something of Ted's fractious outsider personality comes through in both Wade and Aunt Jane. Although some elements in the book appear problematic in our moment, Ted takes on the social problems of South Florida's white-dominated insular society with seriousness.

Some reviewers could see the literary strength of the book when it was published by Little, Brown, and Company in September 1936. The *Mount Vernon Argus* heralded its publication, reminding readers of Ted's having been a reporter for the nearby *Standard Star* and that his new book was recommended by Book-of-the-Month club and was receiving acclaim.[15] The *Philadelphia Inquirer* noted that while novels about southern poor whites were not exactly new in fiction, "pungent characterization makes 'Big Blow' decidedly worthwhile" and the descriptions of Florida local color "the story's major attraction."[16] "Mr. Pratt has done a far better novel than his book of a year or two ago," wrote Kenneth A. Fowler for the New Rochelle *Standard-Star*, explaining that his "description of the capture of Wade and Clay (Clay also was to be chastised) is a vivid and powerful piece of writing as is also the suspensive skill with which he makes the oncoming hurricane a cumulatively catastrophic and terrifying occurrence."[17] Charles Hanson Towne, in the *Buffalo News*, gushed, "Not since Nordhoff and Hall's Hurricane has there been a finer description of a tropical storm. . . . It will hold you breathless."[18] Towne admits there are "harsh and primitive things in this remarkable novel," but if "Mr. Pratt has exaggerated the people he paints, that will be forgiven him, for he knows how to tell a tale, to make his reader see and feel this destitute borderland."

Towne's note of South Florida being a destitute borderland signaled the element that angered Florida-based reviewers. When they began to publish their opinions, Ted could be forgiven for thinking another incident might emerge among natives disgruntled at his depiction of them. While some reviewers might disparage the novel's literary quality, they really had a beef with its content. Vernon Sherwin anticipated this reaction in the Baltimore *Evening Sun*, writing, "'Big Blow' is going to be just that to Florida Chambers of Commerce."[19] Calling the book a "trite little romance," Sherwin concludes that "Mr. Pratt is going to be disappointed in his Miami sales. When you ask a Miamian about that part of the state which is the locale of 'Big Blow,' he'll admit it's there and add, 'But that isn't really Florida.'"

The reviews in Miami followed to form. Rachel Richey writing for the *Miami Tribune* offered some praise with her criticism noting that the novel "presents rather a woeful picture of Florida" but assured readers that "the fascination of Florida strains through" and commended Ted for bringing the non-coastal South Florida to light.[20] When the *Miami Herald* finally got around to reviewing the book in November (after hurricane season ended) the review offered some positive assessment but gave the closing comment, "Aside from the storm scene, the book falls unpleasantly into that category of stories of the South which attempt to picture Southern life in terms of its lowest elements. It is a peculiarity that should pass with the development of writers who can interpret the more complex organisms which make the

South charming."[21] Incidentally, just to the right of the review a column of bestsellers is headed up by *Gone with the Wind*.

The reviewer for the *Palm Beach Post* also waited until November and was less kind, calling the novel "a strange mixture of local color and misconception."[22] The reviewer's own experience living in South Florida for sixteen years and visiting the Everglades had never exhibited the ways of talking and being Ted had created. The reviewer thought Ted must have forged his version of Cracker dialect from a combination of Marjorie Kinnan Rawlings and Jane Peterkin, the result being not believable. Although the descriptions were good, the reviewer wrote, the book was "peopled by puppets" and "will probably be much more popular in the North where it will be accepted as a true picture of South Florida than in Florida."

A number of these reviews referenced the Majorca affair to show that Ted had a knack for upsetting locals. E. D. Lambright, reviewing for the *Tampa Sunday Tribune*, followed suit in this way and denounced the novel for poorly representing Cracker dialect, using the hurricane as a contrivance, and focusing on the state's rogues.[23] In a kind of early complaint about presenting too many "Florida men," Lambright wrote that it was his "impression that this author sought to 'Tobacco Road' Florida." Lambright wished Ted had included some of the decent Florida citizens in his book and frets that the book will scare off prospective newcomers to the state.

The book did receive one somewhat jovial Florida review in the *Stuart News*.[24] In a section called "Ye Editor's Easy Chair," the reviewer blithely calls the book "Big Show" and sometimes misspells "Pratt" as "Platt." Unconcerned as to whether outsiders might look askance at the novel, ye editor simply tells readers, "If you want to see Okeechobee in print, this is it." And "Mr. Platt" knew exactly what he was talking about because he "was a farmer, attended cockfights and Wild Holy Roller meetings, and weathered two hurricanes."

The mixed-to-negative Florida reception continued with Timothy Brace's detective novel. By the time the late Florida reviews of *Big Blow* were appearing, *Murder Goes Fishing* was published by Dutton. Its cover sported a black cloth cover embossed with a man on a hook (the British version, published by Selwyn and Blount, included the same embossing but on a yellow cover). Reviews appeared throughout the country, many of them predictably intrigued with the murder technique. The *New York Times Book Review* well noted the creativity of "a new motive for murder and a new method of destroying human life—so far as we know, both are unique."[25] *The Yachtsman* boasted, "we never before encountered a detective who knew a jib from a jibe. Anthony Adams is this estimable character's name, and the present yarn is a good mystery." And a writer for the *Florida Times-Union* in Jacksonville wrote, "Fish and fishing play an important part in the plot from the start, and the author's intimate knowledge of fish as well as his realistic description of the manner in which they are caught will thrill the most enthusiastic follower of Isaac Walton."

The *Palm Beach Post* reviewer, however, lowered the boom. Suspecting or likely even knowing Ted to be the author, the reviewer groused that Timothy Brace was not to be trusted with local details.[26] Brace did not understand local Florida law enforcement structure, the reviewer opined, nor did the cover artist understand Florida fishing technique. That said, the reviewer was impressed with the method of murder, if not the motive. But even then, the reviewer included a gratuitous and painful write-up from a professional fisherman filled with technicalities about how such a murder just could never happen with the particular tackle described.

Whatever the reviewer criticisms, 1936 proved to be a big year for Ted in setting the course of his writing about Florida. To critics who took him to task for getting details about dialect or culture wrong, Ted surely would have replied that he had not just "visited" the Florida interior but had really spent time there listening to the ways people spoke and witnessing the things they did. Meanwhile, he continued his research efforts and put himself on the road to becoming Florida's "Literary Laureate" in an entirely new way.

CHAPTER 9

Trailers, Dogs, and Florida Onstage (1936–1938)

By the end of the summer in 1936, Ted and Jackie decided they wanted their own home. Renting meant impermanency in someone else's property and the hassle of arranging a seasonal occupancy. How much better it would be to have their own property; better yet if they could move it around wherever they wanted to go as part of taking advantage of the writing lifestyle. They did not need a big place, and they traveled light. Where Ted's sister was expecting a third child—Mary Louise would be born on New Year's Eve—Ted and Jackie had only themselves and the dog, Timmy.

The idea of a trailer presented itself as both economical and portable. Ted especially wanted one with a writing room so he could have it with him at all times and not have to go out looking for one wherever he and Jackie should alight.[1] They went shopping for such a vehicle home. But none, even without an extra room for an "office," could be found for less than one thousand dollars. Only able to afford five hundred dollars, the Pratts determined to build their own.

The problem was that neither Ted nor Jackie had an idea about how to build a trailer. Thankfully, they had a friend who could. His name was Arthur Boyles, Jr., and he was gifted in mechanical and construction skills, including building trailers. He lived in Athens, Ohio, and when he got word of their project, he wrote them, "You're crazy, but you will be crazier unless you build your trailer in my workshop."[2] The couple arrived in the southeast Ohio college town in October planning to build their traveling home in just one month.

Under Boyles's guidance, the Pratts went to work. They framed their trailer in red oak, which they steamed and bent themselves. They ordered in and installed the running gear and painstakingly worked out the placement of the wheels to achieve proper weight distribution. Instead of the often-used linoleum for flooring, they opted for oak, which they discovered would be only marginally heavier. Price-conscious as they were, Ted and Jackie splurged on aluminum for the exterior. It cost almost ninety dollars compared to the then-standard Prestwood at twenty-five dollars. But they wanted quality and durability and understood aluminum to be the way of the future. They found the metal difficult to work with. And the cold November weather, which brought snowfall, slowed the work. But Boyles patiently helped them along. Finally, 1,476 screws later, the trailer was covered.

The couple made the interior as nice as they could afford. They got a great deal on Philippine mahogany plywood for their cabinets. The skills for such work put them on yet another learning curve, but they were pleased with the result. And Ted constructed his writing room to his desired specifications. It was tiny—six feet, two inches, by four feet, six inches—but it worked for him. Two months and a few days later (twice as long as they had planned) the Pratts had their first home. The final cost came in at $453.65. The only thing they could not afford were electric brakes, but those were not necessary.

The couple was immensely proud as they set off for Florida. They were especially gratified when neighbors in trailer parks along the way admired the trailer and offered to buy it. One offered eleven thousand dollars, and a trailer manufacturing representative assured them that such a build would command fifteen hundred dollars minimum. Driving the trailer hitched to their Model A Ford did present challenges: having to crest the Appalachians immediately baptized them in fire. But it was great to have their own home, and they enjoyed the ease of finding either a camp or a gas station to park and hook up for the night.

When they reached Florida, they set up their living in Briny Breezes Trailer Park, which was technically in Boynton but was advertised as being in Delray.[3] Situated on the beach, Briny Breezes offered an especially delicious haven. The weekly rate was a reasonable $2.75 (the most expensive place in the country charged five dollars). The camp featured a community hall that reminded Ted of an airplane hangar, which included a massive fireplace for cool days. Although the Pratts' trailer had a lavatory, the camp featured four toilet buildings. The owner, Ward B. Miller, who had made his fortune as a lumber dealer in Cleveland, believed he could keep trouble down in the community by forbidding alcohol.

Ted quickly fell in love with Briny Breezes. For far less cost than before, he had the trailer, he could walk only a few steps to the beach, and he could play shuffleboard, badminton, and pitch horseshoes.[4] Milk, ice, groceries, and newspapers arrived at the door daily. Most precious to Ted, the camp was quiet, and Ted relished writing in his office parked beneath pine trees and swaying palms. He liked it all so much he wanted to write about it, and he started imagining how a crime might play out there. Doing so would take some work, since it was not an altogether easy thing to do in such a utopia. But then it would not be the first time crime in utopia made for a story that included a variation of the name Adams.

The result was a second Timothy Brace novel, *Murder Goes in a Trailer*. Ted dedicated the book to Miller as well as "all trailerites who, as I, take their houses right along with them." In the novel, Sheriff Chase summons Anthony Adams from Palm Beach to the Seacrest Trailer Park to investigate the murder of retired Army General Franklin Werner. Ted sets up the mystery in the classic "locked-room" style, with the general found dead in his trailer locked from inside.

Since the general had a reputation for being annoying at best and abusive at worst, there are a host of suspects. Because it seems likely that he was poisoned by gas, suspicion falls readily upon his chemist friend, Durbin Judson, with whom he had been collaborating to produce biological weapons as well as another product he believes will save the world. Ted's dedication to research shows in Judson's detailed discussion of gases and their effects. Suspicion also falls on the park's owner (a surly fellow who surely did not resemble the real-life owner of Briny Breezes), the general's wife and her Cuban lover, the general's brother, the general's secretary-chauffeur, and plenty of others living in the park. As with the first Brace novel, Ted eliminates one of the suspects when the park's owner is found stabbed in the back with an ice pick.

The crime and the denouement that reveals it could happen only in a trailer park. Ted knew his subject. He created the ideal trailer park and gave Anthony Adams the most luxurious trailer imaginable. An Aeroyacht, fully furnished with all the best amenities, Adams's trailer sports lush furniture, a telephone, and, most importantly, a gasoline-driven generator that ran lights for when an outside electric connection was not available. It turns out that General Werner's brother also has an Aeroyacht, and when a hose is found running from it to the general's trailer, it becomes clear that his death came from asphyxiation. That method appears to exonerate Judson. But in a final twist, the reader learns that it really was Judson who committed the crime, using asphyxiation instead of the suspected poisonous gas. The chemist improbably admits to the crime rather than frame an innocent party because, as a man of science and equity, he cannot stand to see an innocent person condemned. In the end, Judson kills himself with his own gas, taking the secret of his million-dollar and world-saving biological weapon to the grave.

Dutton published *Murder Goes in a Trailer* in 1937. The finished volume presented an arresting package. The cloth binding was blue with the title embossed in black and red-orange. But it was the dust cover that really caught the eye. It pictured a collection of trailers in blue and black, with some of the windows lit in lurid red and a white Grim Reaper stalking the park. Drawing on one of Adams's own lines, the dust jacket notes, "Babies have been born in trailers, couples have been married in trailers, and now, in Anthony Adams's second mystery, a man is killed in a trailer." The novel's timeliness is a selling point, as this book "has an amusing and novel background suggested by one of the greatest crazes in America today—trailers, trailer camps, and trailer people."

Positive reviews appeared for this second Brace installment. The reviewer for *Providence Journal* observed that "Brace writes well, maintains his suspense, and just when you have picked yourself two culprits he proves conclusively they are innocent and breaks out a brand new murderer, who has been under your nose all the time. Very readable and extremely well done."[5] The *Philadelphia Record* gushed over Adams's fancy trailer and assured readers, "You'll enjoy this yarn." Less enthusiastic, the *New York Times Book Review* observed that the "trailer camp makes a novel background for a mystery story with several unusual features."

Ted and Jackie headed to Hollywood at the beginning of 1938 for not entirely clear reasons.[6] Later, Ted would mention turning down offers for long-term screenwriter contracts, so he may have been shopping a script with the film companies. Certainly, he was returning to dramatic writing, for now he was adapting *Big Blow* for the stage.

It was apparently also in these early months that he whipped out another Brace book, *Murder Goes to the Dogs*. This time the setting is the Everglades Kennel Club in West Palm Beach, represented in the two-tone yellow and black dust jacket of the published volume. One night while Anthony Adams and Sheriff Chase are at the racetrack, a strange event occurs when a greyhound named Sweetheart abruptly stops in an all-but-won race, turns around, and runs in the opposite direction. The track lights go out to prevent Sweetheart from catching the rabbit now hurtling toward instead of away from her. When the lights come back on they reveal that a race track judge has been stabbed. Upon investigation, Adams finds out also that Sweetheart has been shot with pellets from air guns, causing only superficial wounds but adding to the mystery.

By this time in the series, certain conventions have been established. Adams's manservant Thurber continues to be as clueless as Sheriff Chase in finding the murderer, the former taking good-natured but at times bizarre ribbing from the sleuth. Another common thread appears in Adams's sometimes frowning in ways that draw deep furrows making him appear older than his years. And, in a consistent nod to the Nick Charles method, Adams assembles the suspects for the case solution and kicks off the session with his tell-tale phrase,

"And so we come to the end of our fantasy when some of our suspects will live happily ever after and one, perhaps several, will live unhappily."

With a stabbing murder, a great deal of suspicion falls upon an actor, Leo Sunday, who is working with a young female assistant in a knife-throwing act. In a novel full of red herrings, one of the strangest occurs when a female body is recovered from Lake Worth mutilated beyond recognition by shark and fish bites. Sunday strangely worries that it might be the body of his assistant despite the fact that he has himself advised her to go into hiding. This moment and others in which the narrative strains a bit perhaps marked the first signs that Ted's passion for writing detective fiction was waning. Readers were probably underwhelmed to find the perpetrator to be a surly greyhound trainer. The greatest pleasure in the case's solution comes in the relief that Sunday is *not* the murderer. Having made the least suspected character the murderer in the first novel and the most suspected one the murderer in the second, now Ted wanted to exonerate the most obvious suspect.

Some of the most memorable parts of the novel are Ted's use of racetrack and soft drink lingo. The trainer-perpetrator at one point explains such dog-racing terms as "tiger," "ankle-burner," "busting the business," "reaches for his hat," "pushing the pack in," "strictly one-box," and "hamburger." Meanwhile, the curbside waitress offers a range of slang for drinks, the most memorable perhaps being "shoot one with sunshine" for lime in a Coca-Cola. It was to such details, in fact, that Ted's real interest and passion ran. Also, just as Ted loved facts about nature, so does his sleuth. At one point, Adams rips off a list of encyclopedic details about greyhounds no mortal could possibly produce extempore. In an age when supersleuths such as Holmes, Marple, and Pierot ruled on the page and the radio waves, Adams was making his bid.

In the spring of 1938, tragedy struck in real life. On Sunday evening, March 27, Ted's uncle, Eugene, and his wife, Louisa, returned from a visit in Hollywood, Florida, to their home in Dania. Just hours after, Eugene shot himself in the head. According to the newspaper notice, "officers believed he ended his life because of despondency."[7] The suicide affected his brother, Ted's father, who was already battling with emotional and mental struggles. In the middle of the night of April 14, 1938, Thomas went down into his basement and hanged himself. Emma found his body the next morning at nine o'clock.[8] Family stories report that the intense pressure Thomas felt to evict tenants in continuing tough economic times played a role in putting him into a suicidal state.[9]

If Ted was not already in New York trying to work out details for the stage production of *Big Blow*, he hurried there now to comfort his mother. He helped with the arrangements for the funeral, which was held on Monday morning, April 18, in his parents' living room. Candles burned at each end of the coffin. "The whole thing, of course, was a dreadful experience," he wrote Jackie, who could not attend. "But with the knowledge that the man we knew was not the man who had done this, it was possible to get along."[10] When Ted first saw his father in the casket, it looked as if he might speak. "You expected him to," Ted said, "but he didn't." The hours following the funeral were the most difficult for Ted, and after that he struggled emotionally as he helped his mother secure the money from his father's insurance policies. Solace came in work, and he stayed in New Rochelle to get *Big Blow* on stage.

And he succeeded. June saw him hired by the Federal Theater at forty-five dollars to be the director-producer for his dramatized version of *Big Blow*. Ted had hammered his narrative into something suitable for the stage, dividing the action into three acts with two scenes each. The play opens with Wade,

Aunt Jane, and Sarah arriving in Florida but collapses much of the novel's lead-up to that moment.[11] The bad Crackers display much harsher racism in the play, heightened by an early tense exchange between Ony and Wade and an added scene in which Jelks and his followers actually burn an oak hammock to drive Clay out of hiding. Ted also heightened the drama of Sarah's death by having her die at the dinner table. In the following scene, Wade and Jane talk about the funeral in a way that surely felt raw to Ted. Sarah's dying affected Wade in the novel, but he is so down in the play that Aunt Jane tells him, "Listen, boy! the world ain't over on account of your Ma. You always got to go on. No matter how you feel." Perhaps Ted's own mother had said the same words to him, or maybe he had said them to himself after his father's suicide.

Ted also made subtle changes in the drive toward the novel's climax. Where in the novel Wade and Aunt Jane mutually realize their commitment to Florida, Wade makes the decision alone and Aunt Jane decides she must go along with it. Meanwhile, the winds of the coming hurricane have already started blowing when Jelks and his crew come to muscle Wade into selling his property and moving away. When they uncover Clay hidden in a space under the floor, they threaten him in the nastiest ways. The holiness meeting that follows leads not to Celie being dazed and led away by Jelks as in the novel but rather to an attack on Wade, with Celie defending him, while the winds continue to rise. The rising winds element Ted may have been borrowing from the device of the increasing drum beat throughout Eugene O'Neill's *The Emperor Jones* he had seen years earlier.

The final scene sees the blasting arrival of the hurricane, but the play ends quite differently from the novel. The lynching in the novel gives way to a scenario in which Wade permits Jelks and his posse to wait out the storm in his home. When the hurricane passes and the winds start to die down, Jelks tries to get the other Cracker men to lynch Clay. But they resist and kill Jelks instead. Seeing him lying dead, Aunt Jane speaks the play's closing line, "Well, maybe we can live here now."

As the staging came together, Ted refined the script and aided in production. The hurricane required special effects, which were furnished by Hollywood. Ted may have worked some of his connections to get that accomplished. He may also have had the help of the play's producer Morris Nussbaum, who had changed his last name to Ankrum and was himself making his way into the film industry as an actor. Another Hollywood connection came with director Anton Bundsmann, who would also later change his last name simply to Mann and go on to work with Selznick International Pictures, where he worked on such classics as *Gone with the Wind* and *Rebecca* and later still directed westerns starring James Stewart. The cast consisted of actors not often remembered now, with Kendall Clark as Wade, Elizabeth Malone as Aunt Jane, and Amelia Romano as Celie. The name Robert Reed jumps out in the role of Carney Jelks, but this Reed was *not* the one who later portrayed the patriarch of the Brady Bunch.

Even as work on the play's production continued, *Murder Goes in a Trailer* appeared in serialized form beginning August 16, 1938, in the Lewiston, Maine, *Daily Sun*. This run led up to the release of *Murder Goes to the Dogs*, that month. As for the new Brace novel, a reviewer for the *New York Times Book Review* took notice of its distinctive lingo: "Greyhound racing furnishes novelty for a murder mystery, both in scene and in vocabulary."[12] The Montgomery Alabama *Advertiser* ventured, "Anthony Adams rapidly becomes classic in entertaining stories of crime deduction."

Big Blow premiered on October at the Maxine Elliott Theatre on 39th Street in New York, east of Broadway at 8:40 pm, tickets ranging from a quarter to $1.10.[13] Its WPA-designed poster smacked of Modernist stylization that may have irked Ted.[14] Burns Mantle, of the New York *Daily News*, wrote that the play "tells a credible story convincingly, achieves its suspense naturally and is acted and directed with a fine competence."[15] Edgar Price of the *Brooklyn Citizen* gave very high praise: "A lusty, vigorous melodrama of life and death in the inland Florida 'cracker' country, it is one of the finest productions this branch of the New Deal Administration has offered Manhattan theatregoers" and goes on to put it in the same category with the famed *Voodoo Macbeth*, directed by Orson Welles.[16] The *Barnard Bulletin* reviewer was not quite so enthralled, citing Ted's tendency to caricature but also commending it for having "something to say that is not only true but significant."[17] Ernest L. Meyer in the Madison, Wisconsin, *Capital Times* thanked "Elizabeth Malone, Doe Doe Green, and Amelia Romano for contributing especially fine talent to a memorable production."[18]

After years away from the theater scene, Ted finally had a production. It came with bittersweet timing, but it felt real and significant. Ted had gone to Florida to write and now had brought Florida to the New York stage. The next logical step would be to get his adopted state onto the Hollywood motion picture screen.

CHAPTER 10

Florida Mercy and the Movies
(1939–1941)

T he new year, 1939, started off with *Big Blow* in Chicago. By the end of its run, the play had appeared for six months in New York, two in Chicago, and a number of weeks in Boston and Los Angeles. During that time, Ted received a weekly royalty of one hundred dollars.[1]

At the end of February, Ted completed his final mystery novel as Timothy Brace.[2] This one took Anthony Adams out of Florida to New York to coincide with the World's Fair being held there. *Murder Goes to the World's Fair* was published on July 1, and it unfortunately showed Ted's severely flagging enthusiasm for the genre and the topic. It is the most derivative of the four Brace books, lacking the anchoring force of Florida and presenting a cast of flat characters so defined by their ethnicities as to look heavy-handedly racist to most present-day readers. Not that the book does not have interesting points. Ted writes not from a third-person point of view as he does in the other Brace novels, but from the first-person viewpoint of Spike Trevor, a publicist for the fair. He also sets up the intriguing conceit of having Adams receive a message that "Peace is a dinner which it is to be feared will be eaten tomorrow night," a hard-hitter against the backdrop of real-life Nazi aggression. In fact, Ted engaged pointedly with the political machinations of the moment, including Communism.

While Ted may have been about played out with mystery writing and was running afield of his chosen topic of Florida, reviewers actually liked *Murder Goes to the World's Fair*. Positive responses appeared across the country's newspapers. C. E. Mill called it "an altogether pleasing mystery story" in the *Idaho Statesman*.[3] "Plenty of action and a puzzle with a punch in it," wrote Pauline Corley for the *Miami Herald*.[4] *The Buffalo Evening News* called the novel a "real 'must' item for mystery hounds."[5] New Rochelle reviewer Elisabeth Cushman had a little fun with the open "mystery" of the mystery writer's identity: she explained that he hailed from Westchester County—"if you mystery fans could only put two and two together."[6] There was no need to press the mystery further, though—Timothy Brace was being put out to pasture.

It may have been in early March, after sending the manuscript off to the publisher, that Ted took a trip to the Florida Keys. While there, he chartered a sixteen-foot boat with a couple of Conch fisherman out into the Gulf of Mexico from Key West. "Conch" in the present time tends to refer to natives of Key West who may or may not wave the blue flag of the "Conch Republic." In Ted's moment the term specifically designated Bahamians or people of Bahamian descent living the Keys. The Conchs' Cockney accents and fishing expertise fascinated Ted. He saw possibilities for depicting another distinctive group of Floridians in fiction.

While on the excursion, the boat ran out of gas, giving Ted another experience to write about. As he recorded it later, writing of himself in third person, "No hairy Hemingway, this nearly killed him, but he got what he wanted, the talk of the Conchs while they were too busy hauling in fish to notice he was there."[7] The idea of shipwreck in such a beautiful and remote place with Conchs fired Ted's imagination. He envisioned what life could be like amid all those mangrove islands and pale blue water. He was also thinking about death, its cruelties as well as its mercies. Once safely back on land, he set about writing a new novel of Florida he titled *Mercy Island*.

The book starts off in a manner similar to the beginning of Hemingway's *To Have and Have Not* (1937), with a charter boat trip in which a customer conflicts with the captain. High-powered New York attorney Warren Ramsey and his wife Leslie are accompanied by Tennessean Clay Foster aboard the fishing boat *Pilot's Bride*. The boat is captained by a Bahamian named Lowe, who is assisted by a boy called Wiccy, the son of Wica Knowles. Where Ted had tried to capture Cracker dialect in *Big Blow*, in this novel he approximates the Bahamians' Cockney accent and idiom. His admiration for the Bahamians flows in sympathy with both Lowe and Wiccy, and to some extent the book is a coming-of-age story for the boy.

But it is much more. On a plot level, the book drives forward, making for Ted's most engrossing performance yet. After Ramsey loses a massive fish, he pressures Lowe to take him into the less-fished Gulf side. Lowe would rather not because the water levels change so quickly there. Also, going there dangerously takes him out of his normal range, which would mean no one would know where to look for them should something go wrong. But he goes anyway to oblige his customer.

The result of heading into the clear, shallow Gulf waters produces Ted's most lyrical writing yet. "The tremendous brain coral made it look as if the floor of the sea was strewn with the opened skulls of giants," Ted says describing the view through the clear water.[8] In another instance, as the boat weaves among unnamed Keys, Ted writes that a "flock of great white herons rose in delicate flight, stretching their long greenish-yellow legs behind them, and floated away, ghostly shapes drifting silently against the sharp blue sky."[9]

As is to be expected, something does go wrong. The first sign comes when fresh entrails float in these waters, a sign of human life in an area thought to be deserted. Then Leslie hooks a fish that drags the boat into dangerous proximity to one of the uninhabited Keys. When Lowe refuses to continue the fight, Ramsey pushes him out of the way and rams the boat forward, wrecking it. That ramming action fits in line with his personality; his old friend Clay has always called him "Ram." The crash knocks Ramsey out, leaving him with a bad gash on his head. Worse yet, the propeller has been knocked off the boat's engine and lost in the sandy Gulf floor.

The group goes ashore and comes across an unexpected house and garden. They find that it belongs to a man named Richard Powell, who claims he came here six years ago in order to escape civilization after a life at sea. He has a small sailboat that Lowe can take back to the developed Keys to get help. But the boat mysteriously disappears overnight. And that is not the only mystery, for Wiccy seems to know and be known to Powell. Meanwhile, Ramsey thinks he recognizes Powell and suspects the man is actually hiding out to escape punishment for a crime. In the midst of these developments, it becomes clear that Clay and Leslie share a past, which the reader discovers involves Clay's being in unrequited love with her.

More than in any book before, Ted carefully developed each character. Leslie forms a bond with Powell, not romantic but deeply spiritual, producing a vision of what life could be like on a higher plane than her husband's. Ramsey's motivations emerge clear enough and do not change, his selfishness driving through the book, but his personality displays subtleties. Clay struggles with his emotions and ideals of right and wrong. The Bahamians emerge in three dimensions where Ted's

Crackers remained mired in Caldwellian cliché. Through it all, Ted fills the pages with details about the Keys, capturing their paradoxical combination of beauty and danger. He heightens the latter with a ticking clock for the shipwrecked group who face frightening challenges. They must fight dwindling water supply, a season when the crops have not quite made, mosquitoes, extreme heat, and the impending threat that a saltwater crocodile may make its periodic visit to the island and scare all the fish out of the lagoon.

Then another crisis arises. Ramsey finally remembers why he recognizes Powell. It turns out that Powell is actually Dr. Brady Sanderson, a New York surgeon famous for killing a patient. Powell comes clean to the group, explaining that he performed euthanasia for the patient, who was actually his best friend who was terminally ill. When his friend's sister told the media about it, Sanderson-Powell was charged with crime. He fled to this Key he has named "Mercy Island"—the place of mercy for his mercy killing. His whereabouts have been unknown until now where he has been discovered on this Key. With this knowledge, Ramsey declares that he will defend Powell, which will be the trial of the century and will get Powell back to civilization and win Ramsey world fame. But Powell does not want to leave the island, and there is no real assurance that Ramsey will not turn on him once back to civilization.

Certainly, Ramsey means to get back home. Day after day, he goes out into the swamp on the island convinced that Wiccy and Powell have hidden Powell's boat there. It turns out that Wiccy does know Powell because his father actually helped Powell set up his new life on the Key. In his admiration for the doctor, Wiccy defends him at all costs. Ramsey suffers from his search missions, burned by the sun and stung by insects to the point that he begins to grow unrecognizable. When the feared saltwater crocodile arrives on the island, Lowe, Powell, Wiccy, and Clay catch as many fish out of the lagoon as they can before he reaches that body of water. Those catches cannot be smoked, however, so food and water continue to diminish until it looks as if Powell will have to give in. At that point, Wiccy catches a massive jewfish that will feed them all for a long time, an accomplishment that fills the boy with pride. He has explained to Leslie that he wants more than anything to be recognized as "mate" aboard the boat, but he must wait until he has grown into a man.

Seeing defeat now that Powell and the rest of the group can hold out longer, Ramsey plunges back into the swamp to find the boat. There he comes across a conch (the animal inhabitant of the conch shell) that Wiccy had caught and tied to a tree limb. Ramsey arrives at the conch just when the crocodile is about to eat it. The crocodile kills *him* in a gruesome scene, and it becomes clear that Wiccy tied the conch in the swamp to bait the crocodile and the man together. The move comes close to murder, but Powell declares that Ramsey's physical and mental condition made his demise only a matter of time. The crocodile's consuming him merely puts him out of his misery sooner, ironically amounting to a kind of mercy killing. Ramsey's death presumably means preservation of mercy for Powell. As for Wiccy, the novel closes with Lowe calling him "mate" for the first time.

Fully drawn characters, nuanced wrestling with ethical issues, and a compelling plot all add up to a strong novel by any reckoning. By now, Ted had grown sure-handed in capturing the look and feel of Florida's land and sea, the practices of the fishermen, and the wildlife itself. He also captured the south-of-The South viewpoint of people living in the Keys that renders even Clay Foster of Tennessee a northerner and outsider. Ted left off trying to wrestle with the recognizable racial problems of the deep South. Instead, he focused fully on his chosen material—the unique place that is South Florida.

As Ted wrote the book, his nephew Louis Walter was born on July 8, 1939, a sign of moving forward for the family. Notice of Ted's deal for *Mercy Island* with Alfred A. Knopf appeared in May 1940 which was otherwise a quiet year for him. When the novel was published initially in February 1941, only stores and libraries in Florida could carry it.[10] The readers of Florida encountered a handsome green hardback with flowery flourishes. Advertisements at the front of the book announced novels by Willa Cather and Angela Thirkell. The cover featured a full-color painting by illustrator Hy Rubin, best remembered now for his *Saturday Evening Post* work. Floridians were grateful to read a story that, despite its horrors, made the Keys attractive. Where Ted's Cracker characters seemed to bring out the worst in the state when juxtaposed against an upstanding outsider, here the Bahamian Conchs bore themselves nobly against a crass outsider while bonding with good visitors.

Indeed, much had changed since *Big Blow*—now Ted made an effort to celebrate the state. And this time Florida reviewers were appreciative. The *Key West Citizen* carried a feature on Ted, explaining that the combined circulation of the magazines for which he had written articles advocating for the state's attractions had reached twenty-six million.[11] His new book offered a story about a tropical island set not in the Pacific Islands but in the Florida Keys. And Knopf's early Florida release represented the first time a New York publisher had done such a thing. "The man who is doing this is in effect a self-appointed, unpaid, one-man Florida state publicity bureau all by himself," the article stated. Then, noting that Ted would soon be establishing a permanent residency in Lake Worth, the article quoted him:

> *You can breathe here. In Europe, where I lived for five years, you certainly can't breathe any more. And in New York where I come from, it's getting so you can take only short breathes. Florida is my country, especially when it provides me with the unusual material I found for 'Mercy Island.' I wonder if people who live here know how lucky they are?*

Quite a statement for a man to whom home had been elusive. He now thought of himself fully as a Floridian. That identity would not be without ambivalence for him, but moving forward he saw himself as more and more of a "Florida writer."

The book brought even more success when Republic Pictures purchased the film rights for two thousand dollars. The quickly and cheaply made film version was released on October 10. Republic's bread and butter came in the form of B-movies, especially westerns. The company had produced Lone Ranger films the previous few years, and John Wayne was in the middle of his run with the company, slowly building his onscreen persona. Despite the stable of B-level actors, the studio boasted some figures who, along with Wayne, would become well known. One of these was the head of the music department, Cy Feuer, whose future held work on *Guys and Dolls* and *Cabaret*. Feuer went to work with Walter Scharf developing threatening, atmospheric music for *Mercy Island*.

As for the rest of the team and cast, the screenplay fell to Malcolm Stuart Boylan, who had been writing for film since the early 1920s' silent era. William Morgan directed, and producer Armand Schaefer took a turn away from his usual westerns for this Florida picture. Ray Middleton headlined the cast as Ramsey; in his future would come a role in *South Pacific* as well as the distinction of being the first actor ever to don Superman's cape. Portraying Leslie was the up-and-coming young star Gloria Dickson, who in 1937 had been declared "The Luckiest Girl in the World" and "New Star of the Year." Just five years later she would die in a fire in a Los Angeles home rented by Charlie Chan actor Sidney Toler. Donald Douglas, originally from Scotland and later the "fake husband" of Rita Hayworth in *Gilda*, played Clay Foster.

Captain Lowe's character found portrayal by Forrester Harvey, who had made a name for himself as Beamish in Tarzan films with Johnny Weissmuller. Wiccy came to life in the skills of English-born Terry Kilburn, who had appeared in 1939's *Goodbye, Mr. Chips* and famously played Tiny Tim in 1938's *A Christmas Carol*. Perhaps the actor in the film most remembered now was Otto Kruger, who played Powell/Sanderson and would just the next year play the villain Tobin in Hitchcock's *Saboteur* and Douglas Sirk in the 1954 film *Magnificent Obsession*.

Boylan's adaptation placed the focus much more heavily on Conch culture. The film opens with a text statement to that effect, followed by footage of turtles in the Keys and a scene of Conchs in a Key West pub singing lustily. There in the pub Clay happens to meet up with Ramsey by chance after their not seeing one another for a time. The men drive to the dock to board the boat *Pureta* (changed from *Pilot's Bride* in the novel). The outdoor scenes appear actually to have been shot in the Keys, while the underwater scenes were filmed at Silver Springs and bear that location's luminous effects.

Under studio owner Herbert J. Yates's watch, the controversial center of the book was smoothed out as were other disturbing parts. Instead of floating entrails signaling the presence of human life on an island thought to be uninhabited, a can appears on the water. Where in the novel Leslie at one point dons a bathing suit, in the film she remains modestly clothed in her dress. Most significantly, Powell/Sanderson has not actually performed euthanasia. Rather, in his former medical career days, he was given money from an anonymous source to give a death row inmate narcotics to help him face the electric chair. A last-minute reprieve comes, but the drugs by then have overcome the inmate, who died. Although technically still a case of euthanasia, it situates the act somewhat differently, and in a way that most audience members would likely find less offensive.

The film version also downplays Wiccy's coming-of-age journey. Wiccy ties up a fish head in the swamp instead of a conch (and the film avoids any mention of the aphrodisiacal power of conch, which forms a brief but suggestive part of the book). When an alligator (not a crocodile) kills and apparently consumes Ram whole, Wiccy insists he meant no harm but had simply tied the fish head up as a deterrent to Ram, who was searching for the boat engine's distributor cap (instead of Powell's boat).

As was the case with the novel, the film's most memorable parts arguably come in its setting and atmosphere. The lurking creep of the massive alligator, the images of birds, the underwater scenes in which turtles paddle alongside Wiccy swimming, the cloudy photography of Reggie Lanning, and Feuer's moody music all combine to create an uneasy feeling that brings out the beauty of the Keys in a very different way from standard tourist advertisements. The musical score ended up receiving an Academy Award nomination.

A twenty-first-century Keys vacationer-enthusiast may find the characters and situation of both the novel and film difficult to relate to. The culture of the 1930s characters seems remote from those in the pages of James W. Hall or Thomas McGuane. The free-wheeling, cross-dressing, carousing crowd of present-day Key West largely obscures the Conch scene of Ted's time. Those by-gone days appear mainly in the island city's museums, architecture, and ghost tours. On the other hand, the mangroves, sunsets, and fabulous shades of blue water remain. Ted captured them, and so does the film, albeit in a noir look different from the typical tourist experience of the Keys. As Ted would come to realize, the Florida appeal lies more in the land and water than in its characters.

And Ted now had a film adaptation under his belt. That meant not only movie rights money but more exposure for his books. It was a combination Ted could get used to.

CHAPTER 11
Juke Girl
(1941–1942)

A ll this time Ted was publishing books, he also continued to contribute short works to magazines, more and more of them focusing on Florida. One of these pieces appeared in the April 26, 1941, issue of *The Saturday Evening Post*. Entitled "Land of the Jook," it described the dance-hall hangouts typically spelled "jukes" in Palm Beach County.

These jooks gathered both Cracker and African American populations, usually segregated. Ted seemed more interested in the Black joints. Of the nine photographs accompanying the article, seven featured African Americas working the fields or in jooks. In one photo, African American men play a form of poker Ted claims was called "skin game." Along with that game, hangouts were known for having what Ted called "organs," or juke boxes, that played music Ted assumed *Saturday Evening Post* readers knew nothing of. Migratory poor whites also made their way to these places, and one photograph features a group of them at the "Silver Dollar" in Belle Glade. The article also made note of the County Constable, John Kirk, whose "philosophy is to let the people have their fun up to the fighting point.

Then he steps in, and can be harder than any of them."[1] Violence in jooks was common. In one paragraph, Ted describes "jook girls," who worked as a "hostesses," women who implicitly included prostitution in their business enterprises.

Ted developed his research on the jook scene into a screenplay focusing on the jook girls and sold it to Warner Brothers for $5,700.[2] The film company also offered Ted a seven-year contract as script writer at two hundred dollars a week in September, but he declined it because he thought it exploitative.[3] By the end of summer, Ken Gamet and A. I. "Buzz" Bezzerides were working on the screenplay.[4] It was Bezzerides's first, written at the beginning of his own lengthy contract.[5] Adolph Deutsch, later famous for his work with such musicals as *Oklahoma!* and *Seven Brides for Seven Brothers*, began composing music for the film.

Casting continued into the fall of 1941, the same time Warner's head of production Hal Wallis was seeing *The Maltese Falcon* hit the silver screens. Wallis envisioned the Pratt film in the same vein as *King's Row*, a gritty, controversial piece about the hard lives of people in a small town in the Midwest starring Ann Sheridan, Robert Cummings, and rising star Ronald Reagan. For this follow-up film, Reagan, who now stood second only to Errol Flynn among fans, would be the leading man.[6] Wallis and director Curtis Bernhardt envisioned the jook girl role going to Sheridan, but they cast Ida Lupino in the role initially.[7] A month after her casting, Lupino balked and walked off the film even though it meant suspension from the studio.[8] Now Ann Sheridan stepped in. No sooner had that drama passed but another arose, for by the next month, November, controversy arose over whether to the title the film *Juke Girl* or *Jook Girl*.[9] About the same time, news went to the press about adjustments being made for payment of extras in the film.[10]

By December filming had begun, and Ted was in Los Angeles. He had at some point met fellow Floridian and former Columbia student Zora Neale Hurston. In a letter dated December 30, 1941, on Paramount Pictures letterhead, Hurston informed Edwin Osgood Grover (a Minnesota native who taught at and invested heavily in Florida's Rollins College) that she was writing an article for the *Saturday Review of Literature* with Ted. She explained that they were using "his new book as a springboard."[11] She was apparently talking about *Mercy Island*. As for Ted, he hobnobbed with the actors on the Warner Brothers' back lot and in the east end of Moorpark, California, where filming took place.[12] He watched as eighteen antique cars were assembled for the film.

Working with Warner Brothers meant a big step up from Republic, and it brought more publicity. The press took note when Edwin Eugene Lockhart, who had starred in the 1938 *Christmas Carol* as Bob Cratchit, father to Terry Kilburn's Tiny Tim, felt frightened when experiencing his first onscreen killing of co-star George Tobias.[13] Newspapers further reported that after much trouble over censorship in *King's Row*, there seemed little concern about Hays Office problems with a love scene taking place between Sheridan and Reagan in different jail cells.[14] Notice even made it into the paper that filming of one summer scene had to be postponed because cold temperatures were causing vapor to puff out of the actors' mouths.[15] Most dramatic of all, one of the stuntmen, Sailor Vincent, threw a tear gas bomb at some of the cast in retribution for their holding his head in a box of tomatoes to the point of his nearly smothering.[16]

Through the experience, Ted mused on the differences and similarities between California and Florida. Both places offered palm trees, sand, and sun. Yet they differed profoundly. Where South Florida was raw and tinged with the long-established problems of the South, southern California had the fake polish of a movie set and an accompanying array of problems foreign to the east. Being on the set of the fictional South Florida town of Cat Tail in southern California must have felt surreal. The Florida-California contrast would occupy the back—and sometimes front—of Ted's mind the rest of his life. Later, when what he considered overdevelopment encroached on natural Florida, he wondered if California would not suit him better. But he also by then had discovered that the Golden State harbored its own shadows.

The film *Juke Girl* was released in June 1942. It opens with a landscape that at times might pass for Florida. Steve Talbot (Reagan) and Danny Frazier (Richard Whorf) stop at a filling station while those antique cars roll toward the boom-town of Cat Tail. There the two men meet Skeeter, a girl in her early teens portrayed by Betty Brewer. She falls for the older Steve, but both men are more interested in the arrival of two women in a car, Violet Murphy (played by Faye Emerson) and Lola Mears (Sheridan). Danny flirts with Lola but fails to impress her as the women drive off. Meanwhile, the good-natured and upstanding Steve pays for Skeeter's gas, since she lacks money.

Skeeter leads the two men on into Cat Tail, billed as the "Salad Bowl of America." There Steve and Danny meet Jo Mo, played by Willie Best. Where Ted's article had focused mostly on Black populated jooks, in this film Jo Mo is the only Black character. He plays the stereotypical role for which he and Key West native Stepin Fetchit (Lincoln Theodore Monroe Andrew Perry) were famous. Jo Mo tries to convince Steve and Danny to buy lucky rabbits' feet, but a commotion grabs the two men's attention. Trouble has started at the packing and shipping firm of Henry Madden (portrayed by the timorous Lockhart). A Greek farmer, Nick Garcos (George Tobias), fights with Madden's henchman Cully (portrayed by Howard da Silva) and airs his grievances at Madden's exploitative practices. Steve stands up for Nick, but Danny determines to ingratiate himself to Madden in order to get work for himself and his friend. He befriends Yippee (played by Alan Hale, often sidekick to Errol Flynn, whose son would go on to be the Skipper in *Gilligan's Island*) in hopes of advancing his case.

Later that night, the men gather in one of the juke joints owned by Muckeye John (Donald McBride). There, Danny tries again to woo Lola, but with no luck. He fares better with Madden, whom he defends from the irate Nick, who attacks Madden when the shipping magnate lowers his offer for Nick's tomatoes. Disgusted with Danny, Steve goes to help Nick sell his tomatoes, a plan that fails when Madden learns of it and comes to stop the truck and smash the crates. Steve vows to help Nick grow another crop.

In the midst of all this action, Steve and Lola fall in love. Steve stirs the soft core she tries to hide under a hard emotional shell when he speaks of his memories of Kansas, which inspire her memories of Nebraska. As attracted as she is, however, she feels she must stick to her "Nickel for a Dance Girl" line and pushes him away. When Madden has her fired from Muckeye's for helping Steve and Nick recruit bean pickers, Steve brings her to live at Nick's. She helps them in a ruse to escape another attack by Madden, and the three all drive to the Atlanta market. There, they find that Madden has arranged to prevent their selling the crop. Steve takes the dramatic step of blocking traffic until the Atlanta merchant pays up.

Now flush with cash, Nick returns with Steve to Cat Tail while Lola stays in Atlanta, clearly wishing she could stay with Steve but feeling that having lost her innocence she cannot be with the bright-eyed Kansan. Nick celebrates his sale, and in his good-natured drunkenness seeks to make amends with Madden. But Madden shows no interest, which angers Nick. When the farmer starts to beat Madden, the shipping firm owner grabs a wrench and kills him. Hiding Nick's body in the swamp, Madden frames Steve. In order to prove that Steve killed Nick and stole his money, he has an envelope of cash sent to Lola in Atlanta. Cat Tail Sheriff Just (played by Texan Willard Robertson) drives to Atlanta and witnesses Lola open the envelope, taking it as confirmation of Madden's claim. He arrests her and transports her back to Florida.

With Steve and Lola now in those separate jail cells, Cully gets up a lynch mob. Convinced his friend could not commit murder, Danny goes to Madden with Yippee to get the truth. Finally, just as the mob is marching off to hang Steve and Lola, Danny and Yippee pull Madden out of his business to confess to the murder. The film does not show what happens to Madden but rather cuts to Steve and Lola back at the filling station saying goodbye to Danny, who leaves to seek his fortune elsewhere. Meanwhile, Lola has finally relented and agrees to live out Steve's dream of marrying and having a family on a farm.

Juke Girl comes across as less compelling than *Mercy Island*. Both films feature a rawness, but the latter has the advantage of real Florida footage as well as the close-to-the-bone atmosphere of low budget filmmaking. *Juke Girl*, on the other hand, seems comparatively overproduced. The lack of development in certain points leaves the viewer puzzled. What should be made of Skeeter and her crush on Steve? And what happens to Madden? In the end, the film throws together a number of factors that do not quite harmonize, from borrowing the lynch mob from westerns to incorporating the wisecracking of gangster films.

Reviewers saw the film in the same light. Ida Belle Hicks, writing for the Fort Worth *Star-Telegram*, observed that *Juke Girl* sought to capitalize on the theme of *The Grapes of Wrath* but missed it: "It lacks the sociological motivation of the Steinbeck work of art and doesn't have enough substance to go on without it."[17] Hicks admired Sheridan, though, as well as Richard Whorf's performance as Danny. Jay Carmody agreed about Whorf, writing that "he does a fine job of it, too, making himself completely odious."[18] Herbert Cohn declared *Juke Girl* a "winning movie," but also opined that it "lacks poignancy. It makes its characters real and sympathetic only to involve them in a melodrama that is merely incidental to their problem rather than an inherent part of it."[19] In Miami, Bob Fredericks hated the film, calling it a "made-to-measure" stinker, "cut and dried for quick sale to rural and double feature houses, with little to recommend [it] except an alluring or familiar title."[20]

Despite the reviewers' disappointment, the film stayed on screens into September. Perhaps Sheridan's beauty and Reagan's charm provided enough of a draw. Or maybe the tantalizing allure of South Florida grit and sexy edginess kept people coming to the theaters. Best of all, now Ted had two Hollywood films based on his work, this new one featuring bona fide talent. Years later, Ted boasted that he was the "only writer ever to have a Governor of California star in the movie version of one of his Florida stories."[21] Writing of Reagan, Ted described him as "a very fine, gracious, and intelligent man" and added that he saw no reason why actors could not be politicians since he had "known some politicians who are far bigger hams than any actors I ever knew." Ted would not live to see Reagan elected to president of the United States.

Amid all this momentum, Ted had another work on the line. It was a little tale he had written months before that treated of one of his abiding interests—life underwater.

CHAPTER 12
Mr. Limpet
(1941–1942)

Back in the summer months of 1941, Ted had been spending his days fishing and diving. As he plied his way in the Florida waters, he began closely observing fish in their natural habitats. Here he could see their colors in their greatest brilliance, and he could study their graceful movements. The buoyant feel of being in the water, freed from the constricted motions on land, instructed him in a very different way of being. At the same time, the atmosphere of the underwater world, with its particular topography and flora all swaying in an atmosphere as transparent as air, spurred his imagination to a realization of a new way of life. All of this new way of thinking went to work in his subconscious.

One morning, lying in bed half-asleep, half-awake, a dreamlike idea swam up into his consciousness. Ted had always been suspicious of ideas that came to him in dreams because they were "lousy when considered in the cold light of day."[1] He had written his books through a process of research and planning. But this story idea was different, driving him out of his hypnotic state. This time he did not start writing notes in longhand.

Instead, he went straight to his typewriter, clicking away directly on chapter 1 of the new book before breakfast. Even when he did eat a bite or two, he did not stop typing. He worked right on into the day until evening, eighteen hours straight.

This was like nothing he had ever done before. He literally could not stop himself. He knew already that stories could write themselves, but this one did so more intensely than ever. Ted later wrote that he was "just some fingers on the typewriter putting it down" while the hero of the book "wanted to work directly on the machine and he did."[2] Ted slept a few hours and then got up and did it all over again. Jackie quit talking to him. Finally, on the sixth day—as though he were God creating the world—he typed the final pages, 118 in total, adding an inverted pyramid of asterisks to signify its end.[3] He claimed he did "virtually no re-writing." An examination of the original typescript bears out that claim—it is remarkably clean, with only a few sentence-level revisions per page and no major reworking.

Jackie may have been put out with Ted, but she was very much part of the novel. He took the name of his protagonist from the small, conical "limpet" shell in her Florida seashell collection.[4] In life, the limpet housed a snail known to be tenacious. Such a name, he later wrote, "seemed to fit a man turned into a fish and a story told from the angle of the fish rather than the fisherman," a line reminiscent of *Murder Goes Fishing*.[5] Ted also dedicated the book to his wife, using not her full name but "Jackie," with the simple description, "Writer's Wife." It was a fitting dedication for a woman who lived at the center of a story about two unique creatures navigating a difficult world.

Ted imagined his protagonist as a thin, meek, bookish, pop-eyed, bespectacled, fish-looking fellow named Henry Limpet, who is married to a large, strong woman named Bessie. Mr. Limpet has formed a theory that humanity has reached the height of its evolution in a moment of a potential second world war. He believes the entire human race is about to crash backwards, devolving back to the Devonian period when it first emerged from the sea in fish form. Mr. Limpet would far rather be a part of the new form of humanoid that he believed would reemerge from the water than to *Homo sapiens* who are about to go extinct.

The couple goes to Coney Island with a Mr. George Stickle, of the US Navy's destroyer *Starbright* and his second wife. Peering down at the fish while a plane flies overhead, Mr. Limpet thinks, *I wish I were a fish*. About that time, he either falls or jumps into the ocean—it is not clear which. Bessie exclaims because he cannot swim, and Mr. Stickle dives in to save him. Mr. Limpet, meanwhile, has transformed into an actual fish who has excellent vision because he is still wearing his glasses.

After the initial shock in his instant and confusing species change, Mr. Limpet decides to do what so many New Yorkers do—go to Florida. As he swims along the coast, he encounters other fish, but they shun him because he is not of their kind. When a shark tries to eat him, Mr. Limpet cries out, which creates such a shocking sound in the water it scares the shark away. That sound becomes his defense against predators.

Mr. Limpet learns other things too. He cannot bear to eat other fish, so he chooses a diet of seaweed instead. He also learns he can hear and, with his glasses, see better than other fish. He uses these skills along with his knowledge of humans to warn fish away from the bait of fisherman. At first, he makes his fearsome noise to scare fellow fish away from the bait. Later, he actually talks to them and learns that they understand his language, even though they do not reply. At times, newspapers come drifting down into the depths, and he learns to separate the pages and read them. When he finally arrives in Florida, he sidles up to a scantily clad female swimmer and glides by her, prompting her to slap the young man with her.

Despite the many great things about being a fish, Mr. Limpet also feels alone. Other schools of fish avoid him, and he is unsure about exactly what kind of fish he is. Then one day he comes upon a sunken ship and sees himself in the mirror. Pleased with his appearance, he heads out with renewed feelings of benevolence for his fellow fish and immediately sees one hooked. Breaking the line himself, he looks back on the fish and realizes it is a female version of himself. He asks her name, but she has never heard of such a thing, so Mr. Limpet names her "Ladyfish." She feels such gratitude for his saving her that she suggests they go straight to the breeding ground. To his chagrin, Mr. Limpet feels duly loyal to his wife and rejects her.

Ted's description of Ladyfish is particularly effective. He captures the erotic sensuality of undulating fins and the charge of a fish's quivering body. The story recreates the kind of fantasy that historically gave birth to tails of mermaids. Unlike Bessie, Ladyfish feels simple gratitude to Mr. Limpet and uncomplicatedly wants to get right to physical involvement. Even when Mr. Limpet rejects her, she does not lash out but resignedly swims away. When he realizes his mistake, he dashes out to find her but cannot.

Mr. Limpet's bitterness at clinging to lubberly morality gets interrupted when he reads in a newspaper that the United States has entered the war with Hitler, Ted writing about it before it actually happened. Mr. Limpet heads to the north Atlantic to offer his services to the war effort. In the scene in which Limpet makes contact with the Navy, Ted decided to have a little fun at Hemingway's expense. In his 1940 war novel, *For Whom the Bell Tolls*, Hemingway had approximated Spanish cursing by substituting euphemisms such as "I obscenity thee." In *his* novel, Ted has a voice from the Navy ship call out to the voice in the sea, "What the obscenity is this?"[6] When Limpet tells the Navy he is a friend, the sailor asks, "Who the Hemingway are you?" After Limpet demonstrates his ability to help the Navy by locating German submarines, the ship's Commander also asks, "What the obsceneway Heming is this?"[7] and when Limpet asks if he addressing the Commander he replies, "You Hemscene obingway are."

Ted has his underdog (under-fish?) emerge a hero in the end. The Navy promotes Mr. Limpet to the rank of lieutenant, and he now leads a Navy convoy. He *does* encounter a bump in the stream due to a stingray breaking his glasses, but he soon finds new ones on a corpse in a sunken liner. The delay lasts long enough for him to lose the convoy, but Ladyfish shows up just in time to say she wants a relationship on his terms and to tell him where the convoy has gone. He asks her to wait for him as he darts off to serve his tour of duty.

That tour lasts quite a long time. Mr. Limpet aids both the US Navy and the British Royal Navy. He even ends up chatting with Adolf Hitler himself, the Fuhrer trying to cajole him into coming onto the German side in exchange for the Atlantic Ocean. But Mr. Limpet stays true to the Allies and helps them win the war.

With the war over, Mr. Limpet meets with Bessie in order to decide if he needs to go back to her or move on with Ladyfish in his new life as a fish. In an eerie foreshadowing of the post-war atomic time (written, again, even before the United States entered the war), Bessie fears the end of all humans approaches. In the meeting, Mr. Limpet realizes he absolutely must choose Ladyfish, who has patiently waited years for his return. He tells Bessie goodbye and heads off with Ladyfish toward the breeding grounds. The fish they will breed will be unique, having human intelligence, and will provide the best possible start for the new human race that will need to emerge from the sea.

That closing scene is strange, however. Ladyfish swims to the Coney Island pier with Mr. Limpet with the understanding he must choose between the two. Mr. Limpet tries unsuccessfully to explain human morals to her. When Mr. Limpet does finally choose her, she suddenly makes less effort to look attractive and instead hurries him on toward the breeding ground. In this new arrangement, the woman ends up empowered and the man henpecked, even though the woman's power is demeaned as being "shrewish." In a sense, the end of *Mr. Limpet* represents a variation on the Frankenstein story in which the male and female monsters end up happily together. It also recalls the ambiguity of male-female relations at the end of *Big Blow*.

When Ted typed that pyramid of asterisks to conclude the book, it was clear that this one was special. He could not claim the book to be a great work of literature, but it worked well as fantasy. And its inspiration sprang from a sense of patriotism, honor, and duty to a country he expected to play a role in the war in Europe.[8] Although he never said so, perhaps Ted had been inspired by Charlie Chaplin's impassioned speech at the end of *The Great Dictator* (1940). Like Chaplin, Limpet was a quiet little man driven by immense passions—sexual, humanitarian, contrarian—who wrestled with convention, loyal to his wife but keenly aware of the opportunities shining in the large world.

The unique specialness of the book found expression even in the publishing contract for it. Virginia Rice placed the book with Alfred A. Knopf, the contract dated September 2, 1941, with the working title *The Talking Fish*.[9] Rice got him a good deal, not so much on the front as the back end. The advance was only $250, but the royalty rate started higher than the standard at 15 percent through the first five thousand copies sold at a price range fixed between $1.50 and $2.50. The rate jumped to 20 percent on the next ten thousand copies sold and then to 25 percent thereafter. It was to be published in spring 1942. Incidentally, where most copies sold for two dollars then, first editions now regularly sell for over two hundred dollars. A signed copy with its original dust jacket is listed on eBay at the time of this writing for five hundred dollars.

Garrett Price illustrated the book. Born in Kansas and raised and educated in Wyoming, Price had settled in Connecticut as a cartoonist for *The New Yorker*. He contributed sixteen elegantly drawn illustrations that well complemented the comic tone of the book. One of Price's illustrations was embossed on the cover above the title, which was finally set as *Mr. Limpet*. Price may also have devised the fish-scale design that lines the spine. All the embossing was in green ink on orange cloth in a volume that ran 144 pages set in the Linotype face, Caledonia, by W. A. Dwiggins. The dust jacket was framed top and bottom by red stripes, the top with wavy edges to suggest a waterline. A line ran down the center. To its left was the profile of a white-headed, pince-nez-wearing human Mr. Limpet against a blue background. To the right amid lines signifying waves reflected in mirror image was the profile of the fish version of Mr. Limpet.

Ted later said with pride that *Mr. Limpet* was one of the first books to be published after the United States entered World War II. It may be that Knopf felt the subject matter deserved moving the publication date up, for it appeared in January. A reviewer for the *New York Times* wrote that the idea of Lieutenant Limpet leading the United States to victory is "easy to believe as you read, and afterward you wish it were true."[10] The reviewer described the book as "spontaneous and lively, in quite as happy vein as [Ted's] New Yorker pieces" and as "a rare fantasy without a taint of whimsy, a virile, even belligerent fantasy." Of Price's illustrations, the reviewer asserted that while all of them were "humorous," the "meatiest, though perhaps not the funniest, is the heading for Chapter I, showing the steps in the evolution of fish into Mr. Limpet, and the return journey in one big splash."

Other reviews followed suit. Russell Kay gushed in Florida's *Hollywood Herald*, "It is refreshing and delightful and a wonderful tonic for overwrought nerves."[11] Herman Kogan reviewed it along with Groucho Marx's *Many Happy Returns* as part of an omnibus of light-hearted books to help people amid the horrors of wartime.[12] W. J. Hurlow in Ottawa, Canada, called the story "devastatingly clever, excruciatingly funny."[13] "It's a mildly amusing bit of bizarrerie," proclaimed the St. Louis *Globe-Democrat*.[14] E. D. Lambright, changing his tune since his disgust with *Big Blow*, grinned, "Mr. Pratt's clever little story should prove as happy a novelty upon the bookshelves as is his original idea of what a man would do if he suddenly became a fish."[15]

Amid the book's publication and the United States gearing up for war, Ted presented himself to the draft board. He filled out a card on February 15, 1942, at the Palm Beach City Auditorium in Lake Worth. He gave his address as P.O. Box 563, Boca Raton. It is not clear if he and Jackie were renting a house in Boca then—they were known to have been the next year. His height was five feet, six inches, and weight was 121 pounds, eyes brown, hair black, complexion "light." His race was recorded as "White," and a note was added of his having a mole on the left cheek.

Ted would not be drafted, however much he may have wanted to participate in the war effort directly. Where he had been too young for the Great War, now at age forty he was too old for the new one. Moreover, his eyesight kept him out of this new conflict. Also, in an undated letter to her mother-in-law, Jackie mentioned his being classified 3A, which meant a deferral for dependency reasons, evidently meaning there would be economic hardship.[16]

That letter of Jackie's, by the way, offers an insight into her personality. Her husband may have been a professional writer, but Jackie herself was given to writing run-on sentences and not capitalizing the first word of the next sentence when she did bother to include a period. The letter also gives an idea of her practicality, as she writes "mother Pratt," "Thanks for my present both the dog and I liked it a lot. the landlady brought the parcel over to me. I gave it to the dog to keep his mouth shut while I got rid of the landlady, she had a whiskey breath so early in the morning."

There are other interesting aspects to the letter. Jackie tells of their having secured a new home at 117 South Palmway in Lake Worth. They also lived at 313 Third Avenue South at some point during their time in Lake Worth.[17] It may be that they were moving rapidly from place to place at the time. Jackie mentions that the new place costs more but that she does not mind because she is tired of saving money. She also explained that she was making clothes for a department store in Spartanburg, South Carolina. A photograph of her and Ted in their trailer pictures her knitting, suggesting that she regularly helped pay the bills through her own labors. It is also striking that Jackie tells her mother-in-law she is tired of Florida. The day, she writes, "has been so blowy and rainy."

As for Ted, he was away. She did not refer to him as Theo or Ted but Theodore. He had gone to Camp Croft near Spartanburg, a strange comment since he clearly was not in the military. He may have been visiting as part of a trip to deliver the clothes Jackie had made. He also may have been doing research for his new book idea. For, feeling the pang of rejection and stuck at home with a new black cocker spaniel he named Limpet, he was now writing about another unlikely war hero.[18]

CHAPTER 13

Mr. Winkle Goes to War
(1943–1944)

T ed had by now finished another novel that had been ges-
tating for some time. However, when he offered it to his
publisher, he got an immediate rejection. As Ted looked elsewhere, his now-hot typewriter produced something very much
to the times. Writing out of both patriotism and the sting of his
rejection by the military, Ted imagined what it would be like for
someone of his age to be drafted into the Army. In so doing, he
began to prod his feelings about war, killing, death, honor, and
masculinity. From this pondering sprang a new kind of meek
middle-aged man with hidden potential who tellingly shared
Ted's own middle name: Wilbert George Winkle.

In his new book, *Mr. Winkle Goes to War,* Ted created a house-
hold like his own. Over forty years old like Ted, Mr. Winkle has
a wife named Amy and a dog named Penelope. Mr. Winkle is no
fighter: he fought with other boys quite a bit as a child, but when
braces shredded the inside of his mouth in a fight at age ten, he
left off pugilistic ways. He grew up to work an office job as long
as he could stand it, then left it to open a repair shop, which fulfilled his passion for the mechanical. Now, however, the Army

has drafted him. The oldest draftee in town, Mr. Winkle hopes the Army will not take him. He believes his dyspepsia will disqualify him as well as his generally being out of shape. Home is comfortable for him, even if Amy takes him for granted. He takes her henpecking mildly.

But it turns out the Army *does* want Mr. Winkle, and Ted follows his hero's midlife coming-of-age. Surrounding him is a collection of foils. One is Jack Pettigrew, a respectful and homesick young man whose mother worries about him. A little older than Jack is Freddie Tindall, a young fellow about town who disrespects authority and calls Mr. Winkle "Pop." Finally, there is Mr. Tinker, about the same age as Mr. Winkle but, unlike the anti-war Winkle, determined to kill at least one Japanese soldier to avenge the death of his younger brother.

As Mr. Winkle goes through basic training, his dyspepsia vanishes and his paunch compresses into muscle. In the process, he develops confidence and pride. When the Army creates a policy that men of his age can be discharged honorably, Mr. Winkle chooses to stay. He and Mr. Tinker find themselves assigned to the mechanical division, to Mr. Winkle's delight and Mr. Tinker's disappointment since he wants to fight. In writing this new phase of training, Ted could not resist poking fun at the military style of doing business. When Mr. Winkle quickly fixes an engine, his superior makes him break it again and go back through the Army's prescribed process.

Also during this phase of training, Mr. Winkle wrestles with maintaining his fidelity to Amy. Although she has tormented him for years, she worries that her husband will be tempted by women in the hunt for good times with soldiers. Mr. Winkle tries to allay her fears in his letters to her even as women do show interest in him. When he goes home on leave, Amy now respects and appreciates him while Penelope no longer recognizes him and growls at this newly virile human.

This husband-wife dynamic so closely resembles Mr. Limpet's as to be conspicuous—a reader might wonder if Ted was dramatizing his own marital situation, or at least fears he may have had about Jackie.

Soon the military sends Mr. Winkle and his companions (Jack and Freddie's initial rivalry has given way to friendship) to the Pacific island of Talizo. Although not in a combat unit, they wind up engaging with the enemy. At one point, he sees that Mr. Tinker is still alive and is choking an enemy to death just as he had planned to do. When his companions are apparently killed, Mr. Winkle—the "old man" whose shooting skills are terribly suspect and who despises the thought of killing— stands alone shooting Japanese soldiers. As reinforcements arrive, Mr. Winkle leaves off shooting and begins stabbing his assailants with his bayonet. He prevails until a blow to the head knocks him unconscious.

Mr. Winkle wakes up days later to find that Jack has survived, but Mr. Tinker and Freddie have been killed. The newspapers have been declaring Mr. Winkle a war hero, and his injuries are such that he will be sent home. In his newly empowered state, he enjoys a better relationship with Amy, and now Penelope adores him again. Still, his experience leads him to thoughtfulness. Amy asks him if he saw any cannibals on the island, to which he replies "they'd all taken to the hills. There wasn't one of them around. They couldn't stand it."[1] With that comment he has an epiphany: "Cannibals merely killed and ate each other, or what human beings they could find for their meals. When civilized man's war came among them, they were revolted and retired from the scene." Mr. Winkle then thinks that once the civilized fighters have finished and left Talizo, the cannibals will return to their human killing and eating ways. The thought should be deflating, but Mr. Winkle finds it funny.

Ted and Virginia Rice quickly found a publisher for the book. Duell, Sloan, and Pearce drooled over *Mr. Winkle*. But Ted was determined to get his other finished novel published and would only agree to a contract if the publisher printed it too. The press accepted both books and promptly brought out *Mr. Winkle* in March. For the first time ever, a novel of Ted's hit the bestseller list.

Reviews were great. "Mr. Winkle should be to the middle-aged American what Private Hargrove has been to the young squirts. It's a swell book," wrote Meyer Berger for the *New York Times*. Ted Robinson wrote in the *Cleveland Plain Dealer*, "Let me recommend this book without reservation. . . . It is convincing, and yet it is full of deep and understanding humor and charm. There is satire in it and a good measure of genuine entertainment. . . . None but a wise humorist could have written it." The *Infantry Journal* called it "One of the most human tales this war has produced."[2] "There is nothing in this little novel that will arouse the animosity of the United States armed forces," boasted the Washington, DC, *Evening Star*, adding that it "is tender satire at its very best."[3] Newspapers across the country and even in Canada followed in this vein.

The strong sales and timely subject caught the attention of Columbia Pictures, which not only bought the film rights but offered Ted a full-time, short-term job as a screenwriter. This time he accepted, the duration of the job matching up advantageously with the pay. Moving into a rented home in the San Fernando Valley, Ted went to work with a salary. He enjoyed being in an office among those of directors and producers. According to Ted, Columbia bought the rights for Harold Lloyd, who wanted both to produce and star in the film.[4] Lloyd had become so famous and wealthy from his silent movie career that he kept a hired man to witness any of his transactions to protect him from charlatans. Once Ted made it clear he was not out to sue Lloyd, the men became friends. Ted was chagrined when Columbia decided Lloyd was not right for the role and actually moved the star's office into the basement as their way to tell him so. Lloyd withdrew, and Ted took note of Hollywood vicissitudes.

In Lloyd's stead, Columbia snagged none other than Edward G. Robinson. The role did not fit Robinson's fearful screen presence, which had been established when he played Rinco in *Little Caesar* in 1931. On the other hand, Mr. Winkle did resemble Robinson's mild-mannered real-life personality. Ted was under the impression that Robinson wanted to change his image. The reality was more complicated.

Now fifty years old, Robinson's image had *already* changed to the degree that Warner Brothers had begun offering him roles they knew he would refuse.[5] In August 1943, his thirteen-year association with the studio ended, throwing him into freelance. Meanwhile, home life was deteriorating, with his troubled son, Manny, struggling emotionally, and his wife, Gladys, suffering mental illness that included her receiving expensive treatments. Also, although he did not know it at the time, the Federal Bureau of Investigation now watched him. Born Emmanuel Goldberg in Bucharest, as a Jewish immigrant who believed in the opportunities of the United States and had deep compassion for his fellow humans, Robinson had been politically active opposing fascism. But he would become a person of suspicion in his sympathies with Russia. Even his past friendship and mutual admiration with J. Edgar Hoover would not save him when the Red Scare came.

Thus an over-the-hill, out-of-work, cash-strapped, investigation subject of the FBI accepted the offer to make a quick film that at least articulated a kind of heroism. Robinson later wrote that the film, along with others he made at that time, "were all, at the very best, trivial. Yet, deep in my heart I was grateful that anybody could find a role for a fifty-one-year-old man."[6] Little did he know that he was about to play the legendary role of Barton Keyes in *Double Indemnity*, directed by Billy Wilder, which would redefine his image in an entirely new way. For *Mr. Winkle*, however, his humiliation came complete, as he played his meek role as a short man opposite Ruth Warwick, one of the tallest actresses in Hollywood. Negative reviews rolled in upon release.

Yet, in retrospect, *Mr. Winkle Goes to War* showcases Robinson's finesse and range as an actor in a vehicle that actually emerges as a logical point in his career arch. The middle-aged Robinson possessed a gravitas that gave the character dimension. There is no doubt that the whimsical soundtrack and caricatured acting style of some of the surrounding actors affect the film's tone, but a close look at Robinson's performance shows someone plumbing the depths of a man looking for something deeper in life. The film adds an orphaned boy (portrayed by ten-year-old Ted Donaldson) whom the childless Winkle brings into his fix-it shop enterprise with an advertising line that "the world needs fixing," which surely hit the war-grieved audience members' emotions as well as expressing Robinson's own. More than that, an argument could be made that Mr. Winkle's gaining newfound strength prefigures Robinson's own resurgence.

Ted could have done a lot worse than working with a truly great actor. Studio photos show the two looking over the screenplay together backstage. And the film proved timely on multiple levels. Columbia billed it as "Another great 'Mr.'" movie in line with the likes of *Mr. Deeds Goes to Town* and *Mr. Smith Goes to Washington*—hardly shabby peers.[7] The film has since been released on DVD in Columbia's Choice Collection decades later, a performance worthy of Robinson fans and the zeitgeist of the early World War II moment in the United States.

Theodore Pratt's father, Thomas.   *Theodore Pratt's mother, Emma.*
THEODORE PRATT COLLECTION, FLORIDA ATLANTIC UNIVERSITY

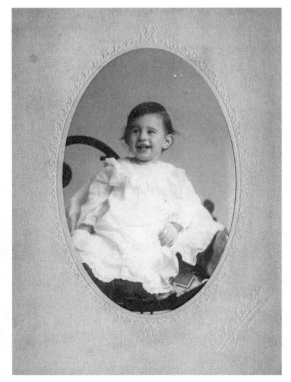

Theodore Pratt as a baby.
THEODORE PRATT COLLECTION,
FLORIDA ATLANTIC UNIVERSITY

*Theo Pratt as a young boy
in Minnesota.*
THEODORE PRATT COLLECTION,
FLORIDA ATLANTIC UNIVERSITY

Theo and his sister Isabel.
THEODORE PRATT COLLECTION,
FLORIDA ATLANTIC UNIVERSITY

Theo paddling on a Minnesota lake with two unidentified girls.
THEODORE PRATT COLLECTION, FLORIDA ATLANTIC UNIVERSITY

A teenage Theo in New Rochelle.
THEODORE PRATT COLLECTION,
FLORIDA ATLANTIC UNIVERSITY

Ted Pratt in 1925, just after his return from his trip in Europe.
THEODORE PRATT COLLECTION,
FLORIDA ATLANTIC UNIVERSITY

Rosabelle Jacqueline Pratt around the time she and Ted met.
THEODORE PRATT COLLECTION,
FLORIDA ATLANTIC UNIVERSITY

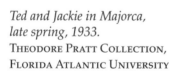

Ted and Jackie in Majorca, late spring, 1933.
THEODORE PRATT COLLECTION,
FLORIDA ATLANTIC UNIVERSITY

OUR HOUSE IN FLORIDA

Ted and Jackie, with their dog Timothy Brace, and the trailer they built.
THEODORE PRATT COLLECTION, FLORIDA ATLANTIC UNIVERSITY

The Pratts in their trailer, 1937.
THEODORE PRATT COLLECTION, FLORIDA ATLANTIC UNIVERSITY

Ted at the Maxine Elliot Theater for the production of Big Blow, *1938.*
THEODORE PRATT COLLECTION,
FLORIDA ATLANTIC UNIVERSITY

Ted with his skiff, The Barefoot Mailman, *circa 1953.*
THEODORE PRATT COLLECTION,
FLORIDA ATLANTIC UNIVERSITY

The Barefoot Mailman Hotel and Restaurant in Pompano Beach
(photograph by George Skadding).
THEODORE PRATT COLLECTION, FLORIDA ATLANTIC UNIVERSITY

Ted and Jerome Courtland signing autographs and promoting
The Barefoot Mailman *book and film at Burdine's in Miami.*
THEODORE PRATT COLLECTION, FLORIDA ATLANTIC UNIVERSITY

Ted showing Jean Flagler Matthews The Flame Tree, *which features her grandfather as a character, at the gala event for the opening of the Flagler Museum on February 6, 1960 (photograph by Sam R. Quincy).* THEODORE PRATT COLLECTION, FLORIDA ATLANTIC UNIVERSITY

The Pratts arriving at the gala event for the opening of the Flagler Museum at Whitehall, Palm Beach, February 6, 1960 (photograph by Bert and Richard Morgan Studio). THEODORE PRATT COLLECTION, FLORIDA ATLANTIC UNIVERSITY

Ted working at his desk in his home in Old Floresta, Boca Raton, Florida.
THEODORE PRATT COLLECTION, FLORIDA ATLANTIC UNIVERSITY

The Literary Laureate of Florida,
circa 1962 (photograph by
Tom Butler).
THEODORE PRATT COLLECTION,
FLORIDA ATLANTIC UNIVERSITY

The Pratt Room at Florida Atlantic University, circa 1969.
THEODORE PRATT COLLECTION, FLORIDA ATLANTIC UNIVERSITY

The final resting place of the Barefoot Mailman and his wife in Delray Beach Memorial Gardens, Delray Beach, Florida.
PHOTOGRAPH BY TAYLOR HAGOOD

*Frank Varga's statue of the Barefoot
Mailman in Hillsboro Beach, Florida.*
PHOTOGRAPH BY TAYLOR HAGOOD

*Detail of the face of the Hillsboro
statue, likely modeled on Ted's.*
PHOTOGRAPH BY TAYLOR HAGOOD

Frank Varga's statue of the Barefoot Mailman in Hypoluxo, Florida.
PHOTOGRAPH BY TAYLOR HAGOOD

CHAPTER 14

The Barefoot Mailman
(1943)

The novel publishers had turned down was one Ted knew to be special. When Duell, Sloan, and Pearce agreed to publish it as part of the Mr. Winkle deal, they had low expectations. Those expectations would be disappointed in the best possible way. The novel, entitled *The Barefoot Mailman*, would enjoy extraordinary longevity in sales and reach of readership. In the process, it became the keystone book of Ted's career. And it would come to define a key aspect of South Florida identity.

Ted anchored the book in extensive research ongoing for about a decade. He had been hearing about late nineteenth-century beach-walking mail carriers from the time he arrived in Florida. Then in 1939, artist Stevan Dohanos was commissioned by the US Treasury Department as part of New Deal programming to paint a series of six murals in the West Palm Beach Post Office. These paintings—now housed in the West Palm's Summit Boulevard post office—depicted the experiences of James E. Hamilton, who died in the line of duty as a beach-walking postman on October 11, 1887. Catching this interest, Ted consulted libraries from Palm Beach to Miami as well as the Florida

Historical Society in St. Augustine and the Library of Congress and New York Public Library.[1]

Along with that archival work, Ted interviewed still-living former mail carriers who had walked the beaches. He made contact with the son of Charles William Pierce, the first to use the term "barefoot mailman." The notes, maps, and sources Ted amassed amounted to over two hundred pages. Finally, Ted took a five-day walk on the beach in the role of mailman himself. In the process, he gained a sense of the mail carriers' experiences and imagined how they dealt with the weather, animals, and even the slanting surface of the beach that required an altered gait.

The idea of such a beach route should be evocative enough, but it is worth giving it a try. Find a less developed stretch—perhaps Blowing Rocks Park on Jupiter Island—and walk it. Allow yourself to feel the many moods of the sea as its waves wash inward along sweeps of foam that chase the scurrying sandpipers. Shut out the twenty-first century and feel the mesmerizing remoteness of the strand, see the shadows on the gray-brown sand, sweat in the heat on your uniform. Danger here becomes beautiful, as it so often does, seducing on a razor edge of promise and destruction. Imagined in the pioneer era, delivering mail on the beach may seem prosaic. Tasting the experience in the now reveals it as a struggle with nature as a combined resistant, stimulant, and narcotic that requires the courage, endurance, and commitment needed in so many necessities of life, much less occupation.

Completing his research, Ted wrote the novel. His mailman's name is Steven Pierton, a young man taking over the route from Palm City (later Palm Beach) to Miami from his friend, Jesse. Steven has been raised by two brothers, Gerald and Cap Jim Bethune, who own a General Merchandise and US Post Office on the banks of Lake Worth. Cap Jim has a sharpie schooner called the *Margaret D*, and the novel opens with his returning from a run up the coast. He brings back goods and a young boy named Adie Titus, who is heading to Miami to care for his sick mother. Although sensing something strange about the boy, Steven agrees to take him along on his first mail delivery trip as a "foot passenger."

Ted takes care early in the novel to develop Steven as a young man of discretion and character. The community of Palm City operates on interdependence, sharing its wealth when goods wash ashore from shipwrecks. When a newcomer named Quimby refuses to share a barrel of lard he has recovered on the beach, the community sends Steven to convince him to change, even if that means fighting. Steven manages to avoid a fight, and the community celebrates as Quimby joins them. Steven's importance to the community becomes even clearer when news comes from the state government that the name "Palm City" has already been taken so a new name is required. It is Steven who suggests the name Palm Beach.

As Steven leads Adie down the coast, he stops at Hypoluxo Island, which has been given to him. He shows Adie his house and rhapsodizes about the island's beauty and his hopes of someday having a wife who will appreciate it. Adie seems surprisingly moved for a boy, and the readers may be less surprised than Steven to learn he is actually a girl. The revelation comes when Adie gets scared by sounds in the night and jumps into Steven's arms. Steven quickly learns the truth, feeling her body against his. Embarrassed and awkward over the situation, Steven and Adie continue to Miami in strained circumstances. Steven feels great relief when Adie's parents show no anger toward him, and he realizes he has fallen in love with the boy-turned-girl.

Into this scenario comes Sylvanus Hurley, a fast-talking "boomer" from up North who plans to develop Miami into a garden spot and encourage wealthy people to immigrate. Hurley becomes Steven's next foot passenger, and he brings the added pressure of stuffing an envelope with one thousand dollars for Steven to carry, guaranteed by the US Postal Service. On the walk to Miami, a band of thugs called "beach combers" attacks and robs Steven and Sylvanus. But Steven harbors suspicions about this northerner and discovers that the man had actually secreted the money in his hat and given Steven a dummy envelope. Hurley's scheme, Steven realizes, was to get the United States to reimburse him for money he would not actually lose. Meanwhile, the beach combers are none too happy with Steven about being tricked.

Things get worse when Sylvanus meets Adie. Where Steven is awkward and inexperienced with women, Sylvanus is a smooth talker who can best Steven at every turn. The rivalry comes to a head at a dance in Miami where the two men vie for Adie's attention only to get caught up in a dance-down in which the last man standing gets to kiss her. Steven wins but grows bashful and paralyzed about taking the prize. While he hesitates, Sylvanus jumps up and kisses Adie himself. Steven responds by knocking him down. Adie runs away, but it is clear to everyone except Steven that she loves him instead of Sylvanus.

In the midst of this love triangle crashes a horrific event. After a storm, casks of wine wash up into the surf. Steven and the rest of the Palm Beach men get drunk. The next day, Steven can barely make it to the refuge station Jesse, his mother, and his expecting wife now occupy. Giving Steven a chance to sleep off his hangover, Jesse heads off with the mail himself on his old route. Little does he know that the beach combers seeking retribution against Steven for foiling their attempted robbery have moved the boat normally used to cross a channel. Worse yet, the storm has disrupted the topography and animals. When Jesse tries to swim across, alligators eat him, leaving only a rib behind for Steven to find.

As Steven and Jesse's family cope with their shock, Sylvanus begins his nefarious program to "update" Miami. He institutes a ferry company to link the two parts of town and makes a land grab that includes Steven's island. Sylvanus also leads Miami citizens to oppose Palm Beach's being named county seat, forcing a vote. Palm Beach wins the vote, but the Miamians refuse to concede or hand over legal documents, including the ones that confirm Steven's ownership of the island.

The novel culminates with a group of armed Palm Beach leaders sailing to Miami to claim the documents. Once they succeed, Steven goes with a Seminole friend to claim Adie, who is ecstatic finally to hear him ask her to marry him. By the time they are paddling away, Sylvanus has caught wind of the doings and chases Steven and Adie with the lead beach comber. Jesse's mother shoots and kills the beach comber for his role in killing her son. She wants to shoot Sylvanus too, but Adie stops her. With the news out that Sylvanus played a role in Jesse's death, meaning it for Steven, everyone is convinced he will leave town as soon as possible. As for Steven and Adie, they are to be married on the boat back to Palm Beach.

The Barefoot Mailman has a peculiar appeal. It is not as ambitious as *Big Blow* nor does it reach the level of gritty detail as *Mercy Island*. It might hit some readers as being adolescent. Some South Floridians, especially historians, challenge Ted for playing loose with historical facts. It has been suggested that the term "barefoot mailman" would have been scorned by the actual barefoot mail carriers.[2] But the novel presents a historical moment with just the right dash of innocence and romance to make it desirable. It distills a romantic version of pioneer Florida that conjures images of a simple life by the beach and in a tiny home on an island where homespun love can blossom.

If the reader imaginatively enters the world Ted creates, it carries special allure. The reader enters an insular community with colorful characters who live in a beautiful, if dangerous, place. You want to conk Steven in the head for not just asking Adie to marry him right away. And you might feel a glow imagining the couple setting up house on their island as a train—the novel includes account of building the "Celestial Railroad"—brings the mail, ending the brief romantic era of the barefoot mailman. More than anything, the book captures the Florida sunshine and breeze, its teeming though dangerous animal life, its fresh and perpetual green. Such is a dream of old Florida that always has the power to entice.

Duell, Sloan, and Pearce released the novel on July 23, 1943. The cover sported a two-color, orange and black dust jacket with artwork by Charles Lolgren featuring Steven and Adie walking the beach. The back of the dust jacket presented a photo of Ted and a two-paragraph biography attesting to the book's historical accuracy. The publishers noted Ted's being the author of the bestseller *Mr. Winkle* just under his name on the front of the dust jacket. The inside front of the dust jacket explained: *"The Barefoot Mailman* pictures vividly the simple, peaceful, yet stirring time of early settlement life in America's only tropics."

Positive reviews rolled in. "This book is calculated to make any reader rush for the nearest beach to take off his shoes," proclaimed *The Atlantic Monthly*. "Delightful, as refreshing as the Gulf Stream," cooed the *Chicago Tribune*. The *New York Times* called it a "unique contribution to the treasury of Americana."[3] "Theodore Pratt is an excellent writer," Dorothy Raymer, of *The Miami News*, wrote.[4] "He has just the right amount of humor, his handling of dialect and colloquialisms is accurate." Raymer doubted the book was as appealing as *Mr. Winkle*, but she thought it would garner a wide readership. Mary-Carter Roberts for the Washington, DC, *Evening Star* described it as "a very pleasant little book which has its charm in a constant irony."[5] "The annals of the U.S. post office will be enriched with the publication of Theodore Pratt's novel," announced *Tulsa Daily World*.[6] Hemingway's old paper, *The Kansas City Star*, observed that the novel "acquires particular distinction from the way in which the author has worked the lore, history and atmosphere of this fascinating region into narrative."[7] The *Asheville Citizen-Times* in North Carolina, where Ted and Jackie liked to spend time in the summer, went so far as to claim him as something of local with a "salty and colorful story."[8]

The sales of the book did not send it to the top of the best-seller list with *Mr. Winkle*, but *The Barefoot Mailman* started selling steadily. Quietly, it sold more and more still, beginning a long journey of finding its way into people's pocketbooks, minds, and hearts. In time, the historical figure it depicted would be adopted as a folk hero of South Florida's pioneer history. And the book would define Ted in his lifetime and beyond.

CHAPTER 15
Hollywood Days
(1943–1947)

Ted was enjoying having a salary at Columbia, and a not-too-shabby one at that. His short-term contract paid him $750 a week.[1] It was a comparatively large amount of money that came regularly instead of episodically as it did with books. And there were perks. Workdays found him in the studio restaurant surrounded by movie producers, directors, and stars. One day he sat at a table next to Rita Hayworth.[2] On days off, he and Jackie would explore California. Their favorite destination was the Sequoia National Park, where they loved to rent a cabin.[3]

Ted witnessed the darker side of Hollywood too. The cynicism of the business seeped into his system like a toxin. When other screenwriters asked him about writing and selling novels, he would reveal how little money he made with them relative to screenwriting. The screenwriters recoiled at such poverty, yet they felt no happiness in their jobs. Jackie told Ted, "This isn't right for you; you don't belong here."[4] He resented her saying it and went on publishing books even as his screenplay writing went largely uncredited.

The first book to appear during Ted's Hollywood era was *Thunder Mountain*. Its narrator, Charles Arrington, has been summoned with his pregnant wife from their Ohio farm to Colorado by his father, Alexander. There, Alexander owns a remote mountain unique for generating winds that spawn extraordinary thunderstorms. He has built a bug-out station atop this place he calls Thunder Mountain and has gathered all of his grown children because in the midst of world war he unsurprisingly believes civilization to be on the brink of collapse. When he tells his family he has built his complex for their protection and preservation, they see him as a controlling megalomaniac. Some of them want to leave right away. In order to keep everyone there, that night Alexander dynamites the natural rock bridge that provides the only access to the mountain.

With everyone stuck on the mountain, troubles and tensions brew. One of the sons, a composer named Norman, chafes when his nymphomaniac wife is drawn to his brother, Mark, who cannot help himself from being attracted to her. Another non-family member, Audrey, feels pressure from Alexander to marry one of his other sons, Mark or Basil. Also on the mountain is a medical doctor named Nelson Pope, who worships Alexander's daughter, Lynne. Finally, in the mix is Zong, Alexander's Chinese cook, whom Ted draws in caricature that mars an otherwise fascinating human study.

The book borrows thematically from William Shakespeare's *King Lear*. Alexander greatly resembles that unwise, self-centered, and dominating monarch. And just as Lear roams the stormy heath in defiance of nature itself, so in the climactic scene Alexander charges outside in the middle of one of the terrible storms calling upon God to decide if his actions have been right or wrong. Readers of the wartime moment surely also saw a connection to Hitler.

In the end, even as his children condemn Alexander's antisocial paranoia, they also find that his actions have brought them to better places in themselves and with one another. The novel ends with tragedies but also some of the family being saved by a new kind of aircraft, a helicopter, which had made its debut only a few years earlier courtesy of Igor Sikorsky. Only so many passengers can travel on the aircraft at a time. As the first group leaves, they can hear in the distance Norman playing a piece called "Thunder Mountain" that reflects his heartbreak and growth.

Duell, Sloan, and Pearce published the book in June 1944. Vera Francis, for *Tulsa Daily World*, declared that Ted "tells a rousing tale in good and dramatic fashion."[5] The *Gazette Montreal* recognized Ted as a "versatile writer" who "demonstrates in this novel that he knows how to write to hold the reader's mind."[6] The versatility did not work quite so well for Mary-Carter Roberts of Washington, DC's, *Evening Star*: "After the genuine charm of 'The Barefoot Mailman' this pretentious effort is particularly sad reading."[7]

Next, Ted wrote a lighthearted novel *about* Hollywood. He imagined a secretary who wants to be a screenwriter. Over twenty years prior, she worked for the fictional Superior Pictures because she believed it would get her on the inside of the business. But the production company never bought any of her screenplays. Finally, she gives up and decides to publish her diary about the inner workings of Hollywood. The book becomes a runaway bestseller, and now every company in town wants the screen rights for it. Things are looking up for her, but there is a problem—as she puts it, she just does not feel like selling the book to be made into a film.

This woman is the titular heroine of *Miss Dilly Says No*, which was published by Duell, Sloan, and Pearce in February 1945. The novel has a Frank Capra feel to it, filled with colorful flat characters. One of these is Mr. Gladstone, head of production, known for his paunch that gleans him the not-striking nicknames of "Glad" and, from Miss Dilly herself, "Potbelly."

There is also Mr. Jonah, the story editor, who bears the nickname "Whale" not only for the connection to the Hebrew prophet but also because of his large girth. There is Mr. Horatio, a rich member of the board who is as shy as Miss Dilly and with whom she is in love and he with her. There is Marilla Marceau, whom Miss Dilly has taken under wing to protect her from the exploitative movie industry. Most memorably, the playwright-turned-screenplay writer Mr. Flora goes by the self-proclaimed name of "The Zombie" and is by far the cleverest character in the novel in terms of repartee.

But Miss Dilly (whose first name is as allegedly hideous as her would-be boyfriend Mr. Horatio's) must not be underestimated. Through her experiences, she has learned every trick the film executives have at their disposal to lure and cheat writers. The novel follows her pure-hearted and sagacious ways of foiling the industry at every turn. A quick read, the book leaves the reader feeling good, so long as the reader accepts its premises, moment, and purpose. *Chicago Tribune* reviewer Will Davidson correctly identified the book as "a lightly amusing potboiler," but the *Hartford Courant*'s review in verse form lampooning the book as "a terrible bore" seems unfair to an escapist book produced in a moment when the war-worn world needed it.[8] The novel's pleasantries found enough acceptance for the *Kansas City Star* to run in it serialized form in September. If *The Barefoot Mailman* captured pioneer Florida from a midcentury viewpoint, *Miss Dilly Says No* caught the feel of midcentury Hollywood.

Ted *did* worry that that Hollywood might disapprove of his novel and never want to make any movies of his books again.[9] When he mentioned his concern to some colleagues, they assured him that he could do his worst and not discourage the studios if they really wanted to buy a book he wrote. *Miss Dilly Says No* itself was not made into a film, but Ted did collaborate with William Mendrek to dramatize it.[10] It reached a stage in Saratoga Springs but flopped and never went any-where after that, although it gained more traction than Ted's efforts to dramatize both *Mercy Island* and *Thunder Mountain*. Concurrent with the doomed dramatization, a producer wanted to adapt *Miss Dilly* into a musical, paying him for the option for two years before that project collapsed as well.[11]

Ted fed the appetite for escapism further by publishing a collection of earlier-written essays based on his experiences in Europe under the title *Perils in Provence*, published also in the winter of 1944. This book struck a different note from *Miss Dilly Says No* by reminding readers of prewar Paris and its charms.

However much Ted may have enjoyed writing about his past in Paris, on June 9, 1945, he officially parted ways with Virginia Rice, the agent who had facilitated his successful run of books. In fact, she had placed two more manuscripts but did not demand that she be paid her commission for the second one despite her legal claim to it.[12] What caused the separation is not known, but the record shows Rice to have been both professional and skillful throughout her working relationship with Ted.

Sometime in 1945 or possibly in the beginning of 1946, Ted's Columbia contract ran out. Upon the advice of his agent, he and Jackie stayed in California long enough to receive his unemploy-ment insurance payments just like other film industry workers. Going each week to the unemployment office stung less when he saw movie stars between films showing up in Rolls-Royces to collect the very same twenty dollar checks he did.[13] Ted failed to secure a job equal to the Columbia one. He also now realized how right Jackie had been about his being a fish out of water (if that phrase may be permitted about the author of *Mr. Limpet*) in California. The time had come to leave.

Fortified financially with Hollywood pay and steady *Bare-foot Mailman* royalties, he and Jackie moved back to South Flor-ida. Instead of renting, they now bought a house at 755 Azalea

Street in the Old Floresta part of Boca Raton. This area was filled with lovely 1920s Spanish style homes embowered among lush foliage. The Pratts had rented one of the houses in this community from Fred Aiken in 1943 when Ted was finishing writing *The Barefoot Mailman*. The house they now bought followed the design of Adison Mizner, a name that would soon become important in Ted's research and writing.

But for now, Ted had some California-related writing to complete, starting with *Valley Boy*. The novel follows ten-year-old Johnny Birch through a summer when life transforms from a largely miserable existence to a bright promise for the future. The setting is a quirky and contentious San Fernando Valley neighborhood where his parents care more for their horses than for him. The story was particularly personal for Ted, as he poured his own ways of seeing the world into his young protagonist. He would always cherish a letter from a reader who told him, "You are *Valley Boy* to me!"[14]

The novel includes other loves and fascinations in Ted's life. One of the female characters is a native of Lake Worth and very homesick for Florida. Ted dedicated an entire chapter, tenuously connected thematically, about her fear of never being able to return to her home state. Then there is the idea of the life lived in water that continually drew Ted. In the Valley's arid summer, Johnny befriends a sea lion named Oscar, and Ted gives a great deal of attention to the lifeways of the amphibious animal. The novel's climax comes with rain, not quite as dramatic as the hurricane of *Big Blow* but strong enough to cause flooding. Johnny's life changes for the better when his father rescues him from drowning. Not only does his father show his love for the boy by doing so, but both parents decide to be more attentive to him.

Darker elements appear in the novel as well. At one point, Johnny tries to commit suicide, and Ted's exploration of the psychological drives and short circuits of that decision surely derived from his thoughts about his father. Also tingeing the novel's atmosphere may have been his mother's death on June 18, 1945. Although the flooding water nurtures and heals, the novel ends with the sad note of Oscar's owner carrying him away from Johnny.

Duell, Sloan, and Pearce continued its association with Ted by publishing *Valley Boy* in 1946. The novel found some success in being chosen as a book of the month by the Retail Bookseller, the closest (as Ted put it) any of his books ever came to winning an award.[15] Universal Studios bought the rights for a film adaptation, but none ever went into production.[16]

The death of Ted's mother may have gotten his mind on matters of faith again because belief took center stage in his next book, *Mr. Thurtle's Trolley*. In his youth, protagonist Andrew Thurtle, manager of a livery stable, hated motorcars so much he made his fiancé, Nettie Parks, vow never to ride in one. When she broke her vow—and with his rival, no less—he left town. His return thirty years later came with a kind of faith-based magic. He had moved to Westchester County, New York, to run a trolley with a partner. Now the trolley had been put out of business by automobiles as completely as trolleys had displaced horses, which finally extinguished what was left of Mr. Thurtle's faith in life. But when he gets on the now-retired trolley in his uniform and prays, he can make it move magically. Mr. Thurtle convinces his partner and his partner's wife to go with him to California instead of Florida (where they had long wanted to retire) so he can reconnect with Nettie along the way. They find her having never married, waiting all this time for Mr. Thurtle's return. She marries him when he confirms that he never actually has lost his faith.

It was a curious book for an author approaching the half-century mark of life, now orphaned and having returned to his adopted home. Ted would not claim to have regained his faith in God. But it may be that he had found a need for faith in something, whether it be South Florida or goodness in people. The second World War had come to an end but at terrible cost that ushered in a new profound anxiety of annihilation peculiar to the dawning atomic era. A fanciful, lighthearted tale of being able to move an outmoded machine simply by faith perhaps offered Ted grounding. He may have felt new optimism with the birth of another niece, Lorraine Ellen Dempsey, on October 8, 1946.

Mr. Thurtle's Trolley was published in September 1947, again by Duell, Sloan, and Pearce. In its review of the novel, the *Indianapolis Star* referred to Ted as a "West Coast writer."[17] But by now Ted had abjured California just as he had Catholicism, and it was time to return to Florida in his fiction. Interestingly, the writer who had abandoned the Trinity now set about to create his own trilogy.

CHAPTER 16

Flagler and the Flame Tree
(1948–1950)

Ted had committed to Florida fully with his return, and it was probably around this time that he and Jackie made some significant literary connections during a trip to St. Augustine. The Virginia writer James Branch Cabell spent his winters there in the nation's oldest city. He was best known for his racy absurdist novel, *Jurgen*. When Ted shook hands with the bestselling author, he said, "This is like meeting God."[1] To that, the Virginian replied, "No one ever met God."

More important to Florida literary history, Ted formed a friendship with Marjorie Kinnan Rawlings. Back in 1941 she had married Norton Baskin, who owned the Castle Warden Hotel in St. Augustine (the building now houses Ripley's Believe It or Not). Although Rawlings and Baskin made their primary home in nearby Crescent Beach, she still maintained her orange grove enterprise inland at Cross Creek. When Ted and Jackie met Norton in St. Augustine, he invited them to go with him to Cross Creek to meet Marjorie. Evidently, he did not bother to tell her ahead of time that he was bringing new friends.[2] Although Marjorie was chilly to the Pratts at first, by the next day her maid Martha had decided they were all right and the writer warmed to them.

With the friendship now begun, Marjorie and Norton took Ted and Jackie with them to Salt Springs, which is known for its blue crabs. The foursome bought a cardboard box full of the live crabs, which they put in the trunk of the car. Then they went to a cookout, where they engaged in heavy drinking and ate yearling deer, literally the animal that she had won a Pulitzer Prize for writing about (and which was apparently by then illegal to eat). When the group finally returned to Marjorie's home around midnight, they opened the trunk and watched the crabs cascade out. Rather stupidly, the cardboard box had been filled with water to keep the crabs alive, and the box had disintegrated. Marjorie warned everybody away from the crustaceans, insisting that only she know how to pick them up without getting pinched.

Ted was not so much looking to write about the Crackers he spent that evening with in the Florida backcountry, but he was ready to write another historical novel about Florida. It made sense to continue the story he had begun with *The Barefoot Mailman*. That book had done him right. Its annual royalties had made him comfortable back in the state he had chosen as home. They helped him purchase a small sailboat he christened *The Barefoot Mailman*. The back of the dust jacket for *Mr. Thurtle's Trolley* featured him with his new vessel. Not only that, people in Florida were starting to call *him* the barefoot mailman.[3]

Ted saw, however, that the strength of the material lay not in furthering the story of Steven and Adie. Instead, the central character was Florida itself. People would come and go, generating new stories of cooperating with or fighting against Florida's land, water, plants, animals, and weather. Those stories took on interest because of Florida itself and because their basic arch never changed. A present-day Floridian can recognize in a Pratt Florida storyline the same conflicts set in any era since the 1880s.

In light of this realization, Ted constructed his sequel around one of the most vivid entities of South Florida. The *Delonix regia*, most commonly called the Royal Poinciana, is a tree native to Madagascar. In the summer months, the wide, canopy-shaped tree bursts into brilliant red-orange bloom. Its vivid, dramatic, almost unreal color had become synonymous with romantic visions of Florida by the middle of the twentieth century. In fact, it had established itself as enough of a fixture in Florida for Coral Gables to hold an annual Royal Poinciana Fiesta starting in 1937 and still held today. Moreover, the tree became a stock element of paintings by midcentury artist Albert "Beanie" Backus and the so-called Highwaymen, a group of African Americans who painted pictures that captured the grandest Florida dreams.

Because the Royal Poinciana seems to blaze like fire when in bloom, it has also been called the Flame Tree. Ted seized on the provocative implications of a tree afire. It surely occurred to him that here was a present-day incarnation of the burning bush Moses encountered, an apt parallel to South Florida's ability to endure but not succumb to human presence and affliction. Ted also saw the way this transplant had become practically native in people's minds. The Flame Tree may not have originated in Florida, but its physical makeup so communed with the state that it thrived. Ted saw himself the same way in his relation to Florida.

He then layered this metaphorical fabric with what he saw as a less sympatico transplant. In 1894, Standard Oil magnate Henry Morrison Flagler built the Royal Poinciana Hotel on Palm Beach Island. In so doing, Flagler not only furthered his railroad (which would ultimately run to Key West) but also established Palm Beach as *the* winter resort of the wealthy. In what is still called "the season," the rich gather in Palm Beach at the beginning of the new year to enjoy the mild weather and beautiful scenery.

By the turn of the twentieth century, the Royal Poinciana had been expanded into the largest hotel in the world. The Palm Beachers who stayed there dined and gambled at Colonel E. R. Bradley's Beach Club and enjoyed extravagant gala events, the most fabulous celebrating George Washington's birthday. But all this glamour pointed up class and race inequity over against the poorer year-round residents of West Palm Beach across Lake Worth. On the island itself, a service class of African Americans drew wheeled carts called "Afrimobiles" as transportation for the Palm Beachers. Furthermore, the hotel and the community around it imposed a degree of artificiality on the Florida land and seascapes.

Ted used these elements to construct a love triangle in a book he entitled *The Flame Tree*. On one hand stood an actual royal poinciana tree; on the other, the Royal Poinciana Hotel. In the middle he installed a woman—a character similar to himself in certain ways—named Jenny Totten. An exceptional beauty from Ohio, Jenny feels an instinctual similarity and draw to the royal poinciana tree. But, having been raised by her aunt since her parents' death from smallpox, she also desires the wealth and status emblematized in the Royal Poinciana Hotel. The resulting scenario features a transplanted woman torn between two other transplants just as Ted himself felt torn between glamorous wealth and the natural world.

Over this triangle Ted spreads another. Jenny's husband, Tip, also hails from Ohio but has a deep affinity with wild Florida. A hunter by trade and inclination, it is he who suggests moving to the state with his new bride so he can take advantage of the teeming wilderness. In resemblance to another side of Ted's personality, Tip embraces the Everglades readily and passionately. He has little use for the intrusion of the wealthy beyond their paying him as a guide on hunting excursions. But the natural environment frightens Jenny, and the call of wealth increases in the form of Cleve Thornton. This member of that rich society has a wandering eye that alights on Jenny. She thrills at his attraction to her and finds herself drawn magnetically to him, his wealth, and his connection to the hotel. Thus, Jenny finds herself in a triangle with Tip and Cleve.

Ted injects this second triangle with a dimension that may have hit close to home for him in another way. Ted and Jackie had no children, and neither did the married couple with the same first-name initials in the novel. Ted had written of child-birth very positively in *Thunder Mountain*. Now nearly in their fifties, the Pratts may have been coming to grips with the reality of being childless, whether intentionally or not. In the novel, childlessness drives Tip and Jenny apart. Maybe the same had been happening to Ted and Jackie.

Although the novel's action starts in St. Augustine with Cleve and Jenny meeting for the first time in front of an immediately jealous Tip, it soon shifts to the familiar South Florida scene. Tip and Jenny sail into Lake Worth on the *Margaret D*, captained by Jim Bethune. Fans of *The Barefoot Mailman* would have recognized the boat and some of the discussion between Jim and others in town. But from that point forward the novel shows no connection to the earlier book. Instead, it follows Tip and Jenny as they purchase a property distinct for its royal poinciana tree with which Jenny falls in love. The tree actually serves her as a crutch. When the walls of Flagler's hotel rise on the island, Jenny shifts her gaze to *that* Royal Poinciana.

A hurricane makes another appearance in a Pratt book, destroying the simple cabbage house in which Tip and Jenny have been initially happy. The larger house they build has bedrooms for children they do not have. As Tip spends more and more time at his hunting camp in the Everglades, Jenny crosses the "Great Divide" of Lake Worth in order to be among the rich of Palm Beach. One day she actually sees Flagler and his young wife, Mary Kenan. She also encounters Cleve Thornton. Now divorced, Cleve pursues her, even when he discovers she is married. To juice up the situation, Ted has Cleve go on a hunting trip with Tip, who brings Jenny along to make clear to Cleve that she belongs to him. The ploy fails to deter Cleve, but when Jenny watches Tip wrestle an alligator she makes him promise he will never do it again.

But Jenny does not follow her own advice of avoiding danger. She exposes herself to marital trouble by deepening her connection with Palm Beach and its famous hotel. First, she gets a job as a telephone operator there. Then she crashes the annual Palm Beach Washington Ball, where she wows the audience with her beauty and brass. Amused by her bold move, Cleve takes up with her. They dance, and he introduces them formally to Mr. and Mrs. Flagler. Jenny even enjoys the pleasure of stealing Cleve away from a beautiful debutante who has caused the most recent scandal of the Palm Beach set. But Jenny and Cleve's cavorting also sets Palm Beach on its ear. Some of the gentlemen go on a hunting excursion with Tip speaking of it, not knowing they speak of his wife.

The incensed Tip goes straight to Palm Beach and challenges Cleve to a fight. Cleve agrees only if Tip will agree to fight round two not with fists but on *his* terms. Tip agrees and promptly beats Cleve up. Cleve insists that their next challenge be a drinking contest. The two men and Jenny go to the Beach Club. Practiced drunk that he is, Cleve nevertheless ends up under the table. Having bested the rich man, Tip tells Jenny she must make up her mind forever between himself and Cleve and the Palm Beach scene he represents. Paralyzed at the thought of losing the Royal Poinciana Hotel, Jenny cannot respond.

Tip stalks off, going back out to his hunting camp still wearing the tuxedo he had to borrow in order to get into Bradleys. After throwing the suit into the Everglades water, he heads off to wrestle an alligator. In his distraction, he makes a wrong move, and the massive creature bites down on his leg and begins dragging him into the water. Tip manages to kill the alligator and escape but only after being nearly mauled to death.

When word of Tip reaches Jenny, she hurries to his side to nurse him, deciding finally to be loyal to him instead of the Royal Poinciana. The doctor explains that Tip can recover but only with her help. She must show him enough love and loyalty for him to recover his will to live. Not only must she nurse him, but the doctor tells her he has discovered a way they could yet have children. He explains that recent research has revealed that diet can play a role in sterility. Changing their way of eating from Ohio to Florida hurt their fertility. Simply consuming the food they grew up on will solve the problem. When Tip recovers consciousness and she tells him the good news, he points out that the Royal Poinciana tree on their property has now grown so tall and big it blocks out their view of the Royal Poinciana Hotel. As with so many of Ted's books, Tip and Jenny will live happily ever after.

Duell, Sloan, and Pearce did not publish *The Flame Tree*. Instead, Dodd, Mead, and Company brought it out in January 1950. The book was not widely reviewed, but the reviews that did appear were largely positive and cognizant of the body of historical fiction Ted was developing. Orville Revelle welcomed the book as a case when "an author and a subject which he makes his life work meet with happy results for both" in the *Fort Lauderdale News*.[4] The *Miami Herald*'s Stephen Trumbull declared the novel "another colorful slice of Florida's yesterday" and predicted it "probably will become a must for the bookshelf in Florida homes where the interest in the home state extends beyond the happenings recorded in today's newspaper."[5]

Non-Florida venues offered more measured responses. Pauline Naylor, reviewing the book for the Fort Worth *Star-Telegram*, offered somewhat clinical praise of the book's presentation of Florida's interior with "a reality and clarity that indicates careful research, as well as enthusiasm" and concludes that "Plot, background and action add up to a vivid picture of a bizarre era in American social history, that may well be termed unique."[6] In a more critical vein, Louise Charles, writing for *Tulsa World*, saw the book as being out of balance. She readily acknowledged Ted's passion for Florida but found it "exasperating that this novel can be so good and yet not so good."[7] Where the story of Palm Beach and the Royal Poinciana was strong in Charles's view, the story of Jenny and Tip just did not pull its weight.

In the end, *The Flame Tree* would never be able to match *The Barefoot Mailman*'s success. But it was doing important work, and as these reviews appeared, Ted applied himself to researching and writing the final installment of his three-part series of Florida historical novels. In the midst of that work, however, a development transpired that would greatly increase his fortune and make him part of a publishing revolution.

CHAPTER 17

Paperback Writer
(1950)

With the midpoint of the century came a golden opportunity. Roscoe Kent Fawcett sought to do something new in publishing. The pocket-sized paperback scene had grown during World War II by reprinting hardbacks in cheap format. Fawcett had the new idea of actually publishing *first editions* in that cheap format. To put it in today's terms, he sought to generate original content. And this content would be designed to move quickly by means of racy titles and covers at bargain prices stocked in drugstores to tempt escapist-minded everyday people.

Fawcett's idea took the form of Gold Medal Books. The line would be edited by Jim Bishop. Al Allard, a native of Minneapolis, served as cover art director. To make the idea appealing to authors, Fawcett paid based on the number of books printed instead of the number sold. Moreover, the payment would be made at the time of the printing instead of months after the book was published. These innovative dimensions in addition to the lease-like arrangement of the rights (as opposed to the lifetime stipulations of standard publishing agreements) gave the author more immediate cash flow and independence. The idea brought a revolutionary dimension to publishing. A host of writers would come into their own financially with Fawcett Gold Medal books, including a fellow Florida writer and soon-to-be friend, John D. MacDonald, whose Travis McGee novels entered the imprint's list.

Ted learned of this new publishing approach from Victor Weybright, who was then starting the New American Library being distributed by Fawcett.[1] In light of the kind of books Fawcett wanted for the Gold Medal line, Ted thought he finally could publish the book on nymphomania he had written when he first came to Florida. By now, the novel had been rejected by thirty-three publishers, largely based on its sexual theme, although the book had, according to Ted, "not a salacious word."[2] Ted decided to try again, and Weybright sent the novel over to Bishop. The editor liked it, but he wanted to make sure it accurately depicted its subject. If Ted could find a respected psychiatrist who could attest to its accuracy, Fawcett would publish the book.

The prospect delighted Ted. He got in contact with New York–based psychiatrist Richard Hoffman, who offered an assessment. "This is an important book," the psychiatrist asserted. "It will be, no doubt, an enlightening, even educational experience for many to read this story. . . . Certainly the wider the knowledge of man's ills, whether they be of the mind or body, the greater the progress toward cure."[3] Armed with this statement, Fawcett put the book in production, walking a curious line between selling the lurid while simultaneously disavowing it. Fawcett had presciently discerned that everyday people dropping a quarter on a cheap book with a racy cover, title, and premise also wanted reassurance about the safety of normal everyday life.

Entitled *The Tormented*, Ted's novel focused on a woman named Zona Dodd, whose sexual appetite overwhelmed her. Ted was surely thinking of his friend Dan as well as the women he had known in Paris. Perhaps he was also struggling with his own appetites. His case subject conspicuously wants to be middle class in her morality: she believes in heterosexual monogamy. But life and her mind and body steer her in a different direction.

Ted traces Zona's life, beginning with her romantic awakening as a teenager in a closet kissing a boy named Jimmie in her hometown of Cranston, New York (a stand-in for New Rochelle). The kiss is so passionate she ignorantly fears it will make her pregnant. When her mother educates her, she feels relieved. She then hurries to Jimmie, however, and they really do consummate their attraction. Embarrassed and confused, Jimmie returns to college and quits speaking to Zona. Crushed, she casually sees a nice boy named Ernest, who, like his name, fervently loves her but fails to ignite her passions. Even when he learns that she fulfills those passions with other men, Ernest forgives her.

But she wants nothing of Ernest and instead marries a successful businessman named Roger. They move to New York City. Unfortunately, Roger cannot keep up with her sexually. In her frustration she allows herself to be wooed away by one of his acquaintances. When Roger uncovers the affair, she tries to patch things up with him only to get drawn into another encounter. Roger divorces her. When she gets pregnant, she gets an abortion.

Her life now in shambles, she starts sleeping with anonymous men she picks up in restaurants and clubs. One night, a man she brings home frames her as part of a corrupt Manhattan scam to accuse women of prostitution and have them pay to avoid jail time. The scam's leader is a man named Waxy Bogart. Zona's downfall takes place against the backdrop of the stock market crash and the Depression. When another framing sting takes place, Zona cannot pay her way out and goes to jail.

As she bemoans her situation, a group of lesbians tries to initiate Zona into their orgies. When she continually refuses, they punish her by lashing her back, leaving a network of scars. Those scars become her ticket out as her unjust story and others come to light amid a city government clean-up. Now free and vindicated but broke, she meets an artist named Henry Dight, who paints a portrait of her. He also sets her up doing the very thing she had been accused of, working as a high-priced call girl. Finding such lucrative labor during the Depression gives her a comfortable life monetarily but an edgy one societally. One of her johns divines that some man has done her wrong and that he would like to work the guy over. When she refuses, he gives her a package of strychnine and tells her he will see that the victim gets a private funeral.

In the midst of this new life, her original love, Jimmie, shows up one night as a customer. Flabbergasted, both Zona and Jimmie express their regrets about not staying together those years ago. Eventually he passes out drunk, and she realizes all her frustrations were built on an idealistic and false illusion of Jimmie as the man who could fulfill her desires. She now sees he is just a man like any other, and her problem will never be solved. The two part forever.

Then one night she sees her enemy, Waxy Bogart. He does not recognize her with her dyed hair. She lures him back to her apartment and kills him with the strychnine. Sitting in the apartment with Bogart's corpse, Zona realizes the final unraveling of her life has begun. She calls the man who gave her the strychnine, but he never answers because he has been sent to jail. She calls her father, who is aghast at what she has done. Finally, she cleans the house up, takes her belongings, and buys passage on a ship to Miami. On the way, she realizes she forgot to take down the portrait of her painted by Dight and that it will lead the police to her.

Upon arriving in Miami, she takes a bus to a small coastal town and checks into a seaside hotel. Not long thereafter she realizes investigators have found her. She walks into the sea to drown herself. But she stops, hesitating, not wanting to die. As the investigators run toward her, the novel ends with her standing ankle-deep in the ocean.

Thus the novel publishers rejected for years. It was the work of a man trying to understand a woman's psychological disorder sympathetically. Ted almost entirely refrained from naming it. The word "nymphomania" does not appear until the last fourth of the novel, and then only a couple of times. The ambiguity of the ending captures all the pain and drama of the character's situation, and Ted cleverly brought the narrative back around to the opening page that featured a newspaper clipping of the baffling murder scene in her apartment. The style might not have been as mellifluous as the now long-deceased Fitzgerald's, but the content and narrative was just as daring as that of Lewis or Hemingway.

The book was published in 1950 and sold out its entire first printing of three hundred thousand copies. Eight more printings followed in quick succession with a total sale of almost 1.75 million copies, putting the book on Alice Hackett's list of all-time bestsellers.[4] The book joined Bruno Fischer's *House of Flesh* to be the first Gold Medal books to sell a million copies.[5] *The Tormented* also sold well in foreign countries. Priced so cheaply, the book did not make Ted a millionaire. But as his sister was fond of saying, he was comfortable.[6]

While most readers paid for the excitement of a cheap thrill, fan mail to Ted showed him many also were grateful for the sex education it brought. One reader wrote, in what looks more dubious in our moment now than it apparently did to Ted, "Now I know what is the matter with my wife, and your book made us go to a doctor who explained it some more so we think we can cope with it. Thank you, Mr. Pratt."[7]

The book received virtually no attention from reviewers, a testimony to just how much Ted had broken the rules in both content and publishing approach. When William Lengel succeeded Jim Bishop as editor of the Gold Medal books, he told Ted the editors of *Publishers Weekly* were wondering why an established author like himself should want to publish in the original paperback scene.[8] Lengel had made a name for himself as an editor long ago and was known for having broken up a fight between Sinclair Lewis and Theodore Dreiser.

Lengel arranged a dinner at the Lotus Club with Ted and the *Publishers Weekly* editors. Ted told them that hardback publishing "was for the most part a fuddy-duddy affair operated by many rules dating from publishing practices used in England hundreds of years ago which hardly applied now" and that they did not "know much about merchandising." The editors disagreed and told him he would "ruin his standing as an author." He said he preferred to be read by millions instead of twenty thousand, and that he had "two thick scrapbooks of mostly good reviews I never looked at any more." Ted even predicted that a time would come when an original paperback would be valued as much as a hardback and that original paperbacks would someday be reissued in hardback.[9]

Ted was all in with this paperback gig. He promptly dashed off another story Fawcett could advertise as being racy. This one, entitled *Cocotte*, drew upon Ted's first time in Paris. The novel tells of Martin Gordon, a nice boy from a nice family who very much resembles the young Ted Pratt. Like Ted, Martin meets a sexually experienced artist named Frank Bizer, who initiates him into Parisian sex life. With Bizer, Martin meets a cocotte named Lucienne after the Lulu Ted himself knew and loved. Overwhelmed by her beauty, Martin falls in love with her and asks her to marry him. The contrast between his innocent devotion and her hardened view of intimacy grows quickly painful to the reader's eyes. She clearly only wants marriage to Martin because he convinces her she will be rich. Martin, meanwhile, wants her to give up her lifestyle.

So far, the story follows Ted's own experience. But when Martin realizes how difficult if not impossible changing must be for Lucienne, he takes her with him to live in the United States. Although Martin's mother graciously tries to bring her into the family, his father disapproves of her and his brother goes to Paris to seek out the truth of Lucienne's past. As for Lucienne herself, she leads a miserable existence living in Martin's family's home. Upon learning the truth of her past, Martin's father delivers an ultimatum and Martin and Lucienne move into a humble apartment while their money dwindles away. She grows more dissatisfied still. Having spurned his family's lucrative diamond business, Martin gets the idea to sell loud-colored and -styled shoes in Harlem. He got the idea from an African American jazz band in Paris.

Martin's business fails to take off right away, and the exasperated Lucienne takes matters into her own hands. She secretly becomes involved with an old employee of Martin's father's, who gives her money in exchange for sexual favors. This activity devastates Martin when he learns about it. His love takes a final crushing blow when he sees Lucienne walking down the street with a man she had denied involvement with in Paris. The novel ends with Lucienne going back to France and her cocotte lifestyle.

In Ted's typical fashion, there is hope for Martin. His shoe business is finally taking off. He writes his mother, who comes to him with new respect to go with her affection. Martin's making something of himself promises reunion with his father and brother. But another curious result occurs as he realizes his heartbreak is "a necessary part of him. He had done many foolish things, but somehow, in a way he did not yet fully understand, he realized that they too had been necessary."[10]

Here in this "cheap" book, Ted articulated something so many people experience in one way or another. The realization that even bad experiences play important roles in life likely was one he himself had come to after his own experiences in Paris. It transforms this book sold as a heavy breather into a coming-of-age tale with wide appeal and real emotional resonance. But Ted had now fully joined the ranks of paperback writer, and the emphasis came down much more heavily on the sex in the book. In fact, Ted was helping swell the chorus of voices driving the country toward a sexual revolution. While it is important not to overstate his role, it is not beyond reason to see Ted's books playing their part in bringing conversation around sexuality into the cultural mainstream.

As important as the theme of human sexuality had become for Ted, the Florida material still defined him and occupied most of his energy. His deep excursion into Florida history was now bearing fruit on key fronts that would solidify his place in the history of Florida's literary and popular culture. He brought this career-defining work to conclusion with a third book and with a project that brought Florida's pioneer era to the screen and himself into greater visibility yet.

CHAPTER 18
Big Bubble:
Florida Trilogy Complete
(1951)

In the midst of researching South Florida's past, Ted wrote a booklet entitled *The Story of Boca Raton*, published in 1950 by the Ford Motor Company. After dedicating a mere page and a half to the epoch from Ponce de Leon to the barefoot mailmen, Ted focused on the twentieth-century birth of the city originally envisioned as the greatest resort in the world. That story set the stage for the final volume of his "Florida Trilogy."

Ted commenced the third novel in the 1920s, picking up the action just as World War I came to a close. He titled the book *Big Bubble*, because it dealt with the rollicking high times of speculation in South Florida that created a massive real estate bubble. As Christopher Knowlton has recently written in *Bubble in the Sun*, that bubble arguably played as big or even bigger a role in precipitating the Great Depression than the iconic stock market crash of 1929.[1]

The remains of that era with which the Pratts were most familiar were those connected to Addison Mizner. An adventurer, writer, artist, and architect, Mizner came to Palm Beach as the guest of Paris Singer, the wealthy son of Isaac Singer, inventor of the Singer sewing machine. A witty raconteur who won over the elite, Mizner mingled with the rich winter guests of Palm Beach. Mizner grew up in California and loved the Spanish architecture there. He also studied architecture during stays in Spain and South America. To his mind, South Florida's landscape called for a Spanish style of building instead of the standard wooden structures—large but perversely called "cottages"—then common on Palm Beach.

Singer provided his friend with his first Palm Beach commission. Having built hospitals in Europe for wounded soldiers, Singer had Mizner design and build one in Palm Beach in 1918. The war soon ended, though, so instead of serving a medical purpose it became the Everglades Club. The Spanish-Mediterranean style of the building so thrilled Palm Beachers that it revolutionized building on the island. This new trend started with *El Mirasol*, a mansion commissioned by Lucretia Stotesbury, wife of wealthy railroad financier Edward T. Stotesbury.

Mizner went on to design and construct a string of mansions, all of them holistic builds inside and out, including furniture and decorations, much like Frank Lloyd Wright's approach. A Mizner house gave a feel of comfort and placidity, with beautiful vistas, old Spanish furniture, and striking blue tile. New as Palm Beach was, Mizner gave his structures an antique feel. He even used worm-eaten "pecky cypress" for his ceilings, transforming the previously useless wood into a highly prized and expensive commodity. Meticulous in his attention to detail but unable to keep up with the demand for actual Spanish antiques, Mizner set up manufacturing facilities in West Palm to generate "antiques" to put in the houses.

From his success in Palm Beach, Mizner wanted to transform from a builder *for* the wealthy to being one *of* the wealthy.

His plan to do so was to design and construct not just mansions and public buildings but an actual city. It would be the greatest resort in the world, carefully laid out with canals, polo fields, a tremendous hotel, and even a castle-like house for its lord and builder. The location: the tiny hamlet called Boca Raton.

Mizner employed writers to produce copy proclaiming the greatness of this future resort city. Carl Fisher had done the same to develop the Miami coast. George Merrick had developed pineapple fields into dreamy Coral Gables, with its tremendous Biltmore Hotel and Venetian Pool. Long before Walt Disney came to the state to build his Magic Kingdom, already South Florida saw entire communities patterned on Old World styles. And South Florida saw the wildness of the Jazz Age in full riotous bloom. Liquor flowed, bathing beauties paraded, and there was a flaunting of any rules or decency among the people who flowed to the region.

The bubble burst when a group of men called "binder boys" came to Miami. Buying and selling properties at increasing rates in rapid fire, they pumped the already ridiculously inflated Florida real estate up to unimaginable heights. When local businessmen executed a pump and dump in retaliation, cracks showed in the Florida real estate armor. The crash came in 1926, and Mizner stood among those holding the bag. Although he did go on to receive other commissions, he died poor in 1933. He had made a start on his dream of building Boca Raton, including the completion of a hotel that now figured largely in Ted's life. But he lost the city and had to watch other developers follow up on his plans, which included building Ted's neighborhood of Old Floresta.

Ted employed Mizner's story in the novel. The main character, Adam Paine, loves Spanish architecture just as Mizner did. He manages to befriend fictional breakfast food tycoon Michael Sumner, who, like the real-life Singer, finds himself intrigued with Adam's vision and commissions a hospital. In Ted's story, neither Adam nor Sumner actually envision the building ever being a hospital; when the war ends, it opens as the Everglades Club's fictional counterpart, the Flamingo Club. Just as the real-life Mizner got his first home commission in Palm Beach from Stotesbury at his wife's insistence, so Adam gets his first commission by impressing Mrs. Bradbury, the social leader of Palm Beach. Like Mizner, Adam sets up manufacturing industries in West Palm to churn out antiqued furniture and items for the houses he builds. And in the same way Mizner attempted to build Boca Raton, Adam begins work on fictional Roca Faro, only to see it go down when the bubble bursts.

Ted's story, however, departs from Mizner's in certain ways. Adam does not much resemble Mizner in terms of personality. Where Mizner was charming, Paine is socially awkward. Where Mizner has often been thought to be gay, Paine is relentlessly heterosexual. Although the fictional Paine's physique matches Mizner's legendary and overwhelming largeness, Ted puts it to use as part of Paine's appeal to women. Finally, where Mizner remained single his entire life, Adam is married to a woman named Eve. This heavy-handed move allows Ted to create a fable of temptation in the paradise that is Florida, a scenario implied in the old Timothy Brace novel *Murder Goes in a Trailer*.

The temptation devolves entirely on the man instead of the woman in Ted's Edenic tale. Where in *The Flame Tree* Jenny feels the alluring call of Palm Beach, in this book it is Adam who cannot resist its glamour. Although he flaunts his independence as an artist, when twice-divorced millionairess and femme fatale Mona Otis sets her sights on him, Adam's impending demise comes clear. A busty blonde temptress given to nude swimming, Mona appears like a character out of Ted's new paperback career. Her physicality overwhelms Adam. He divorces

Eve, who has been running one of the manufacturing companies and obtains it from him as part of the divorce deal. Marrying Mona goes bad from the beginning, as Adam grows quickly suspicious of her young and handsome butler.

Into this mix, Ted throws a 1920s version of Sylvanus Hurley named Gerry Vance. Adam and Eve first encounter him while driving from New Rochelle to Florida in a Rolls Royce Adam obtained in lieu of cash payment from Frank Lloyd Wright. The carnival barker Gerry means to make money fast. He starts his career running rum illegally with the advent of the Volstead Act. He uses his boat to help Adam smuggle antiques from Spain into Florida. From that venture, he moves into real estate, developing his own housing community. He then helps Adam find the land for Roca Farro and lends his barking skills to sell it to hungry Florida speculators. Adam imagines Gerry to be his friend, but as everything crashes around him, he goes home to find Gerry and Mona in a passionate embrace.

The novel ends hopefully as Adam returns to Eve, who takes him back. It seems they will stay in Florida, Eve assuring Adam people will get back to building houses sooner or later and will want him to design them. Unlike the biblical couple they are named after, these two apparently get to stay in paradise. Maybe some readers imagined Adam and Eve were able to stay around until after World War II, when Ted wrote his novel and when Florida building had started back on the upsurge. Perhaps Steven and Adie even lived long enough to see the new building—their names appear in the novel as does the *Margaret D*, the boat that marks the lone solid thread running through all the novels.

Duell, Sloan, and Pearce published *The Big Bubble* in 1951. Its dust jacket featured an abstract gray, white, black, and yellow bubble, a departure from the typical cover art for Ted's Florida books. The Popular Library editions, however, featured Mona in the pool or just out of the pool with a towel barely covering her and the tagline: "She Could Make A Man Or Break Him." The hardback version included a note at its beginning:

My Florida historical trilogy is now complete. In it my main purpose has been to try to present, with candid interest and deep affection the spirit of an exciting and colorful period in what is perhaps the most unique section of our country. That time, from 1887 to 1926, a mere forty years, saw the section grow from a wild frontier to a luxurious civilization. My three stories are of its intense growing pains.[2]

Reviewers all got the memo that this book concluded Ted's trilogy and made that clear to the readers, giving particular attention to the novel's historicity. In his piece for the *Tampa Tribune*, E. D. Lambright laid out the connections between the novel and the real-life Florida bubble.[3] Lillian Blackstone, for the *St. Petersburg Times*, noted that Ted himself would not comment on whether the character Adam was based on Mizner but preferred to leave the matter to the reader's imagination.[4] Pat Price identified the book as the third part of the trilogy for readers of *The Miami News*, adding, "For a stirring romance in an exciting period of Florida history 'The Big Bubble' is high on the entertainment list."[5] Martha Smith celebrated the moral tale at the novel's center in *The Atlanta Journal*, seeing the book as "a pleasant, racy interpretation of what really happened in that sunny Garden of Eden before the snake of financial 'bust' drove out the happy mortals."[6] Beatrice Washburn, in her review for the *Miami Herald*, wrote that the novel lacked the "literary quality" of the first two novels in the trilogy, "but it has an enormous force."[7]

Later, Ted wrote in self-assessment that in *The Flame Tree* and *The Big Bubble* "human emotions are brought to the grown-up stage."[8] He had progressed from creating flat characters to round characters, "but not well rounded," which was his greatest lack. Although Ted did not come right out and call Florida a character, he defended his trilogy in those terms, explaining that he wrote of its "growing pains" with "candid perception, keen knowledge, and deep affection." The little boy who had loved playing in Minnesota waters, visiting the Museum of Natural History, and fishing and sailing the Atlantic Ocean off the Florida coast had, in his own understated way, done something unique and artistic. In the pages of his writing, Florida lurked as quietly but powerfully as a panther slinking through the forest, glimpsed only occasionally for what it is but asserting its presence at all times. Florida was, in fact, Ted's greatest character. And he was steadily becoming one with it.

CHAPTER 19

The Barefoot Mailman Walks Again (1951)

In his constant quest to find places to write away from home, Ted managed to secure a special one in Boca Raton. This place had not only both grandeur and panache but a history close to Ted's own work. Among Addison Mizner's few completed Boca structures was the Ritz-Carlton Cloister Inn (now the Boca Raton Resort) on Camino Real. By the time Ted moved to town, it was owned by J. Myer Schine, who had made a fortune in the hotel and movie theater business. His wife, Hildegarde, was a passionate supporter of the arts, which brought her in contact with Ted. She graciously permitted him to write in one of the cabana bungalows on the property.

In early 1950, Sylvan Simon, production head of Columbia Pictures, was staying at the hotel. According to Hildegarde's faulty memory (she remembered the vacationing producer being Irving Thalberg, who died in 1936), she was reading *The Barefoot Mailman* poolside and began discussing it with Simon.[1] As Ted recalled it, an assistant manager of the hotel came out to his house in Old Floresta (the Pratts refused to have a telephone) and convinced him to come to the hotel with a copy of the novel.[2] Ted did so, and Simon took the book back to Hollywood to read. When he finished it, he called one of Ted's neighbors to inform him that Columbia wanted to make the film so long as Ted served as location director to find a stretch of virgin beach for filming. Ted agreed but doubted he could find such an untouched spot. After searching for weeks, he was about to give up when Key Biscayne in Miami presented itself. Here the beach stretched in a pale virgin strip against the blue water in a last gasp of the past.

Columbia went to work with producer Robert Cohn and director Earl McEvoy at the helm. Through the spring, Alfred Lewis Levitt wrote the screenplay, later joined by James Gunn and Francis Swann. The film would be shot in SuperCinecolor, a newly invented three-color process. As the project developed, Robert Cummings, who had teamed up with Reagan and Sheridan in *King's Row* back in 1942, was cast as Sylvanus Hurley. Cummings was far more established than the actor cast to play Steven Pierton, a young Tennessean named Jerome Courtland. As a result, the script began to cant toward the Sylvanus character, and soon Columbia was clamoring for a title change, suggesting *Blood on the Trail*, *Pioneer Desire*, or *Beach Boy*. Ted leveraged the local South Florida press against that move. Letters and wires flooded Columbia, one Florida theater owner writing to say he would display the book by the original title no matter what the studio decided. Columbia backed down.

The rest of the cast fell into place. In the female lead of Adie Titus was the young starlet Terry Moore, fresh off her role as the friend of the gorilla Mighty Joe Young. Playing Adie's father was Irish character actor Arthur Shields, who next year would play a central role in the John Wayne classic *The Quiet Man*. Playing the beach comber thug leader Theron was John Russell, who would later play in westerns. Percy Helton brought his chipmunk face and squeaky voice to the effort. Arkansan Trevor Bardette offered his particular kind of moustache. Will Geer and Ellen Corby appeared together in this film long before taking on the roles of Grandpa and Grandma Walton in the CBS television series of the 1970s.

Outdoor shooting took place in July. The crew found Key Biscayne's Hurricane Harbor and Crandon Park satisfactory. They caught the landscape on film none too soon: by the time filming wrapped, construction on houses had begun on Key Biscayne. "Boy, we just got in under the line," McEvoy said.[3] The crew still needed footage of alligators. Ted had heard about Ross Allen, the Pittsburgh-born herpetologist who maintained the Reptile Institute in Silver Springs. The crew headed there for alligator filming.[4]

The resulting movie amounted to a kind of western set in South Florida. The scrolling text that opened the film established that: "By 1890 the last frontier of America not in the West, but in Southern Florida." Following this announcement, the first scene features Steven walking on the beach and being attacked by beach combers. Steven hides underwater to escape the thugs only then narrowly to escape alligators. As to be expected in a film adaptation, the plot and focus was simplified from the novel. The business of naming Palm Beach, the presence of Seminoles, and a number of other thematic elements in the novel vanish in the film.

The film does preserve the love story at the book's center. Where in the book Adie pretends to be a boy, the film tries to package Terry Moore up as a twelve-year-old girl in braids and britches. Her being a full-grown young woman gets revealed to the audience before she hits the beach. Then on the trip southward when a bear cub scares her, she runs out in the lingerie she has kept hidden under her "little girl" clothes. Steven in the film is not quite as painfully awkward and paralyzed before Adie as Steven in the novel. But their blossoming love proceeds with innocence and charm.

More three-dimensional in the film is the character of Sylvanus. Cummings well portrays the self-serving flim-flam man as being less odious and more ambivalent than in the novel. Even when he runs a scam of encouraging Miamians to invest in a nonexistent company connected with an imaginary railroad to be built through the area, his conscience really does seem to bother him when the beach combers with whom he has allied attack the town and even threaten to take Adie. He aids Steven and the men of Miami to defeat the beach combers, and when he leaves town he even gives Steven and Adie the deed to his land as a present for their presumed wedding. It does happen to be the case that Sylvanus thinks the land worthless, and immediately after he learns that a railroad really is going to be built he wishes he could get the deed back. But he smiles and heads on away from Florida, everything smoothed over and peaceful by the movie's end.

The Barefoot Mailman is not a great film, but it does manage to capture the Florida history charm of the book. The landscape is authentic. Those in the know would notice that the lake scenes were set in central instead of South Florida, but those scenes present the kind of lush beauty that then and now can draw tourists to rides in glass-bottom boats. The SuperCinecolor juiced the colors of the scenery and of the principal trio of actors with particular appeal, and the visuals of Steven wrestling alligators reach real heights of action. The shoot-outs may not have attained the wagon-circling levels of John Wayne or Jimmy Stewart westerns, but they brought a satisfying enough catharsis when the heavy and his band of robbers get the worst of it.

Columbia released the film on November 5, 1951, with a premiere in Miami. As part of the festivities, the local store

Burdine's held an event in which fans could meet Jerome Court-land and get their books signed by Ted. The book's author sat quietly while bobbysoxers thrilled at meeting the handsome movie star beside him. Most wanted Courtland to sign the books. When one asked if Ted was anybody, he replied no.[5] This event was repeated at Halsey and Griffith, a West Palm Beach store specializing in books, stationary, cards, and other paper products. The shop filled its window with copies of the novel and a painting of the barefoot mailman by Ted's Delray-based artist friend Aaron Smock (the painting was later displayed in the First Bank of Boca Raton). The film still ran months later at Boynton Theater from March 4 to 6, as a co-feature with Robert Mitchum and Shelley Winters in *The Night of the Hunter*. Ted came to the theater to sign any copies of the book theatergoers might bring with them.

Most substantial of all, something of a barefoot mailman craze developed in South Florida. A group of developers received Ted's blessing to build a hotel right on the coast in Pompano Beach named The Barefoot Mailman Hotel. Ted dug the first spade of dirt. Along with being a fine novelty of the moment, its restaurant anticipated Randy Wayne White's present-day Doc Ford's Rum Bar and Grille. More barefoot mailman establishments would follow, including gift shops, a Kiwanis Club, and a camping club.[6] Later, a Barefoot Mailman Hotel on Highway 1 in Lantana, where it still is in operation. And for a time Hypoluxo branded itself as the Home of the Barefoot Mailman.

With this surge of visibility, the image of the barefoot mailman etched itself onto South Florida midcentury iconography. He joined an American pantheon of the folk heroes such as Johnny Appleseed, John Henry, and Minnesota's Paul Bunyan. His landscape is the same as that captured in the paintings of Backus and the Highwaymen. The evocative concept of this unshod beach-walking man appealed to the imagination as readily as Bunny Yeager's cheesecake photographs of Bettie Page posing in cheetah-print bikinis on South Florida beaches. The barefoot mailman exists within a naughtily innocent version of Florida itself part of larger Technicolor era—an era not a few look back on with warm nostalgia. The figure persists even now, perhaps with less force but with staying power nonetheless. As for Ted, his connection with the figure of the barefoot mailman solidified for good.

CHAPTER 20

Of Women and Men
(1951–1953)

While Ted "became" the barefoot mailman, he stayed busy writing paperback novels. Further mining the thematic vein of *The Big Bubble*, he produced a little gem entitled *Handsome* in 1951, the year his fellow Minnesotan Sinclair Lewis passed away. Having found a highly marketable topic, Gold Medal sought another book about sexual unhealthiness. This time Ted dramatized satyriasis, the male counterpart of nymphomania. He approached the material with one of his most clever conceptualizations. Where he had worked with the archetypal Adam and Eve in *The Big Bubble*, he had the sex-sick central character of this novel bear a name signaling his looks—Handsome. The novel never reveals Handsome's real name; later, one of his girlfriends gives him the false but appropriate last name Casanova.

Ted opens the book with an arresting scene in which Handsome is chained up in a bedroom. The house stands in Beantown, a hamlet in the Florida interior where stringbeans are shipped out to the rest of the nation. Handsome's wife, Ellie, keeps him confined in order to protect him from himself. It turns out that although he has a charmingly agreeable personality and extremely good looks, he also has a dangerous side. Tortured by subconscious pain, on the rare occasions when a woman refuses his sexual advances, he becomes homicidal. His condition stems from the traumatic event of seeing his father crash in on his mother having a tryst with another man. At one point in his past, Handsome did actually kill a woman. His rich family covered up the crime. But he landed in an asylum, where Ellie became his nurse, then lover, then wife.

Ellie believes she has Handsome in hand between the chaining and having the ugliest Cracker woman in town watch after him. But Handsome really wants to get away and asks the Cracker woman to help him. She agrees only if he will make love to her, which he does gladly. He does not want to leave Ellie so much as he wants to see the world. Unfortunately, the Cracker woman cannot find the key. They manage to get the chain off, but he retains the metal cuff, which he thereafter calls a bracelet.

With that, Handsome heads off into the wild world, which is to say Florida. His looks get him a long way with women, but his personality wins practically everyone. He shows no vanity at all about his appearance, and he takes great joy in whatever adventures come his way, however low-paying or humble they may be. His likability prevails so powerfully that the few occasions he turns murderous are strangely forgivable. He really is mentally ill.

Like the memoirs of Casanova, there is nothing graphic in the novel. The book is more a picaresque comical tale of a hero encountering racy adventures in the vein of Cabell's *Jurgen*. In fact, Handsome resembles another charming rogue from American literature—Huckleberry Finn. Handsome's Florida becomes Huck's Mississippi. Ted's readers would have recognized the types he encounters. Handsome takes up with a juke girl in Chobee while working a steady job at the bean plant. When Ellie rolls into town, he flees and wanders into a holiness tent meeting, getting a job beating the drum for a scamming husband and wife team. Readers may have been reminded of Sinclair Lewis's Elmer Gantry falling in with Sharon Falconer. Even when these religious cons fleece Handsome in a honeypot scam, he bears them no ill will, happily heading off to more adventures.

Those adventures include commercial fishing, alligator hunting, a stint as the plaything of a rich Palm Beacher, working with an airboat concern outside of Roca Farro (Boca Raton of *The Big Bubble*), handling sales with a medicine show, and selling tickets for a burlesque show in a carnival. Childlike, Handsome never shows animosity to Ellie—every time he escapes her, he simply explains that he has not finished his trip yet but that he loves and cares for her and looks forward to coming home when the right time comes. That time arrives when he gets caught with the burlesque show's premiere dancer and the owner beats Handsome up. Happy to take the beating as expiation for his guilt, Handsome achieves a cure from his condition. Ellie shows up just in time to save him from the pummeling.

Although Fawcett again obtained a statement from Dr. Richard H. Hoffmann testifying to the novel's clinical accuracy, the real power of the book lies less in its presentation of supposed sexual deviance than in its marked absurdity. The relationship and conversation between Handsome and Ellie address his condition without emotion or judgment, which contrasts with the outrageousness of his adventures. The style and tone anticipate the absurdist work of a future Florida writer, Harry Crews, who may have read and absorbed this picaresque story when it hit the drugstore stands. Meanwhile, again Ted deftly evoked Florida life, culture, land, and water. He handles the description of airboating in the Everglades particularly well, capturing that remote place in compelling detail. Handsome even encounters a Seminole, a tribe becoming increasingly interesting to Ted.

Incidentally, where reviewers made much of *The Big Bubble*, they ignored *Handsome*. This despite the fact that the two novels shared many similarities in sexual content and that *Handsome* is arguably a better-written novel. The prejudice against original paperbacks was just too strong, not that Ted's pocketbook cared.

Ted undertook another story of a heartbreaker in *The Golden Sorrow*. This one Fawcett published under the special "Red Seal" category for longer, or "Giant," books. Ted obtained the sonorous title from Shakespeare's *Henry VIII* concerning the pressures that come with success. Perhaps Ted himself was feeling some of these. He had certainly heard about and witnessed them in Hollywood, where this novel was set. The book also evoked Henry VIII's working out his ambitions through a series of wives, as Ted presented a story about a man who uses women to get to the top of the film profession.

Danny Rattigan grew up on the poor side of town in love with Patrice Montgomery, whom he met on his paper route into the rich section. That love goes unrequited, however, setting Danny on a journey to try and impress Patrice enough for her to fall for him. Danny pursues his quest by using women who can help him with money or influence. The process starts with a high school classmate and then proceeds through a wealthy woman in New York, a famous stage actress, a string of film actresses, even a film company owner's daughter. Each case follows a pattern. Danny shows no interest in a woman until he perceives some way in which she can be useful to him. At that point, he becomes strongly attracted to her and enters into a relationship. Once her usefulness has ended, his attraction, interest, and the relationship abruptly end.

Ted followed his now-established groove of exploring psychological causes of sexual deviance. One of the actresses

Danny takes up with explains his condition to him. She herself is obsessed with sex and has a library of erotica. As she learns about Danny's history, she diagnoses his tendencies, explaining that with his mother absent and his father a rumored suicide (Ted's one inclusion of a suicide father in his fiction), he needed a mother figure. Although his sister Maureen tried to be a mother to him, her efforts did not suffice. He found what he wanted in Patrice instead. But Patrice's not loving him back forced him, in his mind, to achieve higher and higher accomplishments in hopes that she would relent. Each time she did not, he went to another woman.

The painfulness of the unrequited love grows keenest when Danny hires Patrice as his business manager. She takes the job only because it will pay for treatments for her husband's alcoholism. When the husband comes to California to live in Danny's mansion, he goads Danny. It finally gets to be too much, and Danny and he fight until the husband loses his footing and falls into an empty pool, striking his head and dying. Although Patrice testifies that Danny did not mean to kill her husband, she never shows any sign of being in love with him. Danny ends up on Skid Row, poor and drunk. One day on the street, a man gives him a dime only when Danny "admits" he is not himself but a poor man begging for money pretending to be the star Danny Rattigan.

The Golden Sorrow closes with a scene in which Danny appears to be rescued from despair by a woman. While it suggests hope that Danny might not just die of drunkenness, the idea that he cannot break out of his pattern with women makes for one of Ted's rare dark endings. Ted's readers surely expected Patrice to break down sooner or later and reveal that she did love Danny and only remains loyal to her husband out of a sense of duty.

The novel reached drugstores, newsstands, and other retailers in September 1952, priced at thirty-five cents. Like Ted's other Fawcett books, it received almost no attention from reviewers. The *Orlando Sentinel* did include a review, but Ted surely rued the fact that the piece was nested within a larger article on Hemingway's *The Old Man and the Sea* along with a photo of the grizzled and gray Papa.[1] The reviewer, Leo Schumaker, noted that as "the author of nineteen hard-cover books, the East Coast authors says he prefers the tremendous readership offered by publication in the paperbacks." It was a graphic contrast between Ted and his quasi-nemesis, the one raking money in with a cheap book while the other reached a popular high with a story of a fisherman on the Atlantic that would win the Pulitzer Prize and help propel him to Nobel Laureate status.

Ted's writing about the stage and film in *The Golden Sorrow* provides a clue to what was on his mind. He had turned back to stage production again, a renewal of the community theater interest of his youth but in a more democratized form that took him deeper into Florida's past than ever. Ted was also expanding his knowledge of Florida's natural scene with new explorations into the Everglades in the south*western* rather than southeastern part of the state. He took a trip with the National Audubon Society to the mangrove coast and enlisted the aid of Everglades National Park Superintendent Daniel B. Beard and biologist Joseph C. Moore. The result came in the form of book published again in paperback by Gold Medal but that also foregrounded his Florida material. The novel was *Escape to Eden*, published in 1953.

In a nod to the Cold War, Ted built his novel around nuclear scientist Angus Martel and his dog, Atom. As one of the developers of the atomic bomb, Angus stumbles across a formula that creates a chain reaction in soil and can thereby destroy the world. Angus flees civilization with his secret, making his way to the remote Pelican River in Florida. Although he envisions living out his life in paradise, his Eden quickly disintegrates.

First, he discovers over half a million dollars' worth of pirate treasure, which exerts a corrupting influence on him. Then into his world comes the beautiful Lise Makin, who has washed into the river after a shipwreck during a storm. At first daunted by her presence, he soon falls in love. But then the bad rains of summer come, bringing mosquitoes and fever. Unable to stand these conditions and with Angus refusing to leave, Lise takes some of the treasure and heads for civilization's air conditioning.

Back in Miami, however, Lise encounters Miami bookie, Clymie Kramer, her former boss and would-be boyfriend who abandoned her during the storm. She refuses to tell him where the rest of the treasure can be found, but he saw her at the Pelican River and heads out to get it. Bitter at Lise's leaving, Angus willingly agrees to give Clymie the treasure. When Clymie shoots and kills an attacking Atom, though, Angus fights and accidentally kills him. Angus cleans up the situation by taking Clymie's body into the gulf and dumping it for the sharks to chew. With Clymie no longer around to pay lackeys to follow her, Lise hurries back to Angus. Realizing she really does love him and that he acted badly in putting her through such terrible conditions in the summer, Angus proclaims that they will cash in on the treasure and sail the world together.

Like Ted's previous Gold Medal books, *Escape to Eden* went largely ignored, but it did have the distinction of gaining positive attention in Palm Beach County. "Theodore Pratt seems to have effected a compromise between his earlier works and his more recent trend into the realm of popular priced paperback fiction," proclaimed *The Palm Beach Post*'s "Book Nook."[2] The cover may have sported a woman in a bathing suit, the reviewer observed, but the inside focused on Florida and themes of escape from society. The reviewer was especially excited to see connections between this novel and *Thunder Mountain*, purring that it "is good to encounter plot, action and even melodrama again in a Pratt novel. 'Escape to Eden' is like a breath of cool air-conditioned air after the heavy, smoky atmosphere of a night club." Whatever backhandedness the review's tone carried, it marked a change, however slight, in at least one reviewer's thinking about what Ted was trying to do with his career.

Escape to Eden closes with Angus offering a speech on the futility of trying to escape civilization, including its air conditioning. "The only paradise that exists," he says, "is to be found in the looking for it."[3] Civilization's discontents and Florida's inability to resist them formed concerns creeping deeper into Ted's mind. He was seeing these problems in Florida's history and now wanted to put them into action on a new kind of stage.

CHAPTER 21
Seminole
(1953–1954)

Over the years, Ted and Jackie had often spent time in the summer in North Carolina. There he saw and became enamored of the outdoor play, *Unto These Hills*, written by Kermit Hunter and first performed in the outdoor Mountainside Theater in Cherokee in 1950. The play presented the tragic story of the Cherokee Indian removal in 1838. Ted envisioned such an outdoor drama about the Florida Seminoles, and he naturally focused on the story of Osceola, whom the US Army captured by dishonest and ignoble means in 1837. Osceola died imprisoned at Fort Moultrie outside Charleston, South Carolina, on January 30, 1838. The story coincided with the Cherokee one in *Unto These Hills*. Ted believed he could do something good for the Seminole tribe and the state of Florida by writing a play for outdoor performance.

Entitled *Seminole: A Drama of the Florida Indian*, the play tells Osceola's story but couches it in a larger celebration of Florida itself. It opens by literally putting stage lights on the landscape while the narrator extolls the state. The play progresses then to the time of young Osceola rebuking the Seminole chiefs for obliging white men's demands. Osceola marries a young maiden named Morning Dew, and they call to each other in the woods via the sound of the chuck-will's-widow bird. That distinctive birdsong forms a means of communication also for a number of Osceola's closest associates, including a Cracker named Gideon Sauny, a scout for the US Army who pleads with the military not to harass the Seminoles.

Another Cracker scout named Blaze Paget hates the Seminoles and wants their land. He captures Morning Dew, calling her a maroon and putting her in slavery with General Wiley Thompson's blessing and over Gideon's protest. By now, Osceola has become a chief, and he leads the fight against the US Army. In one scene, Osceola and his companions kill Paget and Thompson. Later, Gideon comes into the camp via the safe passage of the chuck-will's-widow call and tells Osceola that the Army wishes to negotiate for peace under the white flag. Osceola and his closest friend Wildcat agree to go.

As per the historical reality, General Joseph Hernandez arrests Osceola. The play closes with Gideon finding Morning Dew and bringing her to the dying Osceola in Fort Moultrie. As Osceola dresses one last time for his moment of death, General Hernandez comes to Osceola now out of the army and a private citizen to reveal that he disagreed with his orders, regrets carrying them out, and admires the Seminole chief. Osceola forgives him and declares that all people should find ways to live together and not at war.

As the narrator explains, after his death the magnanimous Seminole chief is celebrated by his very captors as both a warrior and a patriot. Ted caught the irony of the actions well enough, but he also has his narrator celebrate national unity, despite its being problematically won. The narrator concludes the play by pointing out that the Seminoles have never actually signed a peace treaty and thus have technically not been conquered.

Instead, still holding their land, the Seminoles live alongside non-Seminoles. "This, then, is the Seminole and the white man," the narrator says in the play's final words. "This, then, is the land. This is Florida. This, then, is the land of Florida!"

In a rather different publishing approach for Ted, the University of Florida Press published *Seminole* in December 1953. Working with the state's university press may have been a result of Ted's civic motivations. A reviewer for the *Fort Lauderdale News* conveyed Ted's publishing the play as a "grass roots" rather than a commercial project.[1] The published play also got reviewers' attention around Florida in *The Bradenton Herald*, *St. Lucie News Tribune*, *The Tampa Tribune*, and *The Miami Herald*. The *Palm Beach Post* gave the book a particularly lengthy write-up, referring to Ted by what would become his preferred title of Literary Laureate of Florida and warming to even his raciest Fawcett titles.[2] This all amounted to good attention for a university press–published book, a play no less.

For Ted himself, this project was both a throwback to his old playwrighting days and a step forward in civic engagement. He went to work getting the favor and support of Seminole and state government leaders toward the staging of the play. Succeeding on that front, he turned to the all-important step of getting an amphitheater built for the play's performance. There he ran into resistance as it proved difficult to secure funds for the project. Like other fights in his life, this one was going to be long.

In the meantime, Ted adapted the play into a novel of the same name for Fawcett published under the same title in March the next year, 1954. Predictably for the Gold Medal imprint, Fawcett jazzed up the sexuality with John J. Floherty, Jr.'s painting of a half-nude Morning Dew on the slave auction block, a scene Ted added. That scene and attempted rapes by plantation overseer Fergus Dane, a new character Ted created, gave the novel a sufficient amount of torture-porn to help market it as more than a historical work.

But Ted's main concern in the novel was to craft a story that brought history to life in meaningful interpersonal ways. Where the play cannot quite decide whether to focus on Florida or Osceola, the novel fully focuses on the latter, depicting the Seminole chief's growth and hardships on the borders of two conflicting civilizations. Doing so involves greater focus on Gideon, who also navigates those borders. The novel opens not with a rhapsody on Florida or the meeting of Seminole chiefs but the origin of Osceola's relationship with Gideon. When Gideon's father dies. Osceola and Wildcat appear along the road and help him with the burial, which begins the friendship. In between the major scenes that Ted installed with practically verbatim dialogue from the play appear moments of Gideon moving through the Florida landscape between the Seminole world and the white world, his relationship to the Seminoles growing on emotional levels.

Perhaps the most vivid addition in the novel version is the Green Corn Dance. Osceola permits Gideon to become the first white person to attend this grand Seminole event. It may be that Ted himself had witnessed it himself in order to write his descriptions. Ted perhaps envisioned himself as being like Gideon, a white man who befriends Seminoles by showing his deep empathy. Many present-day readers would blanche at Ted or his character believing they can express the viewpoints of nonwhites without exploitation or appropriation. But such optimism characterized white writers and readers of Ted's moment, and he takes pains to show the ways Seminoles never fully trust or accept Gideon.

The cover alone assured sales, and Fawcett's *Seminole* went on to move almost a million copies. Fawcett evidently expected the strong showing, for the third printing did not come until

1960, and then with a new, slightly less provocative cover painting. Of course, the Gold Medal designation precluded the novel's being seen as serious historical fiction. The *Albany Democrat-Herald* included it in its section "Poor Man's Library, or Among the Paperbacks."[3] But although Ted did not claim to expand his Florida trilogy into a Florida tetralogy, *Seminole* could and probably should be seen as part of his Florida history series. It easily falls in line chronologically as a prequel further-ing the theme of Florida development. It was the last time Ted would truly delve into Florida history.

Meanwhile, the play version of *Seminole* saw one of its many disappointments in December 1954. Land had been designated and financing lined up five miles west of Fort Lauderdale in Plantation for an amphitheater to be built solely staging Ted's play. But the airport required that planes take their flights directly over that spot. The idea fell through because the people involved could not see how the play could be performed over the noise of the air traffic.[4]

Amid the excitement of both the play and the novel, Ted took time to participate in an art show as part of his ongoing friendship with Hildegarde Schine. In February, he joined with writers Leslie Charteris (creator of the detective character, the Saint) and Martin Dibner to put on an exhibition at the Art Guild of Boca Raton.[5] Held at the Boca Raton Club from the nineteenth to the twenty-eighth, the exhibition included original paintings by Charteris and Dibner. Ted did not paint, but he had managed to secure original paintings for his book covers. It was an era when such paintings were not considered high art. Many art-ists did not even bother to sign them, and few of the originals were ever returned to the artists themselves, so could be had for the taking. No list from the show has survived, but among the works displayed were likely the unsigned cover painting for *The Tormented*, a powerful painting for Signet's edition of

Thunder Mountain by Stanley Metlzoff, and Floherty's recently finished cover for *Seminole*.

Meanwhile, an interesting insight into Ted's personality might be gleaned from his friend Zora Neale Hurston. On March 28, 1954, Hurston wrote from Eau Gallie, Florida, to William Bradford Huie, a journalist and book author who had, like Ted, written for *American Mercury*. Huie was covering the Florida trial of Ruby McCollum, an African American who had killed a white man she testified to having raped her. A man named Vergil Howard had come to warn her not to help Huie, she believed at Ted's behest.[6] Hurston would get in trouble with the KKK, Howard cautioned, but Hurston offered an opinion on the real motivation. Ted, she wrote, "suffers terribly from professional jealousy" and "is probably suffering aches and pains from what he considers your 'invasion' of Florida and getting all that publicity."

Hurston's opinion may or may not be taken as accurate, but it offers a perspective on Ted. It may well have been the case that he wanted to protect Hurston. It may also have been true that he was possessive of his Florida material. Any possessiveness as well as a desire to protect may have increased in the wake of his friend Marjorie Kinnan Rawlings's death on December 14, 1953. He had defended her earlier that very year against a painful review by Louis Bromfield, prompting her to write him on February 19, "What a friend you are! I am simply delighted that you rared back on your dew-claws and lit into the Saturday Review with such superb, cold efficacy."[7] Ted would remain in contact with her widower, Norton Baskin, a testimony to his friendship and concern. In light of that and the question of whether Ted really did send Howard to warn Hurston, the comments she made seem perhaps unfair and unkind. Her thoughts probably never reached his ears as the two remained friends.

Still, the insight about Ted's "professional jealousy" may contain some truth. Certainly, he felt bitterness toward the publishing industry, which hardly made him unique but may have been sharpened by a sense of frustration when other writers won awards or received recognition. At the same time that Ted cherished his status as *the* writer of Florida history, it bothered him to be discounted as a "regional" writer. He pointed out that such a designation only aided the reputation of Nobel Prize winner William Faulkner.[8] Ted also surely saw that his writing came nowhere near approaching the artistry of Faulkner's. Given that he was competing with such formidable talents as Faulkner, Hemingway, and Hurston herself, Ted could be forgiven for feeling inadequate and at time envious.

CHAPTER 22

Literary Laureate of Florida (1954–1961)

September 1954 saw Ted publishing Gold Medal Title #867, *Smash-Up*, with another fleshy cover by Floherty. Ted drew on his experiences with the heavy traffic in Los Angeles to imagine a story about a deadly car crash. The accident marks the meeting point of several lives that become deeply entwined. A domineering mother driving her daughter whom she wants to turn into a beauty queen causes the wreck by her reckless driving. The other car is driven by the reformed son of a wealthy business owner and the business's manager, who dies in the wreck. An adulterous couple returning from a tryst in a third car witnesses the accident: the man tries to help, but neither he nor the woman want to be exposed. The son of the business owner and the beauty queen daughter wind up in the same hospital and fall in love, which derails the efforts of the domineering mother to sue him.

The novel dealt with a serious crisis. "Whatever reviewers may say about Theodore Pratt's latest novel, 'Smash-Up,' it should be emphasized that it is the first fictionalized treatment of the nationwide problem of automobile accidents," wrote

Paul Jordan-Smith, for *The Los Angeles Times*.[1] Jordan-Smith evidently expected reviewers to say some negative things, but few wrote much of anything and those that did acknowledged that the problem Ted addressed elevated the novel above his typical run of sleazy Gold Medal books. The book caught the attention of director-actor Vincent Sherman, who bought the film rights in October of 1954 but never made the film.[2]

Ted's writing about a car crash would have a prophetic overtone, for a year-to-the-month later he and Jackie would pass actor James Dean on California Route 46 moments before his fatal crash.[3]

Ted spent the summer of 1954 in North Carolina studying the production elements of *Unto These Hills* in order to stage *Seminole* in Florida. But back in Florida he was becoming a celebrity. In February, a feature article on him had appeared in a number of Florida newspapers. A year later, he crowned the queen of the Fiesta del Sol celebration in Lake Worth, one of several occasions of participating in beauty pageants. In April 1955 the Pompano Chamber of Commerce held a banquet honoring him.[4]

Then, on August 12, 1956, an article appeared in the *Palm Beach Post*'s *The All Florida* insert magazine by Howard Wheeler, III, calling Ted "Florida's Literary Laureate."[5] This was not the first time the appellation had been used in print; for example, an aforementioned review in 1953 referenced another newspaper having used the term already. Also, it may have been that general conversation in Palm Beach County bandied the phrase about. But in this feature article, the idea found full expression and definition.

Wheeler was a fifteen-year-old aspiring journalist whose paper route included Ted's house. Ted surely recalled his own days as a teenager dreaming of a career as a writer and reporter. He may also have been amused to see the article published in an insert magazine titled similarly to his own short-lived childhood newspaper, *All News*. He may have been less enchanted with Wheeler's finishing the article with Ted and Jackie leaving Florida and the young journalist hoping Hemingway might move in. Nevertheless, Ted now had a sobriquet he would use the rest of his life.

During that year Ted wrote another play. He had at some point written a novel entitled *The Pensioners* that he could not sell. Now he decided to adapt it into a full-length play. It did not sell either. He would try only one more time to dramatize one of his works, finally admitting defeat as a playwright. He did, however, believe his efforts had helped his fiction: "the large and real benefit to me was to give my a certain facility for writing dialogue in my novels. Perhaps on that sole account it was worthwhile."[6]

The next summer Ted was back in California at the Huntington Hartford Foundation in Pacific Palisades in Los Angeles. An article in the *Miami Herald* announced that he had had surgery but was writing two books.[7] He also continued writing short pieces to keep up his income: one of these, a ten-thousand-word story entitled "When the Bomb Hit" was rejected forty-one times.[8] Such was the writing business, even for those who wrote bestsellers. Before returning to Florida in November, he and Jackie spent time in Arizona as well as California. They had apparently first visited Arizona in 1955, a trip that would prove fruitful.

Back in Florida, Ted quickly grew frustrated with development along the coast. In 1958, he and Jackie moved out of Old Floresta, fleeing westward into what was then still the piney woods west of Delray. They bought a midcentury-style home on Brady Boulevard. In June, he told a *Fort Lauderdale News* reporter that Florida was being turned into an unnatural place.[9] A year later, in March 1959, he equated Delray with the Russian Communist Nikita Khrushchev for trying to annex his area.[10]

Ted was quickly becoming a naturalist-promoting protester of Florida development in the vein of his friend Marjory Stoneman Douglas. He had known Douglas since at least 1952, when he had introduced her as a prospective writer for Fawcett.[11] The two writers shared plenty of common ground, having both been born in Minneapolis, both dedicated their careers to Florida, and now both fighting the encroach of civilization onto what they regarded as paradise.

This new passion played a role in Ted's collecting a selection of his short pieces about Florida in *Florida Roundabout* (1959). The book overall sounded a theme familiar to a lot of Floridians—that the Florida they once knew had vanished before their eyes before the march of progress. Interestingly, the version of Florida Ted decried has since been mourned by later generations who know *it* as the less-developed Florida. In the present moment, plenty (including this author) find themselves wistfully missing the Florida of twenty years ago currently vanishing under the march of further development and change. "Doubtless, in time," Ted accurately predicted, "someone will deplore the passing of the Florida they knew when they arrived to read these, my regrets at the departure of Eden. Thus the cruel and implacable law of relativity operates."[12]

In its stand against development, *Florida Roundabout* offers the greatest single-volume concentration of Florida in Ted's entire body of work. Each essay captures the state in vivid, expert prose and detail. As a pure piece of writing, the book is Ted's best, and it ranks among the classic works of Florida literature. The trappings of fiction—especially plot—fall away before crystalline presentations of midcentury Florida culture, as though Ted freed himself to create his own museum of natural Florida history. Currently out of print, the book practically cannot make it onto syllabi for Florida history and literature courses. But it should be a staple.

Along with *Florida Roundabout*, 1959 saw the printing of a new round of exploits for Ted's Casanova-esque character in *Handsome's Seven Women*. This time, however, the Handsome character seemed not exactly the same. In place of the absurd satyr character of the original *Handsome* novel, this Handsome has a name, Richard MacKinnion, and has fought in the Army in Korea where he learned martial arts. The novel opens with a scene identical to one in the first novel in which Handsome falls in with a crooked holiness preacher and wife. But where the Handsome of the first novel blithely hands over his money and heads off on his merry way, this Handsome judo chops the preacher, ties the unconscious man up, and has sex with his wife before leaving with his money.

In fact, where the first novel's charm lies in Handsome's being benign until women refuse him, this novel carries an edge through a series of male fantasies. Heading westward, Handsome hitches a ride with two women. He sleeps with each in turn and then together at the same time before the police show up to charge the women with stealing the vehicle they drive. From there, Handsome encounters a high-powered female movie director, whom he overpowers physically, his roughing her up causing her to fall in love with him. The ante ups more when Handsome heads to New England and helps an overweight woman reduce in order to get her husband back while Handsome sleeps with her friend. From there, Handsome goes to New York City, where he gets a job in a junk yard and fights the brother of a neighboring junkyard woman in order to help out his own boss and sleep with her. Finally, Handsome goes to Greenwich Village, where he fights off the would-be lesbian lover of a woman who is questioning by showing the latter what a real man is like. All this roaming around Handsome has done to some extent for the purpose of pure adventure (like his counterpart of the earlier novel) but also to obtain funds to buy a charter boat back in Florida, something the other Handsome would never have dreamed of.

The book will hardly jive with many readers today, but in its time it was engaging with dimensions of sexuality then only just coming into wider conversation. Ted champions heteronormativity, without doubt, but he was slipping deeper than ever into less societally sanctioned elements of the sexual theme. And, while he was probably not thinking about it consciously, his way of re-envisioning and re-casting his Casanova-like character approached something akin to postmodernism. That said, Fawcett saw it selling for the sex more than the art at thirty-five cents under the Crest Book imprint. Baryé Phillips, who painted covers for books by Jack Kerouac and William Faulkner, sent the original gouache to Ted for his cover art collection. It was inscribed, "To Ted: The pleasure is all mine! Sincerely, Baryé."[13]

The year 1960 brought a sequence of events stunning and heartbreaking in their contrast and of significance in South Florida history. On the evening of February 6, a Saturday, Ted and Jackie attended the fabulous dedication ball of the newly opened Flagler Museum at Henry Flagler's old home, Whitehall. The event was held by Flagler's granddaughter, Jean Flagler Matthews. Ted received his invitation among the six hundred guests because he had written about Flagler and Palm Beach. It was a heady crowd that included in its number the current governor of Florida, LeRoy Collins. Governor Collins had transformed from a segregationist to a civil rights champion and was only a month away from giving a speech that would catapult him to Democratic National Convention chairmanship and a possible bid for vice president. Music for this gala was provided by the New York Philharmonic, with Leonard Bernstein conducting.

Ted wrote his sister and brother-in-law about it later. He explained that the ball had been held in the old style of the Gilded Age, complete with wigged attendants in knee breeches and an announcer who proclaimed the names of the guests. Flowers abounded along with ice sculptures of Whitehall and a locomotive commemorating Flagler's railroad. The dinner did not get served until 1:30 in the morning. Dancing and drinking continued through the early hours. Ted took particular pride in his tuxedo and Jackie's short evening dress, which she wore instead of a ball gown she had been offered. The Pratts finally got home at five o'clock in the morning.

After a few hours' sleep, Ted and Jackie drove northward to Fort Pierce. Zora Neale Hurston had died on January 28, and her funeral was being held that day. The turnout was good for an African American woman who had died penniless, but the one hundred in attendance came nowhere near the number at the Flagler event. Ted and Jackie were among the sixteen white people in attendance. Ted, who had advocated for Hurston and always would, gave a eulogy. He also proceeded to the gravesite but left no indication of where Hurston was buried.

From the glittering finery of Palm Beach to a small parlor in the Black section of Fort Pierce, Ted felt deeply the vast disparities of race and class in Florida. These disparities were reflected in America at large. He wrote that both "were quite extraordinary experiences, and I am glad I had them."[14]

In the aftermath of Hurston's death, Ted wrote an article about her for the *Florida Historical Quarterly*.[15] He advocated for her and her work, describing her as the only "first-class native-born Florida author." He gave a brief sketch of her life story, including an account of her funeral. He also offered some of his personal experiences with her. When he once asked her what she thought of California during her time working for Paramount Pictures, she replied, "I like my land lying down." He also told of a time when she was visiting him and Jackie at their home and she hid herself when a white visitor came because she "didn't want to take any chance on embarrassing us," which they assured her could not happen. Ted also mentioned a time when he and Hurston had a disagreement: he had convinced some associates to pool money with him to send her so she could pay the fare to New York City where she claimed she had a job offer. But, after taking the money, she stayed in Miami instead. When Ted scolded her, she told him she understood his being out of sorts not because of her but because he was in the middle of a trying publication process. He closed his article with the poignant words, "She is out of circulation and all her books are out of print. One cannot be rectified. The other should be."

Little did Ted know that a few decades after penning these heartfelt and true words, his friend's reputation would be revived. Her published works would come back into print and her unpublished work newly released to the public. Ironically, by that time it was Ted's writings that were falling out of circulation and print. More people know about Hurston than about Pratt now, and she is canonized while he is seen as a lowly middlebrow. A tombstone has since been installed for Hurston at Alice Walker's instigation, and fans and scholars regularly visit. Ted's humble grave, on the other hand, receives nowhere near that attention. But there is every reason to believe—professional jealousy or not—that he would find it fitting for his friend to receive well-deserved adoration and recognition.

In his own time at the beginning of the new decade of the 1960s, though, Ted and his work *were* being celebrated. In May 1960, artist J. Clinton Shepherd sculpted a seventeen-inch clay statue of a barefoot mailman.[16] Originally from the Midwest like Ted, Shepherd had made a name for himself as an illustrator, then a caster of bronze statues for western artist Frederic Remington before moving to Palm Beach County in 1938. He taught at Barry College, then was director of the Norton Gallery School of Art in West Palm Beach. He opened his own gallery in Palm Beach in the late 1940s. Shepherd took his statue to Ted, telling him a life-sized bronze would cost twenty thousand dollars to cast. He and Ted hoped such a statue could be erected in front of a post office.

In August, the *Miami Herald* ran an article extolling Florida as a magnet for writers.[17] Journalist Beatrice Washburn included Ted among two dozen writers who either made their homes in Florida or spent significant time there. Ted surely noticed that Hemingway's photograph appeared first. But also on the list were Robert Frost, John Dewey, and Tennessee Williams, with whom Ted had no direct connection. Then there were Ted's buddies, including Leslie Charteris, Marjorie Kinnan Rawlings, and John D. MacDonald. It was a heady crowd; anyone would be honored to be in it.

Meanwhile, Ted went back to work writing and exactly a year later, February 1961, published a very different kind of historical novel, *The Lovers of Pompeii*, with Monarch Books. By this time, Ted had become almost as deeply committed to writing about sex as he was to writing about Florida. He had played his own role in bringing about the developing sexual revolution with his run of books on the theme. In a statement at the beginning of the book, he claimed to have been among the few people permitted to see the erotic images of Pompeii, then secreted in the museum in Naples. He may have seen them back during his first trip to Europe in 1924 and 1925.

The novel tells the story of Sasia Cinna, a sculptor in ancient Pompeii, who falls in love with his model, the beautiful Clodia Marsyas. Clodia is forbidden fruit in every sense, but Sasia finds a way to gain her, even though it means suffering the loss of his friends and even fighting a gladiator. Like Edward Bulwer-Lytton in *The Last Days of Pompeii*, Ted sets the novel in the year 79 against the backdrop of Vesuvius's steady buildup to eruption. The reader might expect Ted to latch onto the famous figures of lovers dying in embrace, but Ted had a predictably happier idea for the story's end. More importantly, he meant the book to provide mature and relatively frank presentation of physical love, prostitution, and the interrelationships between lust and love, with both being positive, healthy expressions. Running somewhat against that purpose, however, even in lusty ancient Pompeii, with its profusion of phallic graffiti, Ted presented characters conflicting when lust and love do not match up the way they want.

It turns out that Ted toned down the sexual content of *The Lovers of Pompeii*. He actually wrote a full-on erotic version of it entitled *The Amulet* under the penname Peter Steel, published in 1969 by a press with the mysterious initials N. P. as part of its "Playbook Club." Ted referred to it as a book published "in a semi-underground manner" and left strict instructions to keep it hidden from the general public until after his death.[18] He claimed it was not pornographic but his attempt "to enter the field of classic erotic works such as those of Victorian England."

Later in 1961, Ted published another Florida novel with Gold Medal entitled *Tropical Disturbance*. It brought classic Pratt elements into play with further dramatization and exploration of lust and love. Ted enjoyed the good fortune of cover art by Robert McGinnis, the painter of iconic covers for John D. Mac-Donald novels and posters for James Bond films and *Breakfast at Tiffany's*. Set in the fictional seaside town of Coquina Beach, the novel follows a juicy cast of characters through a destructive hurricane named Jane. Ted captures early 1960s Florida perfectly, from lobster diving to the then-relatively new practice of naming hurricanes. Present-day Floridians will recognize the tense experience of following weather bulletin updates as the storm approaches.

The story's true energy, however, lies in the problems of touristic coastal development that so irked Ted. Jay Gatlin is a young man who represents an anti-Cracker, anti-nature attitude—the northern interloper who comes to South Florida with no concern for its land or community but only wishes to exploit the beauties of both. Harold Gifford also comes from this interloping class, but as he sits in his air-conditioned beachside home he reflects on the emptiness of his lifestyle. Gifford's daughter, Nina, may be of that group but does not resemble them. She resists Jay's advances and instead falls for Miley Paget, a Cracker entirely in tune with natural Florida. Pratt readers might have picked up on his having the same surname name as the Cracker villain of *Seminole*, perhaps Ted's subtle way of acknowledging the cyclical nature of Florida's history of development in which the immigrants become the natives.

In many ways, *Tropical Disturbance* retells *Big Blow*. Published a month after Hemingway took his life, the book mentions the brutalities of the 1935 hurricane. The heroes happen to be sexual innocents in this novel as well, but Jay is a complicated heavy. He is unfaithful to Nina, whom he claims to want to marry, spending the summer in sexual encounters with Grace Dunn. Grace constantly lectures the community on Ted's own views about sex. In fact, her late husband died in her arms, and she apparently met Ted's hero Dan. When during the storm Grace outs Jay's involvement with her and everyone leaves the house to save Nina's diabetic mother from insulin shock, Jay goes to her. Doing so clears the way for Nina and Miley and sets the couples right according to their values. Hurricane Jane destroys Jay's house, which was built on a vulnerable spot and represents bad coastal development. But that catastrophe merely symbolizes a destruction of falseness symbolic of Jay's giving up pretense of wanting Nina when he really and naturally longs for Grace. It also recalls Ted's fictional counterpart throwing his manuscript into the sea in "A Visti With the Master."

As a matter of fact, Ted had written a fine novel that did not get entirely lost in the reviewing shuffle. Fred Shaw, writing for *The Miami News*, predicted that "Ted won't mind the disdainful sniffs of those reviewers who think it's safe to ignore any paperback original. Any critic who judges a book by the stiffness of the binding is so obviously a pretzel head that a writer is better of without his support."[19] Still, Shaw noted, Ted had unfortunately developed "a reputation as a manufacturer of sex thrillers" which was inaccurate and not shared across the world, with Ted's book being included (again according to Shaw) in the medical series of the long-established Parisian publishing house, Flammarion. As for *Tropical Disturbance*, it is "an outstanding piece of work—taut, accurate, and masterful in the handling of suspense, as good in its way as the best of Jack London." Ted must have smiled when he read that.

Sadness came to the Pratt family in October when Ted's brother-in-law died. Perhaps his death heightened Ted's concern about himself, bringing his own mortality to mind. He began to think about finding a repository for his papers and to set things in order should he pass away before Jackie. A number of places presented possibilities. He ended up deciding on the newly established Florida Atlantic University in Boca Raton, which would house his papers and display his artworks in a special room where young writers could study. He worked out the details over the remainder of this decade, which would be the last of his life.

CHAPTER 23

Without Consent
(1962)

Throughout the first part of 1962, Ted pressured his views about the unhealthiness of American attitudes toward sex as intensely as he could by writing a novel that took on the emotionally charged matter of rape. *Without Consent* is set in the fictional small city of Poinciana in the also fictional Cypress County, Florida. There, college student Paul Danner rapes high school virgin beauty queen Mildred Dudy. Upon being arrested, Danner admits to committing the crime in full honesty—naïve honesty, in fact, that dismays the attorney who takes his case, John Gimber. The town is outraged, and the case would seem open and shut. The famous and theatrical state prosecutor, a man of Cracker heritage named Ony Weed, has already started gloating.

But into the scene comes Dr. Glenn Talton, who identifies himself as a sexologist. He has recently retired to South Florida from a long career in New York treating people deemed sexually deviant. He urges Gimber and his assistant not to try to defend the indefensible Paul but instead to put American society itself on trial. Paul's crime must be punished, Dr. Talton insists, but other people and forces also have culpability in the crime. These include a state law system that prevents adequate sex education, beauty pageant contests that purposely sexualize young women in order to encourage tourism, and Paul's over-restrictive father who not only has not instructed his son about sex but has been psychologically abusive about it. Ted was apparently drawing on his own upbringing, his comparison of American attitudes toward sex with those of other cultures, and his recent experiences with beauty pageants in South Florida.

Dr. Talton even suggests that Mildred herself has a degree of culpability. She has no consciousness of it, but the extremely short shorts she wears sexually excite by design. All women, Dr. Talton insists, are driven by a fundamental drive to mate. According to his findings, there is evidence that women actually want to be raped—perhaps not violently, but they are on some level aroused by the idea.

Plenty of readers then and now raise their eyebrows at such a litany of asserted guilt, especially the "she wanted it" line. In our present time, a book advocating such concepts would surely be dismissed out of hand. But Ted was after nuance that publishers and readers were then willing to consider. The novel develops a swiftly moving courtroom drama, but it also has the feel of a manifesto. It is difficult not to see Dr. Talton as voicing Ted's own views.

Gimber enters a judicial confession, which causes the case to be argued not before a jury but only the judge and for the sole purpose of determining a sentence. With the question of Paul's guilt and the fact of his being sentenced settled, Ted places the emphasis on the matter of justice. Should the young man who has committed this crime be sentenced to the electric chair or be shown a degree of mercy with only reduced jail time? The answer to the question in the novel depends greatly on how circumstances interact and combine.

Readers in the twenty-first century may find themselves dizzily trying to figure out what view to embrace in such an uncomfortable novel. The policeman who arrests Paul shows no sympathy, but before doing so he shows a mistrust of Mildred and her story that many readers now would see as patriarchally aggressive. Ony Weed condemns Paul and the defense's case, but his own motives and the particular arguments he marshals themselves are ensconced in latent patriarchy. Paul's father would likely appear just as villainous to as many present-day readers as to those in 1962, but it may not be enough to make Paul sympathetic.

Except that Paul *is* sympathetic. The young man's record shows no other blemishes. He cannot explain what impulse overcame him to commit his deed, but he is racked with remorse. He believes he should be punished to the full extent of the law even though he is so horrified of it he attempts suicide in jail. Through the ordeal of arrest and trial, he insists that he loves Mildred and respects her and regrets the terrible harm he has done to her, her parents, the community, and his mother. By the end of the trial, Mildred herself actually begs the court not to punish Paul too harshly.

The novel's conclusion may well be viewed as an exoneration of patriarchy itself and a condoning of rape culture. Paul does receive a sentence, but a far less harsh one that will likely end within a few years. As terrible as Mildred's experience has been, her life has largely returned to normal. She may have lost her old steady boyfriend, but two other boys have asked her out and she has received thunderous applause of support at her graduation ceremony. Gimber even gets her best friend to admit that about half the girls in the high school are no longer virgins, implying that their sexual purity is not actually that sacred to them. As for the rape itself, while Mildred clearly did not give consent and Paul forced himself on her, he did not actually harm her physically aside from the tearing of the hymen. Her only other wound came from bumping her head against the steering wheel of his car. Gimber and Dr. Talton essentially argue that in light of such minor physical harm the deed might not even have been rape at all.

Despite its deeply problematic treatment of a massively vexed topic, *Without Consent* seems not to have made any great stir when it was published by Gold Medal in November 1962. Ted was interviewed on Miami's WTHS television channel.[1] But the book received little notice from reviewers. Perhaps everyone wanted to avert their eyes from a book that surely felt icky then and practically unreadable for most people now. Besides, Ted's name was appearing in the newspapers for a far more innocent project in the works, to be discussed shortly.

As for Ted himself, he had reached a cessation in his passion for writing about Florida. He wrote Marjory Stoneman Douglas in June, "Outside of a new original paperback novel completed and to be issued in the Fall, I have, by the way, nothing of my own I plan to do further on Florida; in fact, after 30 altogether, I'm tired and may not do any more at all except for short things and then, please God, not of an historical nature requiring research. Others go fishing, I'm going traveling."[2] Florida's Literary Laureate was ready to retire.

Three years later, the novel would catch the attention of Desi Arnaz, the former husband and co-star of Lucille Ball who now had his own production company, Desi Arnaz Productions. Arnaz saw what he regarded as truth in Dr. Talton's assertion that society created confusion about sex. He bought the film rights and wrote to Spencer Tracy asking him to read the novel and consider the part of Gimber.[3] It was the kind of role of a brave man bucking society Tracy had played in such films as *Fury*, *Bad Day at Black Rock*, and *Judgment at Nuremberg*. To write the screenplay, Arnaz contracted Ben Maddow, who had written the screenplays for such socially conscious and controversial films as *Asphalt Jungle* and the adaptation of William Faulkner's *Intruder in the Dust*.

An overjoyed Ted salivated at the idea of Spencer Tracy as Gimber and suggested John Carradine for the role of Ony Weed.[4] When Arnaz sent Ted Maddow's screenplay, Ted wrote back with a list of objections and corrections. But he also exclaimed, "It gives me hope that Hollywood . . . is going to make a first-rate picture of one of my books."[5] Ted particularly saw the power of Dr. Talton being rewritten as a female role in a later draft.[6]

Despite the promising start for the project, the timing was all wrong. Tracy's health took a bad turn in the spring of 1965 and continued so until his death in 1967. His final role in *Guess Who's Coming To Dinner* carried on his social conscientiousness, testifying to his appropriateness to the role. But by then Arnaz himself had cooled on the project. He claimed his plate was full with producing a number of television series. He particularly cited *The Mothers-in-Law* as a consuming project.[7] In the end, the film would never be made, the correspondence between Ted and Arnaz concluding in 1967.

It may have been for the best. *Without Consent* is the most cringey of Ted's novels, and it along with *Handsome's Seven Women* and *Lovers of Pompeii* makes a jarring contrast to the far sweeter and more innocent works for which Ted is remembered. One of the most puzzling mysteries of Ted's personality lies in the extreme opposites to which his mind could go, but then those extremes manifest in many people, whether in potential or actuality. Reconciliation of these extremes in Ted may be found in the fact that they derive from his earnest drive to write what he understood as truth. Sometimes truth as he saw it hit in deeply awkward or outright immoral ways. But the more innocent version of Ted made the biggest impact. And even as he wrote of rape and American culture's sexual norms, a lovable figure was arising from his past to hit the movie screen in a big, big way.

CHAPTER 24
Limpet Onscreen
(1964)

The story of the making of the most enduring film adaptation of Ted's works actually began in 1960. *Mr. Limpet* caught the attention of producer John Rose, who had gone independent after a lengthy stint as a producer with Walt Disney. Rose saw possibilities for a Disney-like live-action animation treatment of Ted's story of a man becoming a fish. Rose began corresponding with Ted and working with well-known Disney writer Otto Englander, who had writing credits for *Dumbo, Pinocchio*, and *Snow White and the Seven Dwarfs* under his belt.

Unbeknownst to Ted and Rose, the road to realizing the film would be long. By February 1961, Rose had pitched the project to Columbia and been turned down. Englander was clamoring to have Henry Limpet and Ladyfish turned into porpoises and the title changed to *Mr. Limpet's Secret*.[1] Ted objected, and Rose went about writing the screenplay himself with Jameson Brewer simply titled, "Henry Limpet."[2] Rose expected soon to reach a distributorship deal with Warner Brothers. But by the end of August no deal had been made, and Rose admitted that because Ted's story did not quite conform to "the usual run of Hollywood material" and that they faced "a hard, up hill battle."[3]

Mid-September of 1961 saw Rose delayed on getting the shooting script written.[4] That script got delayed again, not being completed and sent to Ted until after the new year. Ted liked it and was intrigued with the possibility that Fred Astaire might play the title role.[5] Rose later told him he had already pitched the role to Alec Guinness who rejected it. Rose would try Jack Lemmon if Astaire turned the role down.[6] In the meantime, Rose wanted to use Garrett Price's illustrations in the novel as the basis for creating the animated characters in the film.

Finally, in mid-March 1962, Rose could write with confirmation that the contract for distribution with Warner Brothers had reached the final stages (it would be signed on April 18).[7] In the same letter, Rose revealed that the director would be Arthur Lubin, who had directed the *Francis the Talking Mule* films and the *Mister Ed* television series. In other words, Lubin was good for talking animals. As for the title role, Astaire had turned it down and Jack Lemmon was unavailable. Next up were Wally Cox, Henry Jones, Donald O'Connor, and Don Knotts. Rose had some additional ideas for the cast, including envisioning Connie Stevens to voice the animated Ladyfish. He hoped to have the film ready for an Easter 1963 release.

But more battles would be fought. One came with another proposed title, *Be Careful How You Wish*, which Ted roundly rejected. Also, Ted was not so sure about Don Knotts as Henry Limpet.[8] When Knotts signed on for the role in April, Ted gave his approval, but with the caveat, "If Knotts will play it straight, and underplay rather than overplay, which he has a tendency to do, it should be very effective."[9] By the beginning of May, Rose was revising the script under further pressure about the title, this time the studio recommending the "Mr." to be dropped.[10] As Knotts understood it, Rose himself disliked the "Mr." but could not get Ted to budge.[11]

The issue with the title also resulted from yet another wrinkle in the process. By this time, Rose had put a songwriting duo on the job of producing music for the film. One member of the duo was Sammy Fain, a heavy hitter who had written songs for Disney films and had won two Oscars, one for "Love Is a Many Splendored Thing." Fain was teamed with Harold Adamson, whose credits included "An Affair to Remember" and "Comin' In on a Wing and a Prayer" among many others. The duo wrote a catchy number for the Limpet film entitled "Be Careful How You Wish" that Rose and the rest of the crew thought could become a hit.[12] Thus, Rose finally revealed, the main reason for the title change idea. But Ted continued to fight it even as he read the "Estimating Script" that arrived in May.

The process lurched forward. The cast finally fell into place. Limpet's wife would be played by buxom Carole Cook. Jack Weston played Limpet's antagonist-rival-friend, George Stickle. The screenplay added a character not in the novel—an animated hermit crab named Crusty, voiced by Paul Frees, a voice expert whose credits included not only onscreen characters but voiceovers for many Disney attractions, such as the Haunted Mansion. Shooting took place in July on Warner Brothers' Stage 16, one of the most famous studios in movie history where had been filmed *Casablanca*, *My Fair Lady*, *The Big Sleep*, and later such films as *The Perfect Storm* and *Indiana Jones and the Kingdom of the Crystal Skull*.[13] Filming also took place aboard the USS *Maddox*. With this movie being among the first extended live-action animation productions, the actors learned to perform with characters not yet drawn. Cook found herself amused by the novelty of filming for animated insertions, remembering talking to a red ball representing the animated fish version of Mr. Limpet.[14]

The bulk of the filming wrapped on July 26, 1962.[15] Later, in October, some footage was taken of a destroyer at San Diego just before it headed off amid the threat of the Cuban Missile Crisis.[16] By this time, Warner Brothers had confirmed the film's ultimate title, *The Incredible Mr. Limpet*, and had entered the animation process. On that job were Warner Brothers animators Gerry Chiniquy, Hawley Pratt (no relation to Ted), Robert

McKimson, Maurice Noble, and Don Peters, who had brought such characters as Bugs Bunny and Daffy Duck to life.[17] One of the assistant animators was Phil Roman, who would go on to found Film Roman, which would do animation for *The Simpsons*. Meanwhile, Rose and company were displeased with the original voicing of Ladyfish so they brought in Elizabeth McRae, who lent a sultry tone to the role (she later found success in comedy at Gomer Pyle's girlfriend, Lou Ann Poovie).

Rose wrote Ted in mid-May of 1963 to inform him that all the music had been recorded.[18] For one of the four numbers, a ditty entitled "I Wish I Were a Fish," Knotts sang for the first time on film. Rose was ecstatic—every indication pointed to the movie being a smashing success. The studio saw the film as a sleeper, but Rose believed it to be a solid production that would see great box office accomplishment. Of course, Easter had passed, and the film still was not ready, nor would it be for the rest of the year.

The delay did give more time for publicity, and Rose took full advantage. He and Ted worked hard to get a paperback reissue of the novel. Their efforts failed, but others succeeded. One was a comic book version of the book printed by Dell. Another was a recording of "I Wish I Were a Fish" by radio and television star Arthur Godfrey, who released it on a 45 record and made a special commercial advertising his recording to coincide with the movie's release.

The Incredible Mr. Limpet finally premiered on January 17, 1964, in one of the most unique, creative, and purely Floridian styles of all time. Ted and Jackie joined Knotts, Cook, McCrae, and the rest of the crew along with some 250 members of the press at Weeki Wachee Springs on Florida's west coast. The facility boasted a five-hundred-seat underwater theater with 2.5-inch thick glass windows for spectators to watch mermaids perform. Now a screen was installed in the clear spring waters on which to project the film. Over the course of a few days, the actors spoke to the press, took a tour on the Congo Belle III glass bottom boat, watched the mermaid show, and went on fishing excursions.

Then the press and actors gathered with other dignitaries for the underwater screening. Footage was taken of the opening ceremonies, and the camera just caught Ted sitting clean-shaven a row below and just down from McCrae and Knotts.[19] Graciously accepting recognition, Knotts walked to one of the windows and got a "kiss" from one of the mermaids. Then, through an explosion of bubbles and a flurry of swimming mermaids, the film kicked off. In the vibrant blue water, a cartoon Marine Corps helicopter raised a SuperCinecolor banner announcing the movie, followed by a patriotic montage.

The action begins in the bowels of a military building in the present day with George Stickle and Admiral Harlock (played by Andrew Duggan) revisiting Limpet's top secret file. Time then reverts to 1941, when Knotts appears as Limpet wearing the pince nez actor Paul Muni wore in the 1935 film *The Story of Louis Pasteur*. As Bessie and Stickle carry on their flirtation, Henry moons over the fish in his aquarium.

Mr. Limpet's transformation into a fish transpires in a striking animation sequence. Then there follows "Be Careful How You Wish," sung in warm harmony in line with the established Disney style. When Limpet flees into a cave to escape a shark, he meets Crusty, the feisty Yosemite Sam–like crustacean that anticipates the crab Sebastian in Disney's *The Little Mermaid* (1989). Crusty's humor surely got a laugh among the New Yorkers when he calls Limpet "Flatbush" according to the address he gives when asked where he is from. The underwater animation is particularly strong, with undulating warps conveying the environment. Soon Limpet meets Ladyfish and the two swim toward the breeding grounds in an astonishingly sinuous animation sequence to the song "Deep Rapture." The movie follows Mr. Limpet's career with the US Navy but jettisons the meeting with Hitler. It also removes Ladyfish's abrupt change of demeanor once Mr. Limpet chooses her.

Along with departing from the ambivalent ending of the novel, the film zooms back to the present-day scene with Harlock and Stickle. News has surfaced of Limpet's training porpoises for the military (a nod to Englander's idea), which earns him a promotion to the rank of Commodore of the US Naval Reserve. A chorus of male voices sings, "Henry Limpet, your name will live forever. American owes everything to you!" as a setting sun's rays break from clouds over a purple sea.

Despite all the media blitz and good reviews in *Life*, *Variety*, and *Hollywood Reporter*, *The Incredible Mr. Limpet* fell short of box office expectations. Knotts later remembered hearing someone in New York commiserate about news of his lousy film.[20] But over time, with reissues and television airings, the film developed a passionate following and came to be seen as a beloved classic. By the 1990s, there was talk of a remake starring Jim Carrey.[21]

In the decades following the film's release, any time *TV Guide* announced an airing of the movie Ted's many great nieces and nephews would gather in front of the screen waiting for the moment when their accomplished uncle's name would appear. When it did, they clapped.[22] It was a special connection for them: not everyone had an uncle who was responsible for a children's classic. The film remains the most widely known accomplishment of Ted's career, even if people are not always aware of his having written the book on which it is based. It marked a victory at a point that turned out to be late in his life—the kind of happy ending crescendo Ted himself might have written in authoring his own story.

CHAPTER 25
Traveling On
(1963–1969)

During his time in Arizona back in the 1950s Ted became fascinated with the Hohokam Indigenous tribe, which had vanished without a trace. He went to work researching, reading books and magazine files to learn everything he could about the tribe. Based on his research of over sixty sources, he wrote a novel entitled *Quick Arrow* and took the further step of giving it to an archeologist to read.[1] Taking the archeologist's feedback, Ted revised and began sending out his finished product in 1955. By the end of the year, eight publishers had rejected it.[2] The next year twelve rejected it, and Ted saw himself in another experience like that with *The Tormented*. Finally, in January 1962, after sixty-eight rejections, Pyramid Books accepted it under the condition that the title be changed to *White God*.

Published in April 1963, *White God* tells of one of Coronado's men banished from the Spanish conquistador's expedition finding the Hohokam village of Singing Stones in the desert. The natives think him a god, and he proceeds to milk their belief viciously. He takes their turquoise, makes them feed his horse their storage grains, and brutally rapes a young girl. Despite the Spaniard's rapacity, the villagers still believe him to be a god with the exception of the would-be titular character, Quick Arrow. True to his name, this brave challenges the white god and kills him before he can rape Zia, Quick Arrow's lover.

Ted took great pride in his book and envisioned it being sold in museum stores in Arizona. Unfortunately, the store's buyers and managers did not see it the same way. Reviewers also took little interest, Mary Snyder of *The Palm Beach Post* being an exception: she asserted that the "magnificent descriptions flooding each page indicate author Theodore Pratt has done much research for this robust historical novel of a primitive people who meet a semi-civilized man."[3] The book sold fifty thousand copies at fifty cents each, which at 10 percent would have brought Ted twenty-five hundred dollars.

Thankfully for his finances, Ted by then had the distraction of the Limpet film, the possibility of a movie version of *Without Consent*, and a new novel. Published by Duell, Sloan, and Pearce in 1965, the novel *The Money* follows the exploits of a group of neighborhood children who dub themselves the Five Musketeers and build a clubhouse near the rundown home of an old man who rails at them. When the old man dies, they find over two hundred thousand dollars hidden in his basement. Over the course of the novel, the money causes division in their little group until finally they regret ever having found it and want to dispose of it altogether. Reviewer Jan Raby declared that Ted "has provided paced suspense, humor, drama and pathos while creating five young children that you would love to call your own" in her review for the *Tampa Tribune*.[4] Fellow Florida noir-style novelist Charles Willeford felt taken by surprise with Ted's turn in this book, writing in his review for the *Miami News* that "Ted Pratt has dug deeply into child psychology and has come up with some unusual and humorous twists on the perdition road that few adult writers would think of, and, what is more, he makes them plausible."[5]

Ted and Jackie spent the bulk of summer and into fall of 1965 in Europe.[6] He had in the meantime finished a book about the writing life. With noteworthy humility, Ted did not think himself famous or important enough to write an auto-biography. But he did believe that his experiences as a writer who made his income entirely from his words could be useful for young writers. Just as he envisioned his papers at Florida Atlantic University helping young writers through the struggles of their vocation, so he produced a manuscript entitled "Anybody Want to Be An Author?" which he shopped around to presses and continued to work on right up until his death. While he failed to find any takers for the book, he did succeed in placing a historical piece in the *Miami Herald* entitled "That Was Palm Beach" which was later published as an individual volume in 1968.

In that year, 1968, Ted and his friend and fellow Floridian and Fawcett publisher John D. MacDonald became politically active.[7] The two developed an organization called Artists and Writers for Collins, which included also Philip Wylie, campaigning for LeRoy Collins. The politician, whom Ted had met at the Flagler Museum opening event back in 1960, was running for the vacant US Senate seat in Florida. Ted even urged Burt Reynolds, then living in Palm Beach Gardens, to vote for Collins in a letter in which he thanked him for plugging *Seminole* for a possible television series.[8]

Collins lost the race. In the aftermath, Ted wrote MacDonald that maybe they should not have thrown their hat into the ring since Ted had always been on the losing side of any kind of public effort. Besides, artists and writers supporting Collins may have hurt more than helped. Ted thought it likely "that the creative person will never fit into the understanding of the regular world about them. We are apart and forever must remain apart."[9] It was a striking statement by a man settling into quiet capitulation. Ted still understood himself to be an artist, and he had plenty of fight left in him. But his blood had begun to calm. The American involvement in Vietnam failed to move him to write. He accepted defeat in his quest to get *Seminole* staged, at least for the time being. He and Jackie had even quit fighting over the sound of his typewriter. Ted never actually sent the letter to MacDonald.

As for those creative people that cannot fit in, one of the ones who admired Ted met him in February 1968. Harry Crews grew up in Georgia but was living in Fort Lauderdale. He had read Ted's writing along the way and had probably picked up on the absurdism of the character Handsome. After much struggle, he finally published his first novel, *The Gospel Singer*. He inscribed a copy to Ted with "I have long admired your work. I hope there is something here you can like."[10] Unfortunately, Ted did not return the admiration.

Ted's connection with yet another Florida writer, his old friend Marjory Stoneman Douglas, came to an even less fortunate end the next year. In April 1967, Ted had offered her *The Flame Tree* and *Florida Roundabout* for publication with the press she had started called Hurricane House.[11] Douglas chose *The Flame Tree*, paying a rock-bottom price for the plates. All seemed well. But time passed without publication, and Ted pressed her and her assistant Nikki Baere. It *did* bother Ted that the contract seemed poorly constructed, which he took up with the press's third partner, Hodding Carter.[12] Things smoothed over, but more time passed.

When Ted inquired again about when the book would be published, Douglas and Baere asked him for a loan to do so. Outraged as he was, Ted patiently explained that he firmly opposed paying for publication on principle, a decision he had made way back in the debacle of his first novel. Then, in June 1969, he wrote to say that Great Outdoors Publishing Company was willing to purchase the plates for *The Flame Tree* at the same price Hurricane House had paid. It seemed a simple solution. But Baere charged an extra fee over the agreed-upon price.

Great Outdoors pulled out of the deal. By then, the warmth between Ted and Douglas had cooled as the rhetoric heated up. She "reminded" Ted that she had never promised to print the book. He wrote chastising her and Baere and withdrawing their rights to publish. On August 1, 1969, she upbraided him, "Those are harsh words, brother." He wrote back three days later, "I ask you to have another look at them, sister." The file contains no more written words between the two.

On a happier note, Ted did have a South Florida publisher for a new booklet entitled *Florida's Spanish River Area* and his new novel, which was released on December 1, 1969. Wake Brook House, based in Fort Lauderdale, published *Mr. Atom* in a numbered edition, bound in thick splotchy dyed cloth and a dustjacket with an amorphous shape. Ted published with the small local press for a distinct reason—fed up with the publishing industry's exploitative practices that had increased as publishing houses grew bigger through consolidation, he wanted to take a different route. Publishing with a small local concern marked his personal rebellion. In his new foray into publishing innovation, Ted anticipated the twenty-first-century development of ebook publishing, including self-designed and published books on Amazon's Kindle.

The novel presents a science fiction tale that blended Frankenstein with Sleeping Beauty. Ted also revisited the concept he had first written decades ago as a very young man in *Revenge of the Mummies*. Mr. Atom—something akin to what Terry Pratchett would later call an anthropomorphic incarnation—assembles the various other essences of machines, including the wheel, the steam roller, and the computer in an effort to union- ize and attain independence from humans. Mr. Atom leads this effort in part because of the humans' terrifying development of splitting him to create a deadly explosion. Unfortunately, the newly formed union encounters two major impediments—the machines' inability to resist human work orders or to procreate.

While there seems no immediate antidote to the first prob- lem, the second one might be rectified. In the past, a certain inventor, who was fed up with the human race, died while creating a machine simply called Experiment. This hourglass- shaped machine's purpose is to replicate the appeal of a woman and to give birth to machines. When an atomic bomb's detona- tion creates a reaction in Mr. Atom that animates Experiment, his power becomes used for birth instead of death. Now alive, Experiment explains that she needs a mate. The appropriate mate turns out to be Hydraulic Ram, a forgotten, inefficient, and ridiculed machine whose very neglect has caused him to evolve human-like emotions, which machines sorely lack. When the two marry and have their first machine child—it takes these efficient machines nine minutes instead of nine months—the machines see hope for a future of independence from human creation and directive. Mr. Atom explains that humans have claimed they will no longer unleash his destructive power and so gives himself permission to rest, albeit with some doubt that humans will keep their word.

The *Stuart News* announced the new book with pride in Ted's working with a local publisher. This book's publication, the article stated, amounted to a "protest against big business, interested mainly in the quotation figure of its stock, having swallowed so many American publishers lately."[13] Jane Hoff- stetter in the *Fort Lauderdale News* also praised Ted's bucking big business and opting for publishing in Fort Lauderdale, adding,

"No one enjoys writing fantasy more than author Theodore Pratt of Delray Beach."[14]

The novel nature of the book's publication somewhat obscured the story itself. Like so many of Ted's writings, *Mr. Atom* distills middle-class values of heterosexual, nuclear family triumph. It is filled with the expected jokes (a monkey wrench seeks to wreck machinery; a computer cannot think for itself). Lighthearted, quick-moving, it finds a comedic resolution to the deep anxieties of the Atomic Age and the Cold War. It contains Ted's lifelong interest in science, his persistent love of happy endings, and his gift for metaphorically rich flat characters. And it would be his farewell to this world.

Early in the morning of December 15, Ted awoke with serious heart trouble. He hurried to Bethesda Memorial Hospital in Boynton Beach, where he was treated by Dr. Thomas Whitehead.[15] Twelve hours later, Ted passed away at 4:07 in the afternoon. The cause of death was coronary thrombosis, with arteriosclerosis listed as a contributing factor. Ted was sixty-eight years old.

EPILOGUE
Ocean Forever

Ted's physical remains were buried in Delray Beach Memorial Gardens. His simple metal marker was flush with the ground, shaded now by a tree and announcing, "AUTHOR OF THE BAREFOOT MAILMAN AND OTHER BOOKS."

The spirit of Theodore Pratt—the Barefoot Mailman—would have a different future. In 1967, Ted had written his family that a local sculptor planned to use his face as his model for a statue of the Barefoot Mailman. The sculptor wanted to create a bust of Ted, which would then be used for the life-sized statue. Ted did not mention the sculptor's name and stressed that neither he nor the sculptor wanted it to be known that Ted's likeness would be used.

The sculptor apparently was Frank Varga, who would go on to sculpt two such statues. One, in bronze, depicts the Barefoot Mailman walking with a hiking stick and now stands in Hypoluxo Scrub Park in Hypoluxo, Florida. The other was sculpted of Athena stone and erected at the entrance of Hillsboro Beach, Florida. Both statues featured mustached men who could easily pass for Ted. Whether Varga actually ended up using Ted's likeness, the statues ended up being perfect incarnations of Ted as the Barefoot Mailman so many had thought him actually to be.

And there was another, even more fitting chapter to come for one of the statues. After the Athena stone statue deteriorated and was restored by Varga, in 2012 it was remade in a bronze version and installed at the foot of the Hillsboro lighthouse.[1] Meanwhile, the old statue was restored again by Dixie Divers, who anchored it on the ocean floor just north of the Deerfield Beach Fishing Pier as a diving destination.[2] Thus the "Barefoot Mailman" who had been born in one watery state and adopted another while so often imagining what it would be like to live underwater found a lasting resting place in the sea.

All this time, *The Barefoot Mailman* novel kept being reprinted. It had entered its fifteenth printing at the time of Ted's death. Eventually, other presses picked it up until in 1993, Port Salerno–based Florida Classics Library printed a fiftieth anniversary edition. Jackie carried on the business of her late husband in various ways, including seeing this book through these printings. In the end, she outlived not only her husband but her sister-in-law, Isabel, who passed away on February 7, 1987. Jackie died June 26, 1998, and was buried next to her husband. To his marker was added the words, "HIS WIFE JACKIE."

Ted was given another landmark in Palm Beach County a few years after his death. On September 14, 1971, the Boca Raton City Council discussed renaming 40th Street and the 40th Street Bridge over the Intracoastal Waterway.[3] The City Council decided to rename the street itself Spanish River Trail, although the City Engineer J. P. Vansant pointed out that "Trail" should be changed to "Boulevard" in order to comply with state code. A placard would be placed on the 40th Street Bridge memorializing Ted's patrons Mr. and Mrs. Schine. As for the bridge itself—it would be renamed the Theodore Pratt Memorial Bridge. Back in 1935, Ted and Jackie had been unable to get back to the mainland because the Lake Worth drawbridge was up when the Labor Day Hurricane struck. Now the city of Boca wanted to honor Ted by naming a bridge after him.

Ted's influence would be felt for a time. *The Barefoot Mailman* obviously continued to be read. Harry Crews would go on to write more Florida novels with echoes of Ted's work, from *Karate Is a Thing of the Spirit* to *Body*. Randy Wayne White lists Ted among the "many gifted and workmanlike pros from that era [who were] collectively a major influence," including Richard Powell, Philip Wylie, Patrick Smith, John Keasler, MacKinlay Kantor, and John D. MacDonald.[4]

To the larger world of literary criticism, however, Ted was soon all but forgotten. By the early twenty-first century, his work had vanished into the abyss with scores of other middlebrow midcentury writers of paperbacks with lurid covers. Aside from a stray scholarly essay or two, no literary critic has written about Ted. Along with his reputation and readership, the Florida Ted knew and felt slipping away has since become more difficult to locate now than ever. The tacky jouissance of the 1980s through the early 2000s of Palm Beach County down through the Keys has given way to something more austere while urban sprawl has continued its progress. The pioneer days find remembrance in historical societies in the area, but the postpandemic waves of new immigrants seem hardly in touch with the Miami cocaine-cowboy era, much less Ted's midcentury one. The barefoot mailman figure has faded somewhat from South Florida identity.

But now, in the third decade of the century, literary criticism has changed. The menu for literary critics has expanded to allow analysis of everything from comic books to video games. More than ever, it makes sense to revisit a middlebrow writer in whose work can be discerned the tumult of midcentury America. Marjorie Kinnan Rawlings might be a cut above middlebrow, but her most famous novel being for adolescents has kept her largely out of the critical eye. Yet the opening years of this decade have seen a new biography of her as well as her middlebrow contemporary and earlier-mentioned antagonist Louis Bromfield. Perhaps now Ted's turn for attention approaches.

In fact, Ted may get the last laugh. The difficult Modernist style of writing he so disliked and resisted has now fallen out of favor while his straightforward and easily readable prose has come back into vogue. His sexual themes now seem outmoded and problematic, but his fiction offers perspective on them. Some of his views on race can look racist in our time, yet his condemnation of racist-driven violence and earnest promotion of Zora Neale Hurston make him seem a hero, however problematically. More than anything, there is a lot to learn and relearn about the middle of the twentieth century in Florida and generally. Ted presented its unique beauties and problems. Interestingly, his ideas about euthanasia, situation ethics, and breaking sexual taboo have now become mainstream.

For readers now as well as in his lifetime, Ted's writing becomes most appealing when offering the escape of the state it embodies. Just as the recently departed Jimmy Buffett captured Florida's lazy, slow-time, out-of-the-way tropical appeal, so Ted's writing offers a great read for someone who wants to let go and drift off on the orange waters of a Florida sunset or in the delicious shadows of its coastal glades. There you might find people with flaws but an endearing simplicity of life. There you will find the ghosts of Mizner and Flagler and Steven and Adie. There the royal poinciana blossoms without interruption. There you might just see the barefoot mailman's footsteps lingering in the sand. There you can find a happy ending.

BOOKS BY THEODORE PRATT

Spring From Downward, London: Selywn and Blount, 1933

Not Without the Wedding, New York: Dutton, 1935 (London: Selywn and Blount, 1934)

Big Blow, New York: Little, Brown, 1936

Murder Goes Fishing, New York: Dutton, 1936

Murder Goes in a Trailer, New York: Dutton, 1937

Murder Goes to the Dogs, New York: Dutton, 1938

Murder Goes to the World's Fair, New York: Dutton, 1939

Mercy Island, New York: Knopf, 1941

Mr. Limpet, New York: Knopf, 1942

Mr. Winkle Goes to War, New York: Duell, Sloan, and Pearce, 1943

The Barefoot Mailman, New York: Duell, Sloan, and Pearce, 1943

Thunder Mountain, New York: Duell, Sloan, and Pearce, 1944

Perils in Provence, New York: Duell, Sloan, and Pearce, 1944

Miss Dilly Says No, New York: Duell, Sloan, and Pearce, 1945

Valley Boy, New York: Duell, Sloan, and Pearce, 1946

Mr. Thurtle's Trolley, New York: Duell, Sloan, and Pearce, 1947

The Flame Tree, New York: Dodd, Mead, 1948

The Big Bubble, New York: Duell, Sloan, and Pearce, 1949

The Tormented, New York: Fawcett Gold Medal, 1950

The Story of Boca Raton, Ford Motor Company, 1950

Cocotte, New York: Fawcett Gold Medal, 1951

Handsome, New York: Fawcett Gold Medal, 1951

The Golden Sorrow, New York: Fawcett Red Seal, 1952

Escape to Eden, New York: Fawcett Gold Medal, 1953

Seminole (play), Gainesville: University Press of Florida, 1953

Seminole (novel), New York: Fawcett Gold Medal, 1954 (Duell, Sloan, and Pearce, 1954)

Smash-Up, New York: Fawcett Gold Medal, 1954

Handsome's Seven Women, New York: Fawcett Gold Medal, 1959

Florida Roundabout, New York: Duell, Sloan, and Pearce, 1959

The Lovers of Pompeii, Derby, CT: Monarch Books, 1961

Tropical Disturbance, New York: Fawcett Gold Medal, 1961

Without Consent, New York: Fawcett Gold Medal, 1962

The White God, New York: Pyramid Books, 1963

The Money, New York: Duell, Sloan, and Pearce, 1965

That Was Palm Beach, St. Petersburg, FL: Great Outdoors, 1968

Florida's Spanish River Area, Highland Beach, FL: Boca-Hi, 1969

Mr. Atom, Fort Lauderdale, FL: Wake Brook House, 1969

ACKNOWLEDGMENTS

Seventy-one years after Theodore Pratt first moved to Florida, I did the same, accepting a professorial position at Florida Atlantic University (FAU), which houses the Theodore Pratt Collection. I must thank the university for nearly twenty years of employment, during which time I have grown tremendously. My colleagues in the Department of English and the Dorothy F. Schmidt College of Arts and Letters are very dear to me, and I am grateful to them. The various chairs and deans over the years have supported me tremendously. I must mention the late Gabrielle Gutting, a fellow Faulkner scholar who preceded me in writing about Pratt. I am also grateful to Andrew Furman, who was chair of the English Department when I was hired and has inspired me to reach beyond literary critical writing. Mark Scroggins has inspired me in the same way and many others. To Mary Faraci, my mentor, I express my deepest and abiding gratitude and affection. She has been sweeter and kinder to me than I could possibly deserve. It is my honor to dedicate this book to her.

FAU's S. E. Wimberly Library has been central to this project. I am deeply indebted to Victoria Thur, assistant dean for Special Collections, Archives, and Distinctive Collections at FAU, for her encouragement and aid. She has been wonderful to work with, and I count her a friend. The same goes for Robert Feeney, manuscript and archives assistant in the Special Collections, who has made each request for material and each session a collegial and enlightening experience. Alethea Perez, Wimberly Library's manager of digital recorded sound archives, digitized old audio media from the collection, for which I am grateful.

Thank you to Kayleigh Howald, archivist, Delray Beach Historical Society. Thank you to the Palm Beach County Historical Society, with special gratitude to Rose Guerrero, research director, for so kindly allowing me to work there even when I got the appointment date wrong and for patiently taking me into the depths of the archives. An equally special thank you to Debi Murray, chief curator, for conversation about Pratt and for connecting me with Pineapple Press, which I had long admired.

Thank you to Barbara Davis, city historian of New Rochelle, New York, and co-director of the Westchester County Historical Society, for generously providing information about Pratt's time in New Rochelle.

Thank you to Susan Gillis, curator of the Schmidt Boca Raton History Museum, who has offered tremendous direction and insight for this project. The museum and its archive were especially great resources.

Thank you to John DeSando and Wayne Miller for film history guidance.

I am very happy to have made contact with Pratt's relatives. Noreen Regan, one of his great-nieces, shared some lovely stories. Stephanie Dempsey, another great-niece, applied her fabulous energy and enthusiasm to track down things I could not have discovered in a hundred years.

It is a special honor to me to work with Pineapple Press. I first learned about it when I moved to Florida and read Patrick D. Smith's *A Land Remembered*. Although now an imprint of Globe Pequot, Pineapple Press continues to embody the focus on locality and attention to the author Pratt believed presses should. It has been a great pleasure to work with Lauren Younker and Debra Murphy, both of whom I hold in the highest esteem. I am grateful for their guidance and warmth, and I have the deepest respect, admiration, and affection for them. It has been an equally great pleasure to work with production editor Meaghan Menzel and marketing manager Alyssa Griffin.

One of the special monthly zoom meetings of my life since the pandemic has been the LIFE (Learning Is Forever) group of Rochester Community and Technical College in Minnesota. Everyone in the program is precious to me. I am especially grateful to Chrisanne Pieper for bringing me to it and to Jamie Schroeder for facilitating everything so smoothly (and thank you to both for their friendship). Thanks also to Frank Lossi, Tom Gaffey, and everyone who has been so kind to me. This connection has helped me gain an understanding of Pratt's birthplace I could not have gained otherwise. I very much appreciate also the special literary and architectural tour of St. Paul and Minneapolis provided by Dr. Kristin M. Anderson of Augsburg University.

I want to say a big thank you to a couple of Florida writers whom I admire greatly. Thank you to Randy Wayne White for generously taking the time to talk to me about Pratt and also for his warmth and encouragement. Thanks also to James W. Hall for his encouragement, who has also been a role model from afar. I should probably also thank Doc Ford and Thorn.

Thank you as always to the people who support me. You know your names, and the fact is that each of you deserve a paragraph, chapter, or book at least to begin to express adequately how much you mean to me. Space permits only a sentence. Thank you to Barbara Dahlem always. Thank you Chris Bundrick for all the conversation. Thank you David Ramm for the emails, the podcast talk, and for being the closest thing I have ever had to a big brother. Thank you to Hope Goodsite for keeping faith in me. Thanks to Marianna de Tollis for patience and interest and all the other things brought to my life. Thank you to Warren Kelly for all the talks and support and laughter. Thanks to Laura Cade for everything, most recently the paradigm change.

I do want to mention a few other South Floridians who mean more to me than they know. The first is Victoria Fedden, whose support, conversations, suggestions, and excitement have inspired me tremendously. And a special thank you to Skye Cervone and Dan Creed, who have for quite a few years now been quiet rocks of Gibraltar for me (which will probably surprise them to hear).

My family is and always has been at the very core of my life. Thank you to my father and mother for all the millions of ways they believe in me. Thank you to my sister and brother-in-law, my nephews, Emory, Everett, and Hildebrando, all of whom have learned to love Florida along the way. Thank you to my Aunt Nancy and her love of Florida's piracy. Thank you to my aunts, uncles, and cousins in Mississippi and Tennessee.

I would be remiss not to include a bittersweet thank you to Trisha Marie Dewey, who first opened my eyes to the wonders of South Florida.

And I must acknowledge that state. It has both filled and broken my heart at times. Over a lifetime in which home has been elusive for me, I feel very happy and fortunate for it to be so. I love it dearly, and this project has been fueled by my desire to stake some small claim in its history.

NOTES

PROLOGUE

1. "Transcript from WPTV Peter Donald Program," February 26, 1963, Pratt Collection, Florida Atlantic University S. E. Wimberly Library Special Collections, Box 106, File 1. (Pratt Collection, Florida Atlantic University S. E. Wimberly Library Special Collections is hereafter PC.)

2. Elizabeth Bishop, "Florida," *The Complete Poems: 1927-1979*, New York: Farrar, Straus, and Giroux, 1983, 23.

CHAPTER 1

1. Caitlin Dempsey, "Which States Have the Highest Percentage of Water Area?" *Physical Geography* November 10, 2015; *Geography Realm*, accessed July 10, 2023, https://www.geographyrealm.com/which-states -have-the-highest-percentage-of-water-area/#:~:text=Minnesota%2C%20 known%20by%20the%20nickname%20%E2%80%9CLand%20of%20 10%2C000,state%20with%20the%20ninth%20largest%20totay%20 water%20area.

2. Geoffrey Lynfield, "Theodore Pratt (1901-1969): A Reassessment," *The Spanish River Papers*, volume 12, number 3, 1984, nonpaginated (hereafter GL).

3. "A Writer's Life," unpublished notes by Theodore Pratt, Pratt Collection, Box 106, File 33 (hereafter WL). The name of the company appears in the obituary, "Thomas A. Pratt," *Star Tribune* Sunday, April 17, 1938, 8.

4. Description based on a photograph in PC, Box 139.

5. PC, Box 139, Item 13.

6. PC, Box 103, File 4.

7. "Biographical Notes," unpublished notes by Theodore Pratt, Pratt Collection, Box 106, File 30 (hereafter BN).

8. "Anybody Want to Be an Author?" unpublished manuscript by Theodore Pratt, Pratt Collection, Box 38 (hereafter AWTBA), 8.

9. Caitlin Dempsey, "Which States Have the Highest Percentage of Water Area?" *Physical Geography* November 10, 2015; *Geography Realm*, accessed July 10, 2023, https://www.geographyrealm.com/which-states

-have-the-highest-percentage-of-water-area/#:~:text=Minnesota%2C%20
known%20by%20the%20nickname%20%E2%80%9CLand%20of%2010
%2C000,state%20with%20the%20ninth%20largest%20totay%20water%20
area.

10. "Lake Harriet Park," Minneapolis Park and Recreation Board,
accessed April 25, 2022, https://www.minneapolisparks.org/parks
_destinations/parks_lakes/lake_harriet_park/

11. BN.

12. "The Barefoot Mailman Walks Again," Teleprompter script, PC,
Box 106, File 3.

13. BN.

14. WL.

15. WL; AWTBA, 4.

16. Theodore Pratt, "A New York Childhood," PC, Box 70, Folder 22.
Subsequent quotes until otherwise noted are taken from this nonpaginated source.

17. AWTBA, 9.

18. WL.

19. In AWTBA, Pratt identified this school as DeWitt Clinton High
School.

20. AWTBA, 10.

21. Information on New Rochelle is based on emails between Taylor
Hagood and New Rochelle City Historian, Barbara Davis, and Davis's
books, *Images of New Rochelle*, Arcadia Publishing, 2009, and *Postcard History Series: New Rochelle*, Arcadia Publishing, 2012.

CHAPTER 2

1. The issues of *The All News* described are deposited as part of
"Scrapbook 1916-1923," PC, Box 102, Folder 11.

2. AWTBA, 12.

3. Barbara Davis email to Taylor Hagood, July 5, 2022.

4. AWTBA, 12.

5. AWTBA, 16.

6. AWTBA, 17.

7. Theodore Pratt, "I Wouldn't Go to War," PC, Box 70, File 11.

8. AWTBA, 20.

9. AWTBA, 20–21.

10. Theodore Pratt, "Here and There With Society," *Minneapolis Sunday
Tribune*, November 2, 1924, 6.

11. PC, Box 101, Folder 59.

12. AWTBA.

13. AWTBA, 21.

14. AWTBA, 22–23.

15. Pratt's high school diploma is in PC, Box 103, Folder 20.

CHAPTER 3

1. BN.
2. Colgate University Students' Record, PC, Box 103, Folder 13.
3. BN.
4. AWTBA, 23–24.
5. AWTBA, 25.
6. AWTBA, 26–27.
7. Playbill in PC, Box 102, Folder 11.
8. Article clipping undated in PC, Box 102, Folder 11.
9. Transcript of Record, Columbia University, PC, Box 103, Folder 13.
10. AWTBA, 29.
11. Pratt, "Here and There with Society," *Minneapolis Sunday Tribune*, November 2, 1924, 6.
12. AWTBA, 32.
13. Ted's playbills for these productions are in PC, Box 101, Folder 62.
14. *Revolt of the Mummies* Typescript, PC, Box 65, Folder 3.
15. "Ted Pratt, Local Boy, Writes Play" article clippings in "Scrapbook (1916-1923)," PC, Box 102, Folder 11.
16. PC, Box 65, Folder 3.
17. PC, Box 65, Folder 3.
18. AWTBA, 32.
19. Ted provides the information about these plays in AWTBA, 92–93.
20. AWTBA, 90.
21. AWTBA, 91–92.
22. Advertisement for the play is in PC, Box 102, Folder 11.
23. BN.
24. AWTBA, 34.
25. AWTBA, 34.
26. AWTBA, 32.
27. "Pratt to Study Literature This Winter in Paris," undated newspaper clipping in "Scrapbook (1916-1923)," PC, Box 102, Folder 11.
28. AWTBA, 34.
29. AWTBA, 37.

CHAPTER 4

1. AWTBA, 38.
2. PC, Box 106, Folder 28.
3. AWTBA, 42.
4. AWTBA, 43.
5. AWTBA, 43–44.
6. AWTBA, 53.
7. AWTBA, 56.
8. AWTBA, 65.
9. AWTBA, 65.

10. AWTBA, 69.

11. AWTBA, 75.

12. AWTBA, 67.

13. AWTBA, 87.

14. AWTBA, 76–77.

15. AWTBA, 76–77.

16. AWTBA, 77–78.

17. AWTBA, 77–78.

18. WL.

19. AWTBA, 80.

20. AWTBA, 79.

21. AWTBA, 99.

22. Massachusetts Vital Records, 1840–1911. New England Historic Genealogical Society, Boston, Massachusetts.

23. Thirteenth Census of the United States, 1910 [Sterling, Worcester, Massachusetts; Roll: T624_630; Page: 15A; Enumeration District: 1822].

24. GL records their meeting on a blind date. I am speculating that mutual friends in the theater/film business set the date.

25. Letter from Theodore Pratt to Rosabelle Jacques, June 9, 1927, PC, Box 89, Folder 22.

26. Letter from Theodore Pratt to Rosabelle Jacques, May 10, 1928, PC, Box 89, Folder 22.

27. Letter from Theodore Pratt to Rosabelle Jacques, June 1, 1928, PC, Box 89, Folder 19.

28. Letter from Theodore Pratt to Rosabelle Jacques, September 1, 1929, PC, Box 89, Folder 19.

29. AWTBA, 100.

30. The following account of the novel's doomed publication is recorded in AWTBA, 95–100.

31. Pratt explained the circumstances in AWTBA, 104. The New York, New York, Marriage License Index lists the License Number as 28075.

32. AWTBA, 104.

CHAPTER 5

1. AWTBA, 104.

2. AWTBA, 108.

3. AWTBA, 107.

4. AWTBA, 108.

5. AWTBA, 110.

6. AWTBA, 113.

7. AWTBA, 110–11.

8. AWTBA, 111.

9. AWTBA, 111.

10. AWTBA, 119–20.

11. AWTBA, 123.

12. New York State Marriage Index, 1881–1967, #9726.

13. George Sand, *Winter in Majorca*, translated and annotated by Robert Graves, Valldemosa Edition, Valldemosa, Majorca, 1956.

14. AWTBA, 125.

15. "Agatha Christie in Mallorca," *The Mallorca Photo Blog*, September 15, 2012.

16. AWTBA, 125.

17. Victoria De Silverio, "Mallorca, Spain: Three Perfect Days," *Hemispheres*, May 2023, 56.

18. AWTBA, 132.

19. AWTBA, 132.

20. AWTBA, 130.

21. AWTBA, 135.

22. AWTBA, 137–38.

23. AWTBA, 140.

24. AWTBA, 142.

25. AWTBA, 143.

26. AWTBA, 144.

CHAPTER 6

1. These clippings are included in an scrapbook dedicated to the Majorca affair, PC, Box 106, Folder 19.

2. These descriptions are based on photos and clippings in the PC, Box 106, Folder 19.

3. AWTBA, 146.

4. AWTBA, 5.

5. AWTBA, 7.

6. AWTBA, 135.

7. "Spring from Downward," *Times Literary Supplement*, Thursday, October 26, 1933, 733.

8. Undated clipping in PC, Box 64, Folder 67.

9. AWTBA, 147.

10. AWTBA, 147.

11. This vehicle is pictured in photographs and Jackie mentioned in GL. Pratt himself wrote of it in *Florida Roundabout*, New York: Duell, Sloan, and Pearce, 1959.

12. Theodore Pratt, "New York to Florida," *New Yorker* January 5, 1935, 86–87.

13. Pratt, *Florida Roundabout*, 3.

14. Pratt, *Florida Roundabout*, 3.

15. Pratt, *Florida Roundabout*, 4.

16. BN.

17. GL.

18. AWTBA, 175.

CHAPTER 7

1. AWTBA, 147.
2. AWTBA, 148.
3. Timothy Brace [Theodore Pratt], *Murder Goes Fishing*, New York: Dutton, 1936, 220.
4. AWTBA, 147.
5. L. McC., "Majorca," *Evening Sun*, Sunday, January 26, 1935, 8.
6. Jay Bee, "Serious Comedy, Light Tragedy in Spain," *Star Tribune*, Sunday, January 27, 1935, 46.
7. The *Star Tribune* does not attribute the drawing, but when it was thusly attributed when printed in the *Birmingham News* (Alabama), Sunday, February 10, 1935, 49.
8. "No Excuse for It," *Miami Herald*, Sunday, January 27, 1935, 8F.
9. "The Book Nook," *Palm Beach Post*, Sunday, February 3, 1935, 2.
10. Kenneth A. Fowler, "Turning Over a New Leaf," *Star-Standard*, Saturday, February 2, 1935, 2
11. Pratt, *Florida Roundabout*, 5.

CHAPTER 8

1. Pratt, *Florida Roundabout*, 7.
2. Pratt, *Florida Roundabout*, 45.
3. W. G. Hippler, "A Line on Books," *Buffalo News* July 13, 1935, 3.
4. "Former Resident Waits Hurricane," *Standard Star* September 4, 1935, 1, 10.
5. *Daily Times*, September 5, 1935, 5.
6. Ernest Hemingway, "Who Murdered the Vets? A First-Hand Report on the Florida Hurricane," *The New Masses* September 17, 1935, 9–10.
7. Pratt letter to Ernest Hemingway, September 27, 1935, PC, Box 82, Folder 25.
8. Theodore Pratt, *Big Blow*, New York: Little, Brown, 1936, 288.
9. Pratt, *Big Blow*, 288.
10. Pratt, *Big Blow*, 295.
11. Pratt, *Big Blow*, 295.
12. Pratt, *Big Blow*, 295–96.
13. Pratt, *Big Blow*, 296.
14. Pratt, *Big Blow*, 296.
15. "Theodore Pratt of New Rochelle Author of Book," *Mount Vernon Argus*, Friday, September 11, 1936, 18.
16. "Two Novels of Country Life in the South," *Philadelphia Inquirer*, Saturday morning, September 12, 1936, 13.
17. Kenneth A. Fowler, "Turning Over a New Leaf," *Standard-Star*, Saturday, September 19, 1936, 3.
18. Charles Hanson Towne, "Description of Storm a Thriller," *Buffalo News*, Friday, September 11, 1936, 27.

19. Vernon Sherwin, "Not Really Florida," *Evening Sun* (Baltimore), Saturday, September 12, 1936, 6.
20. Rachel Richey, "Books," *Miami Tribune*, Monday, September 14, 1936, 10.
21. J. K. B., "The Hurricane Roars," *Miami Herald*, Sunday, November 22, 1936, 13G.
22. "The Book Nook," *Palm Beach Post-Times*, Sunday, November 1, 1936, 8.
23. E. D. Lambright, "Books and Bookmen," *Tampa Sunday Tribune* Sunday, September 27, 1936, Part 1, 10.
24. Edwin A. Menninger, "Ye Editor's Easy Chair," *Stuart Daily News*, Saturday, November 7, 1936, 2.
25. This quote and the following ones are included in the frontmatter of *Murder Goes in a Trailer*, New York: Dutton, 1937.
26. E. C. K., "The Book Nook," *Palm Beach Post*, Sunday, October 4, 1936, 7. That Ted's authorship may have been known finds support in an article in the New Rochelle *Standard-Star* (Kay Ross, "County Society," Saturday, October 17, 1936, 7), which actually offers a light account of Ted introducing the writer to his pet, Timothy Bra.

CHAPTER 9

1. Theodore Pratt, "Building Our First Home—A Trailer," PC, 1936, Box 76, Folder 10.
2. Theodore Pratt, "Building Our First Home—A Trailer," 3–4 PC.
3. Theodore Pratt, "Our Footloose Correspondent," *New Yorker* March 13, 1937, 85.
4. Theodore Pratt, "Building Our First Home—A Trailer," PC, 17, 1936, Box 76, Folder 10.
5. These review quotes are taken from the dust jacket of *Murder Goes to the Dogs*, New York: Dutton, 1938.
6. Notice in Mount Vernon *Daily Argus*, Friday, January 7, 1938, 16.
7. "Self Inflicted Bullet Kills Dania Man," *South Broward Tattler* (Hollywood, Florida), April 1, 1938, 11.
8. "New Rochelle Man, Ill, Hangs Himself," *Herald Statesman* (Yonkers, New York), April 15, 1938, 2.
9. Taylor Hagood phone interview with Stephanie Dempsey, January 31, 2023.
10. Letter from Theodore Pratt to Jackie Pratt, April 18, 1938, PC, Box 89, Folder 18.
11. Theodore Pratt, *Big Blow: Dramatized From the Novel*, National Service Bureau, Federal Theatre Project, Works Progress Administration, December 5, 1938.
12. These review quotes are taken from the dust jacket of *Murder Goes to the World's Fair*, New York: Dutton, 1939.

13. Advertisement in *New York Daily News*, Wednesday, November 30, 1938, 57.

14. *Big Blow* poster, Library of Congress Prints and Photographs Division, https://www.loc.gov/resource/cph.3b49014/.

15. Burns Mantle, "'The Big Blow,' Tense and Exciting Drama; It Stars a Hurricane," *Daily News* Monday, October 3, 1938, 33.

16. Edgar Price, "The Premiere," *Brooklyn Citizen* Monday, October 3, 1938, 14.

17. M. W., "*Big Blow*—Maxine Elliott Theatre," *Barnard Bulletin* Friday, October 14, 1938, 2.

18. Ernest L. Meyer, "'Making Light of the Times," *Capital Times*, Tuesday, October 11, 1938, 22.

CHAPTER 10

1. BN.

2. "The Book Nook," *Palm Beach Post*, Sunday, March 5, 1939, 2.

3. C. E. Mill, "Trouble at the Fair," *Idaho Statesman*, Sunday, August 13, 1939, 4.

4. Pauline Corley, "Three for the Mystery Fans," Sunday, July 23, 1939, 4.

5. N. C. N., "Here's a Tangle for Mystery Fans," *Buffalo Evening News*, Saturday, July 15, 1939, 3.

6. Elisabeth Cushman, "County Mystery Writer Remains—A Mystery! Who is Timmy Brace?" *The Daily Argus*, Saturday, July 8, 1939, 6.

7. BN.

8. Theodore Pratt, *Mercy Island*, New York: Knopf, 1941, 10.

9. Pratt, *Mercy Island*, 16.

10. "Writes About Florida's Attractions," *Key West Citizen* Friday, February 21, 1941, 4.

11. "Young Author Carrying Word of Florida to 26,000,000 People," *Key West Citizen*, Friday, February 12, 1941, 4.

CHAPTER 11

1. Theodore Pratt, "Land of the Jook," *Saturday Evening Post* April 26, 1941, 43.

2. BN.

3. BN.

4. "Ida Lupino in 'Juke Girl,'" *Dixon Evening Telegraph* (Dixon, Illinois), Friday, September 12, 1941, 41.

5. "A. I. Bezzerides," *Inquirer*, January 15, 2007.

6. Edwin Schallert, "Reagan Second to Flynn in Fan Popularity," *Los Angeles Times*, Tuesday, December 2, 1941, 10.

7. "Ida Lupino in 'Juke Girl,'" *Dixon* (Illinois) *Evening Telegraph*, Friday, September 12, 1941, 41.

8. "Ida Lupino Takes Suspension Rather Than Play Juke Girl," *The Modesto Bee*, Saturday, October 4, 1941, 5; Louello O. Parsons, "Ann Sheridan Replaces Balking Ida Lupino in Picture," *Pittsburgh Sun-Telegraph*, Monday, October 6, 1941, 8.

9. "Even Court Can't Change 'Juke Girl,'" *Times Herald* (Port Huron, Michigan), Thursday, November 13, 1941, 14. A number of papers carried this article.

10. "'Adjustments' Mean More Pay for Film Extras," *St. Louis Globe-Democrat*, Thursday, November 20, 1941, 1K.

11. Zora Neale Hurston, *Zora Neale Hurston: A Life in Letters*, collected and edited by Carla Kaplan, New York: Doubleday, 2002, 463.

12. "'Cat Tail' Town on Warner's Busy Back Lot," *Salt Lake Tribune*, Tuesday, December 16, 1941, 20; "The Juke Girl," *Simi Valley Star*, Thursday, December 4, 1941, 1.

13. John Chapman, "Hollywood," *New York Daily News*, Saturday, December 6, 1941, 22; "Screen Killing Leaves Gene in Real Dither," *Salt Lake Tribune*, Wednesday, December 17, 1941, 11.

14. Erskine Johnson, "Hollywood," *Monrovia News Post* (California), Wednesday, December 24, 1941, 6.

15. "Summer Scene Filmed With Coating of Ice," *Norfolk Ledger Dispatch*, Thursday, November 27, 1941, 18.

16. Paul Harrison, "Pays to Be Dull Witted," *The Calgary Albertan*, Thursday, December 11, 1941, 5.

17. Ida Belle Hicks, "'Juke Girl' Depicts Life in Florida Farming Area," *Fort Worth Star-Telegram*, Saturday, June 6, 1942, 5.

18. Jay Carmody, "Gang Loses Another Battle With Heroes in 'Juke Girl,'" *Evening Star* (Washington, DC), Saturday, May 30, 1942, B-12.

19. Herbert Cohn, "'Juke Girl' Screened at the N. Y. Strand," *Brooklyn Eagle*, Saturday, June 20, 1942, 14.

20. Bob Fredericks, "'Juke Girl' at Sheridan, Paramount and Beach," *Miami Herald*, Wednesday, May 20, 1942, 10-A.

21. AWTBA, 157.

CHAPTER 12

1. BN.
2. BN.
3. PC, Box 49, Folder 3.
4. BN.
5. BN.
6. Theodore Pratt, *Mr. Limpet*, New York: Knopf, 60.
7. Pratt, *Mr. Limpet*, 70.
8. Pratt wrote of this expectation on the front cover of his handbound original typescript (PC, Box 49, Folder 3).
9. "Mr. Limpet" contract, PC, Box 101, Folder 18.

10. "Of Fish and Men: *Mr. Limpet*. By Theodore Pratt. Drawings by Garrett," *New York Times*, January 18, 1942.

11. Russell Kay, "Too Late to Classify," *Hollywood Herald*, Friday, January 20, 1942, 2.

12. Herman Kogan, "Humor Books Offer Pleasant War Antidotes," *Chicago Tribune*, Wednesday, February 18, 1942, 15.

13. W. J. Hurlow, "On the Book Table," *The Citizen* (Ottowa), Saturday, February 7, 1942, 18.

14. "Epic of the Poor Fish," St. Louis *Globe-Democrat*, Saturday, January 17, 1942, 1-B.

15. E. D. Lambright, "Books and Bookmen," *Tampa Sunday Tribune*, Sunday, February 1, 1942, Part 1, 12.

16. Letter from Jackie Pratt to Emma Pratt, date unknown, PC, Box 89, Folder 6.

17. GL.

18. BN.

CHAPTER 13

1. Theodore Pratt, *Mr. Winkle Goes to War*, New York, Duell, Sloan, and Pearce, 1943, 198.

2. These three first reviews are quoted on the dust jacket of a later edition of *The Barefoot Mailman*, New York: Duell, Sloan, and Pearce, 1943.

3. J.W.R., Jr., "Mr. Winkle Goes to War," *Evening Star* (Washington, DC), Sunday, April 4, 1943, E-6.

4. AWTBA, 152.

5. Alan L. Gansberg, *Little Caesar: A Biography of Edward G. Robinson*, London: New English Library, 1983, 125–28.

6. Edward G. Robinson, with Leonard Spigelgass, *All My Yesterdays: An Autobiography*, New York: Hawthorn Books, 1973, 235.

7. Ad in PC, Box 64, Folder 23.

CHAPTER 14

1. The exact details of Ted's research have not been officially documented. He apparently told Dorothy Raymer, of *The Miami News*, about his research efforts (Dorothy Raymer, "The Reviewing Stand," *Miami News*, Sunday, July 11, 1943, 8-D).

2. The historical problems of Pratt's using the term "barefoot mailman" have been elucidated to me by Palm Beach County historian Debi Murray.

3. These first three quotes are included on dust jackets of later printings of the novel.

4. Dorothy Raymer, "The Reviewing Stand," *Miami News*, Sunday, July 11, 1943, 8-D.

5. Mary-Carter Roberts, "Current Books," *Evening Star*, Sunday, August 8, 1943, 37.

6. "The Sunday World Page of Books and Art," *Tulsa Daily World*, Sunday, August 22, 1943, Section 5, 5.

7. "Barefoot Mailman on Route to Miami," *Kansas City Star*, Saturday, August 7, 1943, 3.

8. "'Barefoot Mailman' Is Yarn of Early Florida," *Asheville Citizen-Times*, Sunday, September 26, 1943, 6-A.

CHAPTER 15

1. AWTBA, 152.

2. AWTBA, 152.

3. AWTBA, 155.

4. AWTBA, 155.

5. Vera Francis, "Drama Atop a Mountain," *Tulsa Daily World*, Sunday, May 21, 1944, Section 5, 3.

6. "Pratt Has New Story On Old Theme," *The Gazette Montreal*, Saturday, June 3, 1944, 11.

7. Mary-Carter Roberts, "The New Books," *Evening Star* (Washington, DC), Sunday, May 7, 1944, C-3.

8. Will Davidson, "Hollywood Antics Provide Setting of Escapist Tale," *Chicago Tribune*, Sunday, February 18, 1945, 12. The review in verse form was signed "Japsie," and presented under the title, "Unfunny Funniment," *Hartford Courant Magazine*, Sunday, March 4, 1945, 14.

9. The information concerning *Miss Dilly Says No* and Pratt's concerns about Hollywood and the potential *Dilly* musical are in AWTBA, 156.

10. AWTBA, 94.

11. AWTBA, 156.

12. Letter from Virginia Rice to Theodore Pratt, June 9, 1945, Pratt Collection, Box 97, Folder 10.

13. AWTBA, 155.

14. AWTBA, 156.

15. Theodore Pratt, "An Author Looks at Himself," 9, PC, Box 76, Folder 6.

16. AWTBA, 156.

17. "Theodore Pratt Again Exhibits Gift for Story," *Indianapolis Star*, Sunday, September 7, 1947, 28.

CHAPTER 16

1. AWTBA, 157.

2. AWTBA, 158.

3. Ted would make mention of the phenomenon of his being referred to as the barefoot mailman throughout the 1950s and 1960s. The first claim of that happening that I have been able to find is in Orville Revelle,

"Florida's Author," *Fort Lauderdale News*, Thursday, January 12, 1950, 4. It is unclear whether Revelle actually had heard such references or if Ted simply made that claim to him.

4. Orville Revelle, "Florida's Author," *Fort Lauderdale Daily News*, Thursday, January 12, 1950, 4.

5. Stephen Trumbull, "Pratt Recaptures Flagler's Florida," *Miami Herald*, Sunday, January 8, 1950, 4F.

6. Pauline Naylor, "Bizarre Era Painted in Palm Beach Story," *Fort Worth Star-Telegram*, Sunday, April 2, 1950, Section 2, 9.

7. Louise Charles, "Theodore Pratt Pens Sequel To Classic 'Barefoot Mailman'" *Tulsa World*, Sunday, February 19, 1950, Section 5, 9.

CHAPTER 17

1. AWTBA, 175.

2. AWTBA, 175.

3. Richard Hoffman qtd. in Theodore Pratt, *The Tormented*, New York: Fawcett Gold Medal, 1950.

4. AWTBA, 176.

5. Piet Schreuders, *Paperbacks, U.S.A.: A Graphic History, 1939-1959*, translated by Josh Pachter, San Diego: Blue Dolphin Enterprises, 1981, 98.

6. Noreen Reagan Phone interview with Taylor Hagood, January 13, 2023.

7. AWTBA, 177.

8. AWTBA, 178.

9. AWTBA, 178.

10. Theodore Pratt, *Cocotte*, New York: Gold Medal Books, 1951, 173.

CHAPTER 18

1. Christopher Knowlton, *Bubble in the Sun: The Florida Boom of the 1920s and How It Brought on the Great Depression*, New York: Simon and Schuster, 2021.

2. Theodore Pratt, *Big Bubble*, Duell, Sloan, and Pearce, 1951, 6.

3. E. D. Lambright, "Books and Bookmen," *Tampa Tribune*, Sunday, December 9, 1952, 28-A.

4. Lillian Blackstone, "Author Theodore Pratt Finishes Trilogy on State's History With 'The Big Bubble,'" *St. Petersburg Times*, Sunday, November 25, 1951, 57.

5. Pat Price, "Pratt's Trilogy Complete With Story of '26 Boom," *Miami News*, Sunday, December 23, 1951, 14.

6. Martha Smith, "Story of Creation: Florida Land Bubble Bursts in Pratt Novel," *Atlanta Journal*, Sunday, December 2, 1951, 12-E.

7. Beatrice Washburn, "Big Bubble Forceful But Not Up to Pratt's Two Earlier Volumes," *Miami Herald*, Sunday, December 9, 1951, 7F.

8. Pratt, "An Author Looks at Himself," 10, PC, Box 76, Folder 6.

CHAPTER 19

1. Interview with Hildegard Schine by Ruth Reitz Balish for Boca Raton Historical Society, March 1981.
2. AWTBA, 160.
3. AWTBA, 161.
4. Article clipping in PC, Box 75, File 22.
5. AWTBA, 162.
6. AWTBA, 163.

CHAPTER 20

1. Leo Schumaker, "Book Reviews," *Orlando Sentinel*, Sunday, September 7, 1952, 39.
2. "The Book Nook," *Palm Beach Post*, Sunday, November 29, 1953, 22.
3. Theodore Pratt, *Escape to Eden*, Greenwich, CT: Fawcett, 1953, 266.

CHAPTER 21

1. "New Play 'Seminole' Tells Story of Osceola," *Fort Lauderdale News*, Sunday, December 20, 1953, 23.
2. "Theodore Pratt's Latest Book Is Another About Florida," *Palm Beach Post*, Sunday, November 15, 1953, 20.
3. Charles Alexander, "Poor Man's Library, or Among the Paperbacks," *Albany Democrat-Herald*, Saturday, March 13, 1954, 7.
4. Philip Weidling, "Building In Review," *Fort Lauderdale News*, Saturday, December 4, 1954, 1-C.
5. "Arts and Crafts Show at Boca Raton," *Fort Lauderdale News*, Sunday, January 31, 1954, 4-E.
6. Zora Neale Hurston, *Zora Neale Hurston: A Life in Letters*, collected and edited by Carla Kaplan, New York: Doubleday, 2002, 705.
7. Letter from Marjorie Kinnan Rawlings to Theodore Pratt, February 19, 1953, PC, Box 81, Folder 11.
8. Pratt, "An Author Looks at Himself," 10, PC, Box 76, Folder 6.

CHAPTER 22

1. Paul Jordan-Smith, "Books and Authors: Summer in L.A. Impels Author to Write Analytical Study of Auto Accidents!" *Los Angeles Times*, Sunday, September 26, 1954, 94.
2. "In the News," *Los Angeles Evening Sun*, Monday, October 25, 1954, 14.
3. AWTBA, 155.
4. "Fiesta Crown Won by Carolyn Guignet," *Miami Herald*, Saturday, February 19, 1955, 1-B; "Pompano Beach C of C Honors Author Theodore Pratt," *Fort Lauderdale News*, April 18, 1955, 3-B.

5. Howard Wheeler III, "Florida's Literary Laureate," *Palm Beach Post* "All Florida Magazine," Sunday, August 12, 1956, 6.

6. AWTBA, 94.

7. George Bourke, "Ted Pratt Recovering After Surgery," *Miami Herald* Sunday, September 29, 1957, 29-E.

8. Theodore Pratt, "When the Bomb Hit," PC, Box 65, File 21.

9. Anne Kolb, "State Disillusions Writer," *Fort Lauderdale News*, Sunday, June 13, 1958, 8-A.

10. "Quit Being a Kruschev," *Fort Lauderdale News*, Tuesday, March 10, 1959, 1-B.

11. This correspondence can be found in the PC, Box 82, Folder 43.

12. Theodore Pratt, *Florida Roundabout*, Duel, Sloan, and Pearce, 1959, 14.

13. Original cover art in PC, Box 125.

14. Letter from Theodore Pratt to Isabel and Walter Dempsey, February 8, 1960, PC, Box 89, Folder 31.

15. Theodore Pratt, "Zora Neale Hurston," *Florida Historical Quarterly* 40.1 (1961): 35–40.

16. "'Mailman' Statue Site Wanted, " *Palm Beach Post*, Monday, May 16, 1960, 7.

17. Beatrice Washburn, "Florida—It's a Magnet for Writers," *Miami Herald*, Sunday, August 14, 1960, 5-F.

18. AWTBA, 249.

19. Fred Shaw, "Weather Prophets, Please Note!" *Miami News* Sunday, September 10, 1961, 6B.

CHAPTER 23

1. "Novelist Theodore Pratt Is Dr. Robert Hively's Guest," *Miami Herald*, December 2, 1962, 4.

2. Letter from Theodore Pratt to Marjory Stoneman Douglas, June 27, 1962, PC, Box 82, Folder 43.

3. Letter from Desi Arnaz to Spencer Tracy, March 1, 1965, PC, Box 84, Folder 12.

4. Letter from Theodore Pratt to Desi Arnaz, November 13, 1965, PC, Box 84, Folder 11.

5. Letter from Theodore Pratt to Desi Arnaz, November 13, 1965, PC, Box 84, Folder 11.

6. Letter from Theodore Pratt to Desi Arnaz, April 3, 1966, PC, Box 84, Folder 11.

7. Letter from Desi Arnaz to Theodore Pratt, June 7, 1967, PC, Box 84, Folder 11.

CHAPTER 24

1. Letter from John Rose to Theodore Pratt, February 3, 1961, PC, Box 85, Folder 37.

2. Typescript in PC, Box 39.

3. Letter from John Rose to Theodore Pratt, August 25, 1961, PC, Box 85, Folder 37.

4. Letter from John Rose to Theodore Pratt, September 15, 1961, PC, Box 85, Folder 37.

5. Letter from Theodore Pratt to John Rose, February 9, 1962, PC, Box 85, Folder 37.

6. Letter from John Rose to Theodore Pratt, February 12, 1962, PC, Box 85, Folder 37.

7. Letter from John Rose to Theodore Pratt, March 11, 1962, PC, Box 85, Folder 38. For the signing date for distributorship, Letter from John Rose to Theodore Pratt, April 20, 1962, PC, Box 85, Folder, 38.

8. Letter from Theodore Pratt to John Rose, March 15, 1962, PC, Box 85, Folder 37.

9. Letter from Theodore Pratt to John Rose, April 21, 1962, PC, Box 85, Folder 37.

10. Letter from John Rose to Theodore Pratt, May 1, 1962, PC, Box 85, Folder 37.

11. Don Knotts, with Robert Metz, *Barney Fife and Other Characters I Have Known*, New York: Berkley Books, 1999, 137.

12. Letter from John Rose to Theodore Pratt, May 8, 1962, PC, Box 85, Folder 38.

13. Stephen Cox and Kevin Marhanka, *The Incredible Mr. Don Knotts: An Eye-Popping Look at His Movies*, Nashville: Cumberland House, 2008, 49.

14. Cox and Marhanka, 50.

15. Cox and Marhanka, 45.

16. Letter from John Rose to Theodore Pratt, October 28, 1962, PC, Box 85, Folder 38.

17. Cox and Marhanka, 47.

18. Letter from John Rose to Theodore Pratt, May 14, 1963, PC, Box 85, Folder 39.

19. This footage can be found as part of the extras on the DVD of the film.

20. Knotts, 138.

21. Knotts, 138.

22. Taylor Hagood phone conversation with Noreen Regan, January 13, 2023.

CHAPTER 25

1. AWTBA, 166.

2. The story of the rejections of the novel appear in AWTBA, 168.

3. Mary Synder, "When 'The White God' Found Singing Stones," *Palm Beach Post*, Sunday, July 21, 1963, E-4.

4. Jan Raby, "Problems of Cash," *Tampa Tribune*, Sunday, October 24, 1965, 31.

5. Charles Willeford, "Take the Cash and Let the Kiddies Go," *Miami News*, Sunday, October 10, 1965, 12.

6. Theodore Pratt Passport, PC, Box 103, Folder 16.

7. Correspondence and documents pertaining to Pratt and MacDonald's campaigning are in the PC, Box 84, Folder 81.

8. Letter from Theodore Pratt to Burt Reynolds, September 30, 1968, PC, Box 84, Folder 8.

9. Letter from Theodore Pratt to John D. MacDonald, November 6, 1968, PC, Box 84, Folder 81.

10. The inscribed volume is in PC.

11. Letter from Theodore Pratt to Marjory Stoneman Douglas, April 15, 1967, PC, Box 82, Folder 43.

12. Correspondence between Theodore Pratt and Hodding Carter, PC, Box 82, Folder 43.

13. "Theodore Pratt Writes New Book: 'Mr. Atom,'" *Stuart News*, Sunday, November 9, 1969, 2-A.

14. Jane Hoffstetter, "Pratt Unwraps New One in His Series of Fantasies," *Fort Lauderdale News*, Sunday, December 7, 1969, 9H.

15. Palm Beach County Health Department Certificate of Death, Theodore George Pratt, Registrar Number 3955.

EPILOGUE

1. "Bronze Barefoot Mailman Statue Unveiled at March Light Station Tour," *Big Diamond: Hillsboro Lighthouse Preservation Society* 15.1 (Spring/ Summer 2012): 1, 6.

2. Carmen McGarry, "A Restaurant, a Sculpture and the Boy Scouts; The History of Honoring and Preserving the Barefoot Mailman," *New Pelican*, September 30, 2020.

3. "Minutes of the Regular Meeting of the City Council of the City of Boca Raton, Florida, Held on the 14th Day of September, 1971, 5996–99.

4. Email from Randy Wayne White to Taylor Hagood, October 4, 2023.

INDEX

promotes Zora Neale Hurston, 187–88; and *The Purple and White* high school newspaper, 14; reads authors independently in Colgate library, 18–19; recognizes Florida as a character, 136–37; relationship with Lulu, 26–27; researches for *Barefoot Mailman*, 119–20; response to Hemingway's *New Masses* article, 63–64; takes fiction writing courses at Columbia (1919), 15–16; trip to Camp Croft, South Carolina, 111; as unconventional artist, 28–29; views of Modernism, 29; visit with Marjorie Kinnan Rawlings, 135–36; witnesses 1935 Labor Day hurricane, 61–62; works as reader for movie companies, 23, 29; works for Pathe Motion Picture Company, 29–30; works for *Variety*, 22, 29; worries about Hollywood disapproval of *Miss Dilly*, 130; writes at Ritz-Carlton Cloister Inn, 159; writes first novel (unpublished), 32; writes first play for Little Theater, 19; writes one-act plays, 21–22; writes papers for fraternity brothers, 18; writes pieces for New York magazines, 30–31. *See also names of family members and titles of written works*
Pratt, Thomas Amede (father of Theodore Pratt): accepts job in silk manufacturing, 8; birth and background of, 5; buys passage for Theodore's trip to Paris, 23; commits suicide, 80; funeral of, 80; laughs off New York City rent, 9; marriage to Emma Hineline, 5–6
Price, Garrett, 109, 200

Puerto de Pollensa, Majorca, Spain, 40, 46,
Pyramid Books, 205

Rawlings, Marjorie Kinnan: and Cracker dialect, 70; current literary standing of, 215–16; death of, 178; listed as Florida writer in *Miami Herald*, 189; Pratts' visit with at Cross Creek, 135–36; writing about orange groves, 60
Reagan, Ronald, 3, 96–101, 160
The Revolt of the Mummies (play), 20–21
Republic Pictures, 92, 97
Reynolds, Burt, 4, 207
Rice, Virginia: end of professional relationship with Pratt, 131; and *Mr. Limpet*, 108; and *Mr. Winkle Goes to War*, 116; and *Not Without the Wedding*, 47; and *Spring From Downward*, 42; and *The Tormented*, 52
Ritz-Carlton Cloister Inn, Boca Raton, Florida, 159
Robertson, Willard, 100
Robinson, Edward G., 117–18
Rockwell, Norman, 4, 14–15, 41–42
Roman, Phil, 202
Rose, John, 199–202
Ross, Harold, 30
Royal Poinciana Hotel, 137–42
Royal Poinciana tree (*Delonix regia*), 137–42, 216
Russell, John, 160–61

Saratoga Springs, New York, 131
Scharf, Walter, 92
Schine, Hildegarde, 159, 177, 214
Schine, J. Myer, 159
Selwyn and Blount, 42, 47, 56, 71
Seminole (novel), 175–77
Seminole (play), 173–75, 177